T0393072

Green Magic

With a Preface and biographies from Jack Zipes, as well as the original illustrations by Violet Brunton, this collection of fairy tales originally published by the award-winning Romer Wilson – *Green Magic* (1928), *Silver Magic* (1929), and *Red Magic* (1930) – offers a combination of classic fairy tales, alongside lesser-known global and diverse tales.

Green Magic contains many traditional fairy tales, including "Rapunzel" by Grimm, "Ali Baba" by Diyab and Galland, and "Puss in Boots" by Perrault, as well as previously unknown tales, such as "The Golden Twins" by Iperescu and "The Brotherless Girl" by an anonymous author. It was Romer Wilson's intention to combine the familiar with the unknown, and introduce authors and cultures from a variety of countries. As a researcher, she uncovered a remarkable amount of stories from other countries that remain unknown today. The collection gives voice to unique and intriguing tales that inspire children to have a better understanding of how people and their stories are alike despite major differences.

Through his Preface and commentary, Jack Zipes shows how all three books are a means to bring people together in the name of peace and justice. These books will therefore be of interest to anyone researching or studying fairy tales, folklore, and children's literature, as well as global or comparative literature and social justice.

Jack Zipes is Professor Emeritus of German and comparative literature at the University of Minnesota. In addition to his scholarly work, he is an active storyteller in public schools and has written and translated fairy tales for children and adults. Some of his recent publications include: *Grimm Legacies: The Magic Power of Fairy Tales* (2014) and *The Sorcerer's Apprentice: An Anthology of Magical Tales* (2017). In 2019, he founded his own press called Little Mole and Honey Bear and has published *The Giant Ohl and Tiny Tim* (2019), *Johnny Breadless* (2020), *Yussuf the Ostrich* (2020), *Keedle the Great and All You Want to Know about Fascism* (2020) and *Tistou, The Boy with the Green Thumbs of Peace* (2021).

Green Magic

The World's Best Fairy Tales Collected and
Arranged by Romer Wilson

Edited by
Jack Zipes

Illustrated by Violet Brunton

Routledge
Taylor & Francis Group

LONDON AND NEW YORK

Designed cover image: Anastasiia_Guseva, Getty

First published 2023
by Routledge
4 Park Square, Milton Park, Abingdon, Oxon OX14 4RN

and by Routledge
605 Third Avenue, New York, NY 10158

Routledge is an imprint of the Taylor & Francis Group, an informa business

British Library Cataloguing-in-Publication Data
A catalogue record for this book is available from the British Library

Library of Congress Cataloging-in-Publication Data
Names: Wilson, Romer, 1891–1930, compiler | Zipes, Jack, 1937– editor. |
Brunton, Violet, illustrator.
Title: Green magic : the world's best fairy tales / collected and arranged
by Romer Wilson ; edited by Jack Zipes ; illustrated by Violet Brunton.
Description: New York, NY : Routledge, 2023. |
Summary: A collection of familiar as well as lesser-known fairy tales.
Identifiers: LCCN 2022027805 (print) | LCCN 2022027806 (ebook) |
ISBN 9781032285818 (hbk) | ISBN 9781032285832 (pbk) |
ISBN 9781003297536 (ebk)
Subjects: LCSH: Fairy tales. |
CYAC: Fairy tales. | Folklore. | LCGFT: Fairy tales.
Classification: LCC PZ8 .G827 2023 (print) |
LCC PZ8 (ebook) | DDC 398.2–dc23/eng/20220802
LC record available at https://lccn.loc.gov/2022027805
LC ebook record available at https://lccn.loc.gov/202202780

ISBN: 978-1-032-28581-8 (hbk)
ISBN: 978-1-032-28583-2 (pbk)
ISBN: 978-1-003-29753-6 (ebk)

DOI: 10.4324/9781003297536

Typeset in Sabon
by Newgen Publishing UK

Contents

Preface

Jack Zipes

The Startling Romer Wilson

Considered one of the foremost young novelists in England during the 1920s, Romer Wilson (Florence Roma Muir Wilson, 1891–1930) never had the opportunity to realize her potential. She died from a severe case of uterine cancer when she was only thirty-nine. She lived for her writing, but life was not kind to her. Nor was history, for she has been neglected in most histories of English literature. So have her fascinating collections of unusual tales, *Green Magic* (1928), *Silver Magic* (1929), and *Red Magic* (1930).

Born in Sheffield, England, she was educated first at the prestigious West Heath School, and in 1910, she enrolled at Girten College, Cambridge, one of the first higher-educational establishments to accept women, to study law. However, after four years, she left college in 1914 to devote herself to writing and also to making contributions to war work against the Germans.

Indeed, Wilson was greatly affected by World War I, and most of her early novels deal with the impact of war not only in England but also in Europe. Her first novel, *Martin Schüler* (1918) deals with an ambitious young German composer, who tramples on other people's lives to fulfill has dreams. Her second novel, *If All These Your Men* (1919), is a reflection on the devastating effects of World War I on people's lives and on how chaos becomes the norm in England. Wilson's third novel, *The Death of Society* (1921), involves a former British major in World War I who stumbles upon an enchanted forest in Norway. His love affair with a Norwegian married woman frees him briefly from the fetters of conventional society. But he leaves the forest empty-handed and alone.

Wilson's trip to Europe in 1921 led to the publication of *The Grand Tour*, an epistolary novel, which concerns the Parisian sculptor, Alphonse Marichaud, who flounders because he can no longer determine the meaning of life and art. This novel was part of Wilson's philosophical exploration of existence and ethics at a time when civilization appeared to be disintegrating, and the theme of despair can be found in her other novels, *Dragon's Blood* (1926), *Latterday Symphony* (1927), and *Greenlow* (1927).

In 1923, on a second trip to Europe, Wilson met the American writer, Edward J. O'Brien, in Italy, and they were married that same year. From this point on, until her death, Wilson and O'Brien lived in a number of Italian cities, and finally they moved to Locarno, Switzerland, in 1928 due in large part to her contracting uterine cancer. She had numerous treatments for this disease and eventually died in Lausanne in 1930.

Why and how Wilson developed her series of fairy-tale anthologies in 1928 is unknown. In fact, she had even planned a fourth anthology titled *Blue Magic*, which never came to fruition. In her first anthology, *Green Magic*, she dedicated the tales "To the Children of England, Good, Bad and Indifferent," but this dedication is missing in the other two collections and remains puzzling because the tales were not primarily for children. Her selection of the stories in all three volumes reflects an erudite mind bent on displaying cultural treasures – namely fairy tales to challenge readers. Wilson was by no means a folklorist; however, she was very knowledgeable about folklore and the difference between literary fairy tales and oral folktales. Her collections include both, though the majority of the stories are more literary than oral. There is no standard that defines her choice of the tales, and the witty words at the beginning of each tale do not explain her choice. Nevertheless, to her credit, Wilson was one of the first anthologists of fairy tales to include major and minor fairy tales from all over the world with an evident intention to demonstrate the "dazzling" power of the narratives she selected. It is not possible to categorize or codify the tales she selected, but there is clear evidence that the ethics and mystery of the tales drew her to them.

Green Magic tends to favor tales by well-known writers and folklorists such as Charles Perrault, the Brothers Grimm, Peter Asbjörnsen, and Jørgen Moe. Yet Wilson also surprisingly includes known authors and translators such as Herbert Giles' Chinese tale, "The Lake Princess," Diamond Jenness's "The Wolf's Bride," a complex story that emanated from the indigenous people in Canada, William Ralston's Russian version of "The Water King and Vasilissa the Wise." Charles' Coxwell's Siberian story, "The Man Who Understood Animals' Conversation," and Elodie Mijatovich's "The Gold Tree and the Nine Peahens." The major tale in this collection is "The History of Ali Baba," which Antoine Galland translated while listening to the storyteller Hanna Diyab.

Silver Magic contains a miraculous barrel of fairy tales, some of which are Apuleius's "The Marriage of Cupid Psyche," The Grimms' "The Twelve Dancing Princesses," Madame Villeneuve's "Beauty and the Beast," and Perrault's "Cinderella, or, The Little Glass Slipper" are well known. However, these classic versions are much different from contemporary literary translations because Wilson chose lengthened examples and may have changed some of the tales herself. Interestingly, Wilson also included an American fairy tale, "The Miraculous Pitcher" by Nathaniel Hawthorne and two delightful Irish tales by F. R. Davies. Finally, this book is typical of Wilson's intent to include world-wide tales from ancient times to the present as can be seen in Petronius's "The Werewolf," "Eight Tales from the *Gesta Romanorum*," and the Irish "Two Stories about Finn MacCool."

Red Magic also includes tales from ancient Greece and Italy such as Aesop's "The Country Mouse and the Town Mouse" and Percy's "St. George and the Dragon" as well as tales from nineteenth-century Europe and America, notably Robert Southey's "The Story of the Three Bears," Charles Dickens's "A Child's Dream of a Star," Charles Nodier's "Bean Flower and Pea Blossom," and Nathaniel Hawthorne's "The Chimaera." What is surprising in this volume are tales by unknown authors such as Taddeo Ricciardi's "The Reward of Virtue," Cholmondeley Pennell's "King Uggermugger, or the Princess Silver-Silk," Puss Brambula Compton's "At the Door," and Elodie Mijatovic's "Bash-Chalek; or True Steel." Wilson had an incredible magic touch in forming her three anthologies, and she was fortunate to find two fabulous illustrators, Violet Brunton and Kay Nielsen, who added luster to the stories.

As I have stated before, Romer Wilson lived for her writing, but she also lived for the writing of others, namely the fairy tales which she published in her three anthologies, *Green Magic, Silver Magic,* and *Red Magic.* In the process of re-publishing the tales in these three books, I have edited some of the archaic grammar and words, and I have deleted three long and boring stories. I believe that Wilson would not have minded this. I believe that she had an extraordinary eye for choosing only the best tales for the world, and this re-publication contains only the best of her best tales.

Introduction

Romer Wilson

Do you believe in fairies? I will tell you what I have heard from full-grown men and women on the subject. When I have told you what I have heard, you can read these stories, and after that please judge for yourselves. I won't have anything to do with it one way or another, because if I say "There are fairies," certainly elderly people might say "Nonsense!", people of thirty or so, who have reached a ripe old age, and whose memories of their fairy-tale years are long ago decayed. If I say "There are no fairies," I might get on the wrong side of the Good Folk. You know what happened to the Sleeping Beauty because her mother forgot to ask a fairy to her christening! Something like that might happen to me if I offended their High Mightinesses, or worse (to sleep for one hundred years is not too bad) for I might be stolen away, and only sent home after seven long years with my toes danced off like the Woman of Hart Lake, that Mr. Yeats calls to mind. Or those Small Gentry might "turn me into an ugly worm and bid me toddle about a tree," which sad fate befell more than one young gentleman who offended the Little People. Well, be there fairies, or be there none, I will tell you of some which have been seen. In order to keep on the safe side, I will give you the words of people who cannot be supposed to think twice about fairies in the ordinary course of events: curates, learned Englishmen, and persons of reputation from both England and America, people who one might infer were born with a strong disbelief in fairies, or were certainly brought up to despise them.

These are the words of a curate, a Mr. Hart, who lived at Yatten Keynel in Sussex: In the year 1633, he saw one night on the Sussex Downs, "innumerable quantities of pigmies dancing in a fairy ring, making all manner of small odd noises."

In 1691, the Reverend Robert Kirke, Minister of Aberfoyle, Perthshire, printed at Edinburgh a book entitled *Essay on the Subterranean, and for the most part Invisible People, Heretofore going under the Name of Elves, Faunes, and Fairies, or the lyke.* In it he describes fairies as "A sort of astral spirits – betwixt humanity and angels," – they have, he says, "children, nurses, marriages, deaths, and burials."

Sir Walter Scott reports that this Reverend Gentleman, from all accounts never died, but was carried away to fairyland for meddling with the fairies.

Mr. William Blake, the English poet, born in 1757, once saw a fairy's funeral. He says, "I was walking alone in my garden, there was a great stillness among the branches and flowers, and a more than common sweetness in the air; I heard a low

DOI: 10.4324/9781003297536-1

and pleasant sound, and I didn't know where it came from. At last, I saw the broad leaf of a flower move, and underneath I saw a procession of people of the size and color of green and gray grasshoppers, bearing a body laid out on a rose-leaf, which they buried with songs, and then disappeared. It was a fairy funeral."

In a book called Hollingsworth's *History of Stowmarket*, you may read a record of sober decent people having seen fairies in Suffolk at a much more recent date. The fairies, on one occasion, were seen dancing in a field, "the biggest about 3 ft. high, the small ones like dolls. Their dresses sparkled as if with spangles – they were moving hand in hand in a ring. No noise came from them. They seemed light and shadowy, not like solid bodies."

In the year 1855, Mr. Thomas Quiller Couch, of Cornwall, states that an old friend of his knew the fairies well, that they were "about the height of a span, clad in green, and having little straw hats, or little red caps on their heads." He, further, says that "Our piskies (as fairies are called in Cornwall) are little beings standing midway between the purely spiritual and the material – they have a power of making themselves seen, heard and felt." He adds that they are governed by a king.

Now I come down to modern times, and will put down here evidence I have gathered from living people. I promise you that the description of fairies, which I shall now relate to you, are not hearsay, but the real words of people I know very well.

A friend of mine, Mrs. Salaman, a clergyman's daughter wrote this very charming description of fairies she has seen especially for this book.

"I have always believed in Fairies, and can certainly testify to the fact of having seen them as a child in the garden of my old Yorkshire home. It is many years ago now, but I have a vivid recollection of the immense pleasure I had in watching them dancing and flitting in and out of the bushes. Very dainty lovely little creatures they were, and though so tiny, quite perfect. I used to watch with breathless interest so as not to startle them. They always seemed very, very happy, and would appear and disappear quite suddenly."

Then Mr. O'Brien, a Boston man, an American, one day saw fairies dancing on the sea at sunset. They were little flimsy creatures. He told me himself they were neither good nor bad, nor mortal nor angels, and took no earthly notice of anybody but themselves. Two other grown-up people were with him who saw the fairies at the same time.

American fairies have been reported to me. They are said to wear little red caps and to be jovial little creatures. Another man I know, who often sees fairies, went on a fairy hunt with his little girl one day. I don't mean they went out with butterfly nets to catch them, but merely set off to try and spy them out. Now fairies don't show themselves to prying eyes, but as my friend walked under a particular tree where they used to dance, he *felt* them. The air was thick with them, as if thousands of cobwebs had gathered in a cloud.

I could talk a great while on this subject, but the printer will allow me no more room. He says it is time to tell proper tales now with real princesses, dragons, giants, dwarfs, ogres, witches, and whatnot in them. So I will stop and give way to his importunity, for his fingers are itching to be done with this introduction and to set the "True and Marvelous History of Puss in Boots," that the machine may print it for your edification. I hope that you may all be as clever as Puss, and become in time, as he did, ornaments to your country, Prime Ministers, Presidents, or Secretaries of State at the very least, not to mention Ambassadors and Ambassadresses, whose lives I believe are passed in splendid palaces, and who give balls and parties every night of their lives.

THE MILLER FEARED NOTHING

Puss in Boots

Charles Perrault

From the French of Charles Perrault, as read to the Court of Louis XIV. The costumes and manners of this narrative are those prevailing in fashionable French circles in 1700, so you must imagine Puss with a great ostrich feather in his hat, and the Marquis of Carabas in a wig down to his waist, and a velvet coat loaded with gold lace and buttons. Puss's boots had high red heels and silver-gilt spurs.

The fairies, the water-spirits, and the loup-garoux, or men-wolves, lingered longer in Brittany than in any other of France, and the forest which was close to the village where Pierre Armand, the miller, lived was more haunted by these airy and fantastic beings than any other place in that ancient duchy.

Once upon a time, the miller, who was a brave, shrewd man, and feared nothing, was carrying some sacks to the market, and as the way to the town through the forest was much nearer than that by the high road, he resolved to go by it, in spite of the remonstrances of his neighbors, who would on no account have penetrated its gloomy depths. But the miller laughed at their fears, and when he found himself sheltered from the midsummer sun under the arching branches of the grand old oaks, he rejoiced greatly that he was not such a coward as to care for shadows.

He had a delightful journey; the ringdoves cooed in the trees, the bees and dragonflies flitted about, and the ground was all enameled with brilliant wild flowers. As he was glancing around in admiration of all this sylvan beauty, he perceived a very large and handsome cat struggling to free itself from a large water snake, which had coiled around its throat and nearly choked it; poor Puss could not even mew for help.

The miller was kind to animals, of course, because he was a brave man, so he rushed forward, seized the snake by the throat, and unwound it, releasing the cat from its coils, and throwing the creature with all his force back into the deep river running through the wood, from which he believed it had emerged.

The cat, thus delivered from its dangerous enemy, came fawning around the feet of the miller, purring and rubbing itself against his boots, so that he could not advance a step for it. Laughing, he tried to put him on one side and said:

"Get out of my path and go home, Puss; you should not be wandering in the wood."

Puss looked up, to his surprise, and replied: "Kind master, I have no home. I thought that I should like to live in this wood, but I find it would not be safe to do so. I have offended the spirits called 'Washerwomen of the Night,' and I believe they sent that snake, from which you so bravely saved me, in order to destroy me."

DOI: 10.4324/9781003297536-2

PEOPLE SAID THAT WOOD WAS HAUNTED

"Then you had better come and live with me," said the miller. "I shall be very glad to have your company at the mill, for the rats and the mice give me a great deal of trouble."

Puss was quite delighted. He ran along by the side of the miller, arching his tail and purring with satisfaction. The miller was about to return by the same road at night, after he had sold his flour, but Puss persuaded him not to do so.

"The water-spirits are very malicious in this country," he said, "and you have offended them by delivering me from their vengeance. It would be very unsafe to traverse the wood after dusk. We had better go home by the road. A short cut often proves in the end longer than a long one."

So, the miller, his ass, and his cat, came home by the high road. When they reached the mill, three boys rushed shouting out to welcome their father home. The miller's wife was dead and those, his sons, lived under the care of a kind old peasant who kept his house for him. The eldest was called Antoine, the next Oliver, the third, Gabriel, and they all began to talk at once when they saw the cat.

"Father, father! What a fine cat! Where did you get it?"

"In the wood, boys. He wishes to live with us. Therefore be kind to him."

"I will," said little Gabriel, the youngest son stroking Puss; "he shall have half my milk for supper."

And so he had; and many another little kindness did Puss receive from Gabriel. The other brothers were not so kind. They would never give the least morsel of anything they had to him, for they were greedy, selfish lads, and cruel also, and, of course, sly; so very often when the miller and Gabriel were both out of the way, they would kick or hunt the cat.

Years passed. The three boys grew into young men; the two elder still selfish and cruel; the youngest generous, kind, and unselfish. People were not surprised that he was his father's favorite, and that the miller was seldom seen unaccompanied by Gabriel and the cat, which never seemed to grow a day older.

At last, the poor miller was taken very ill, and lay at the point of death. Gabriel nursed him with the tenderness and care of a woman, while the elder brothers gave all their attention to getting grist for the mill. The cat shared the youngest son's devoted watch beside the miller's bed, and held long conversations with the miller when they were alone, for Puss never spoke to the boys. One day Puss was missing from his usual post by the sick man's pillow, and he asked his father where the cat had gone.

"My dear son," replied Pierre, "I am dying; it is only right that I make my will. Puss has gone to fetch a notary to draw it up."

The notary returned with the cat shortly afterward; and the miller requested his son to leave him and to send up old Margot and the lad to be the witnesses to his will.

Gabriel was very unhappy, for he dearly loved his father; and while this business was going on he sat by the hearth and wept. He went up to the old chamber in which his father had died and sat down to think, while the autumn wind wailed through the trees, and the poplars bent down and tapped against the lattice, as if to give him speechless tokens of sympathy,

"What shall I do? What will become of me?" said Gabriel talking to himself aloud. "My brothers will live together at the mill, but J shall be homeless. I know Antoine so well; he will let Oliver live in the old place, because he can't do without the ass, but they will not tolerate me living with them. What am I to do with poor Puss? Unless he can find food for himself, he will starve, and if I somehow survive, I shall, perhaps, be obliged to kill him and sell his skin, which I really think I could not do."

There was a slight noise from an old walnut-press close by, and the miller's cat jumped on the table.

"My dear young master," said he, tapping Gabriel's arm affectionately with his paw, "Do not grieve. Our seeming troubles often prove to be blessings in disguise. Only get me a nice pair of boots, and a bag, and you will find that I am no despicable legacy."

Gabriel was mute with amazement when he heard the cat talk. He had at times fancied that he heard voices in his father's room, when the cat alone was with him, but he had fully believed it was a mere delusion, for Puss had requested the miller on their way home (the night of his arrival at the mill), not to tell the children that he (Puss) was more highly gifted than ordinary cats; and the miller, who was naturally prudent and silent, complied.

"What is the meaning of this?" exclaimed Gabriel. "Who and what are you?"

"Your father's old cat, and now yours, master," replied Puss, bowing low.

"But who would have ever thought you were able to talk like a man!" exclaimed the youth.

"Ah!" said the cat. "We are often ignorant of the best qualities of those who live in the same house with us until circumstances develop them, but will you buy me a pair of boots?"

"Yes," replied Gabriel. "I shall do it with this piece of gold which is all the money I possess. It was given me 'for luck' (having a hole in it) by my grandma when I was christened."

"And luck it shall bring you my dear young master!" cried the cat. "Now cease weeping and look hopefully toward the morrow."

Gabriel set off that very evening into the next town and bought a splendid pair of boots for the cat, and a large, handsome leather bag, for he thought there must be something mysterious in that sort of talking animal.

Just as the unfortunate young man expected, his selfish brothers demanded that he leave the mill the very next day, and he had to seek a dwelling-place. He found one in a broken-down, ruined lodge, which stood unoccupied at the entrance to an ogre's park, which was situated in that neighborhood. He had been told terrible stories of his gigantic neighbor; but he was as brave as his father, and thought it was worth some risk to get a shelter for his head. So he and Puss took up their abode on a spot that everybody was afraid to approach. The next day Puss made his appearance before his master in top-boots, and with his bag slung over his shoulder. He was so proud of his boots, that he could not resist showing them before he went out.

"Don't you think," he asked, "that they give me a very military appearance?"

Gabriel laughed, and said jestingly that he thought even the ogre would be afraid to attack him. And so Puss set out on his expedition.

Now he had put some bran and parsley into his bag, and trotting on until he came to a rabbit-warren, he put it down open (retaining, however, the strings of it), and hid himself among the ferns and the bushes. Meanwhile, two fat giddy rabbits fell into the bag.

Puss instantly drew the strings tightly, and then hurried off until he reached the king's palace. Arriving at the gate, he demanded an audience with the sovereign. The attendants were so amazed at hearing a cat talk, that they reported the demand to the king, and the royal curiosity was aroused so greatly by the story of a talking cat, that he at once told them to admit Puss.

PUSS GOES TO COURT

Puss walked through the palace with graceful nonchalance, stroking his moustache, and casting civil glances of contempt on everything around him, until he stood in the royal presence. Then he bowed very low; and on the king's asking from whence he came, and what his business was, he replied: "Please your majesty, my master, the Marquis of Carabas" (this was the title he chose to confer on Gabriel) "sends me with these rabbits as a present to your majesty, with the assurance of his entire devotion."

"Tell my lord marquis," replied the astonished king, "that I am much obliged for his gift; and especially pleased that he should have sent it by such a courteous messenger. Pray may I ask what country produced so accomplished a feline courtier."

"Your majesty is too good! I am a native of Katland; only a poor cat, in fact. But my master is exceedingly *recherché* in his tastes, and since he thinks that footmen have grown vulgar, he has engaged my services instead."

"Indeed! Does he have a household composed of talking cats, then?"

"No, my liege. His servants are all invisible, except myself. He thinks it more elegant to have repose and little show in his dwelling than visible attendants."

"A man of first-rate taste!" exclaimed the king. "Why does he not come to court?"

Puss stroked his moustache.

"Really. Ahem! Your majesty is doomed by your royal state to endure it; and moreover, you are too great to be affected by such contact – but there is such a mixture at courts!"

Now the king of that country, happening to be rather foolish, thought that the Marquis of Carabas must be a very grand person. So, he dismissed Puss with many compliments, and a purse of gold.

The cat went directly to a cook's shop, bought a fricassee for his master's dinner, and some meat for himself, and went home quite joyful.

The next day he went into the ogre's preserves, which were wonderfully well kept, as no one ever dared go into them; and baiting his bag with wheat this time, he contrived to catch two partridges. Then he quickly took them to the palace, where he was admitted once again, and delivered the same message.

The king detained him so he could have a chat, for, as his majesty justly observed, you may talk to a man any day, but a cat is a different thing; indeed, he was quite charmed by Puss and said he did not have so witty and sensible a person in his court like the cat, nor one who made himself so intelligible to him.

One day he sent for his daughter to see the wonderful Puss in Boots. She was a very beautiful lady and was so very kind and amiable to Puss that he was charmed, and purred out his admiration so warmly, that she said she had never met with his equal for intelligence and grace.

"Ah!" said Puss, turning up his eyes, "what would you say then to my good master, the Marquis of Carabas?"

"I wish the worthy noble would come to court," said the king. "Tell him I greatly desire his acquaintance."

The cat went home walking quite proudly, and related his conversation to his master, who shook his head, and said: "What folly, my dear Puss! How can you be so very absurd? And how is it all to end?"

"We shall see," said Puss, stroking his moustache.

Meantime, the courtiers had grown quite jealous of the cat. And there were whispers that he was to be admitted to the king's room when he was dressing in the morning, which was, I assure you, a great honor. The king *did* tie a piece of red ribbon around his neck with his own hands; and everybody talked of the good fortune of Puss in Boots.

And the courtiers tried to win his favor by giving him presents, on which the miller's son and he lived quite comfortably. One day, the cat heard the king tell his daughter that he would take her for a long drive by the river's side the next day. And then he asked Puss (in strict confidence) if he thought it would be nice driving inside the ogre's park-gates.

Now Puss was certain that the courtiers had tracked him there, and that the king was coming to discover where the Marquis of Carabas lived, and in what style. So he ran home, and said to his master: "If you will take my advice, your fortune is certainly made. Go and bathe in the river, at the place I will show you, and leave the rest to me."

The "marquis" did as he was told; and as soon as he was in the stream, the cunning cat took away his clothes, and hid them under a large stone.

While the young man was bathing, the royal carriage and attendants came in sight. As soon as he saw the procession, Puss began to utter a succession of the most alarming cries:

"Help, help! Or my lord Marquis of Carabas will be drowned!"

The king looked out of the carriage window and saw his favorite, the cat, and immediately called for two of his attendants to go to his assistance.

The young man was pulled out of the water and asked if he had his clothes. Then the cunning Puss in Boots ran here and there and everywhere to find them, and pretending not to be able to find them, he cried out that they were certainly stolen, and that his master would catch his death of cold.

Then the king said that by a lucky accident a dress suit of his was in the carriage. The attendants wondered how the clothes managed to be there! (I dare say Puss could have told them.) And he begged the Marquis of Carabas to honor him by putting on the dress suit.

So the "marquis" was dressed in the king's clothes, and looked exceedingly handsome in them; and the king, pleased with his frank, good looks, insisted that Gabriel join them in the carriage and take a drive with the princess and himself.

The cat, enchanted at the success of his cunning trick, ran hastily on before them, and coming to a large field, in which reapers were at work, he told them that if they did not tell the king (should he ask) that those fields belonged to the Marquis of Carabas, they would be chopped up as small as mincemeat.

The poor peasants were dreadfully terrified by the fierce looks of the cat and so amazed at hearing him talk, and seeing him walk in boots, that they dared not even think of refusing. So, when the king, looking out over the rich wheat-fields, asked, "Whose noble harvest is this?" they replied, "It belongs to our lord the Marquis of Carabas."

In the meantime the cat ran on, and came to some verdant pastures covered with flocks of sheep; and he said to the shepherds: "If the king asks you, by-and-by, who owns these pastures, you are to say they belong to the Marquis of Carabas, or you will be cut up as small as mincemeat."

These shepherds, also, were so terrified by the singular apparition in boots that they said they would be sure to obey his commands. And so, when the king leaned from his window and asked the peasants: "Who owns these fair pastures and herds of sheep?" they replied "Our lord Marquis of Carabas."

By-and-by the cat came to the gamekeepers' and woodmen's lodges, and he said: "If the king asks you whose broad lands these are you must say they belong to the Marquis of Carabas, or you will be chopped up as small as mincemeat."

When the king beheld the wide forest glades and the deer bounding by, he looked out of the window, and asked: "To whom do these fair lands belong?"

And the woodsmen answered: "To our lord Marquis of Carabas."

And, the king smiled and said to the young man, "Monsieur le Marquis, you have a fair estate. Let us drive through these charming arcades. Just imagine the blunders people make. I had always understood that these extensive domains belonged to an ogre. The idea of calling you by such a name!"

And the marquis cast his eyes down modestly, and replied:

"There is no knowing what people say of one!"

The cat had run on with the speed of the wind in the meanwhile, and had reached a magnificent castle, which he knew was the abode of the cruel ogre, who ate children. However, as he had not heard that the gigantic potentate indulged in eating cats also, he boldly rang the bell.

The door was opened by the ogre himself, who, seeing a little person in boots coming up to the castle, and not being able to make out who it was, thought it must be some nice little boy who would make a delightful supper. So he went to the door himself, and behold, instead of a young boy, he found Puss in Boots.

"Do you call yourself a cat?" growled the ogre in a rage – not that he expected an answer to his question.

"No! I am Puss in Boots," said the cat, with dignity. "Prime minister to the Marquis of Carabas, and favorite Ordinary to the King of the Cannibal Islands!"

"Oh!" said the ogre, much impressed. "Your king ought to be a friend of mine! What do you want?"

"To make your acquaintance, most magnificent ogre," said the cat, who saw that the ogre was stupid. Therefore, he used all the longest words he knew. "To make your acquaintance, and to enjoy the felicity of a little ratiocination with you!"

Now the ogre could not understand these long words, so he looked very wise, and said:

"Come in."

He thought that was the safest answer. And Puss entered the castle, which was a most magnificent place, full of costly furniture and great treasures.

"Is it true, may I presume to inquire," asked the cat, bowing down to the ground. "May I presume to ask, can your wonderful ogreship turn into any kind of very large animal that you desire?"

"I can, Oh cat," replied the ogre, for Puss quite tamed him by such lofty courtesy: "I certainly can. Would you like to see me do so?"

"Oh! really," purred the cat, "you are too good. I should be delighted, if not enchanted."

All of a sudden, an elephant stood in the ogre's place, and Puss uttered a cry of amazement.

"Most wonderful!" he said; "the world has no second ogre like your lordship."

"That's nothing," said the ogre; and suddenly the elephant turned into a lion, and Puss was really very much alarmed. He climbed up to the rafters of the hall, and would not come down until the ogre had assumed his original shape.

"I must say," observed Puss, recovering himself, "that all which report says of your great powers, most gracious ogre, is true! But I suppose you cannot (being of such very noble proportions yourself) change yourself into a small animal like a dog or a rat?"

"You shall see," replied the ogre, greatly flattered by Puss's admiration, "you shall see!"

And then he became a dog, and flew at the cat, and Puss scratched his face; whereby the ogre turned into a rat and then into a mouse, and the moment Puss in Boots saw him capering in the latter form on the floor, he made a dart at him and killed him right away.

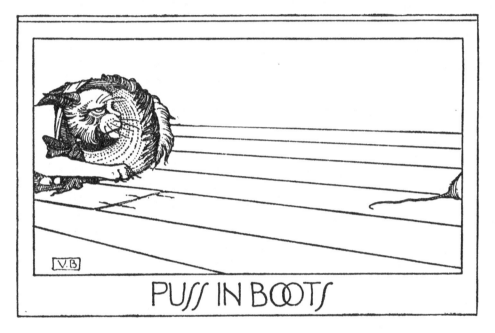

PUSS IN BOOTS

Now the ogre lived in a house all by himself, for no one liked to hire to him as a servant, for fear someday he might grow hungry and eat everyone up. So, Puss's old stories of invisible servants did not run the risk of being contradicted.

Puss now perceived from the hall window the king's carriage driving by, and so he ran out and cried: "My lord, Marquis of Carabas, won't you ask his majesty to enter and take a little refreshment?"

"You presume," said his master, with a frown. "Such an honor is too great for a humble person like myself."

"Nay, my lord," said the king, laughing, "We like the rough loyalty of your servant, and will not disappoint the honest fellow." So he ordered the carriage to be driven up to the castle door, and they all entered.

And there on the hall table was spread out the ogre's every day luncheon – not a feast of stewed babies, luckily, but a boar's head, and a turkey, and a chine, and a goose, and four fowls, and two tongues, and a haunch of venison, and a baron of beef, not to speak of jellies and tarts and custards, and all kinds of sweets, all of which the ogre used to consume daily.

"Your majesty will excuse our having next to nothing," said Puss, bowing profoundly. "This was just a trifle for my lord Marquis of Carabas alone."

"Oh," cried the king, "what magnificent housekeeping!"

And they sat down to the meal; and the king ate and drank, and, as his journey had made him hungry, he declared that he had never met with such a good cook as the invisible chef de cuisine of the Marquis of Carabas.

In an hour or two they had finished luncheon, and the king expressed a wish to see the castle. Puss was in readiness, and if you had seen him exhibiting the wonders and riches of that abode to the king, you would have thought that he had lived in it all his life and knew all its contents by heart.

The king went home greatly impressed by the wealth and charming appearance of his neighbor, and resolved to make him his son-in-law. And Puss and Gabriel remained masters of the ogre's lordly castle.

Gabriel then asked Puss to tell him all that he had done and to explain what all this trickery meant, and he could not help laughing as he listened.

"You have been a very clever contriver, Puss, and I suppose are honest enough for a cat! But I don't want to keep this castle and estate, which don't belong to me, but to the ogre's relations."

"His relations!" said Puss arching his back angrily. "He had none; he ate them all up a long time ago. And if it isn't yours, it will go to the chief of Chanceryland, and then who will be the better for it? It will all go to decay and ruin, and the peasants will starve. No, no! The castle is yours; I won it by my prowess, and I give it to you."

Gabriel was at last induced to accept it, and became a very rich man. Then he sent for his brothers and repaid their unkindness by great generosity and a noble forgiveness.

Gradually, the king, who came frequently to the castle, made proposals of marriage for the princess to Gabriel.

Now, the young man loved the lady very much, for she was sweet and gentle and kind, and Puss adored her. But he felt he ought to tell the king the truth because, as he said to Puss, "It did not become a gentleman to tell or to act a falsehood."

So, when his sovereign mentioned the subject of marrying with his daughter to him, Gabriel answered:

"My liege, I am not a fit match for a great princess. I was once a very poor man and a miller."

The king thought he must be mad and begged him to explain himself; and then Gabriel told him the whole story just as I have told it to you, and the king laughed until he felt quite exhausted.

"But," said he, when he could speak again, "this castle and all these noble domains are really yours, are they not?"

"They are, sire, thanks to Puss in Boots."

"He ought to educate all my diplomats," laughed the king. "Well, Gabriel, your honesty and truth show me that you are a real gentleman of Nature's making, and

I will still give you my daughter, and we need say nothing about the past. I anoint you Marquis of Carabas from this day onward, and your arms shall be a cat in boots *passant gardant*, just like the heralds say. As to your cat, I shall make him my prime minister."

So the Marquis of Carabas married the princess, and lived as happily as is possible; and the cat was made prime minister with the title of Baron Katz, and it was generally agreed that no kingdom was better governed than the one ruled by the wisdom of Puss in Boots.

Fortunatus and the Wishing Cap

Laura Valentine

This tale is a very old Eastern Tale, told to please the Court of Louis XIV. Poor Scotch Lords, such as the Noble Loch Fitty, seem to have been pensioners of the French Court since the earliest times. There were certainly several of them attendant on the exiled Stuarts in Louis XIV's reign, one of whom probably sat for the portrait of Loch Fitty in this tale. I may add that the title of Lord Loch Fitty is now extinct.

In the city of Famagosta, on the island of Cyprus, there lived a gentleman possessed of immense riches. His name was Theodorus. Well, he married the most beautiful lady in Cyprus, and she was as rich as Theodorus himself. She was called Graciana. They thought themselves extremely happy in being able to keep the finest house and gardens imaginable, and in entertaining their friends not only with the most delicate repasts, but with diversions of every kind. Aside from all this, they rode out on the most stately horses ever beheld which were covered with the richest housings; they had pleasure-boats painted with the finest colors to take them on the water when the weather was not too hot; and had besides all sorts of musical instruments.

In addition to all this, they possessed a fine little son, so that one would think nothing could have prevented Theodorus and the lady Graciana from being the happiest and most content people in all the world.

This, however, was not long the case. The lady Graciana, it is true, was as content as could be; but Theodorus, when he had enjoyed all those gratifications for some time, grew tired of them. Not even the smiles of the cute little Fortunatus – for he was christened by that name – could prevent him from thinking he should find more pleasure in the most cheerful society of Famagosta.

Theodorus accordingly became acquainted with some young noblemen of the court with whom he sat up all night drinking and playing cards, and in a few years spent his whole fortune so that he was obliged to send away his servants, and finally he no longer had the means of providing his family with even a loaf of bread.

He was now very sorry for what he had done; but it was too late, and there was no remedy for his foolish conduct but to work at some trade to support his wife and child.

In spite of all this, the lady Graciana never said an unkind word to him but continued to love her husband as before. At one point, she said, "Dear Theodorus, I do not know, it is true how to work at any trade, but, if I cannot help you in acquiring money, I shall help you to save it. Indeed, for I shall clean the house, and make the bread and wash our clothes, all with my own hands. Though they've not been used to

DOI: 10.4324/9781003297536-3

such hard work, they will soon be able to bear it, if you will but love your Graciana and your Fortunatus."

So, Theodorus set to work, and the lady Graciana, who had always been accustomed to call for everything she wanted, now scoured the kettles and washed the clothes with her own hands.

They went on in this manner for several years, until Fortunatus was sixteen years of age. One day, when they were all seated at dinner, Theodorus fixed his eyes very sorrowfully on his son and sighed deeply.

"What ails you, my father?" said Fortunatus.

"Ah! My boy," replied Theodorus, "I have reason enough to be sorrowful when I think of the noble fortune I have squandered, and that my folly will be the means of obliging you to work as I do for subsistence."

"Father," replied Fortunatus, "never grieve about it. I have often thought that it is time I should do something for myself, and, though I have not been brought up to practice any kind of trade, yet I trust I can learn how to gain a subsistence in some way or other."

When Fortunatus had finished his dinner, he took his hat and wandered to the seaside, determined to think over what steps he could pursue, so as to be no longer a burden to his father and mother.

It happened that just as he had reached the seashore, the Earl of Flanders, who had been to Jerusalem, and on his return had touched at Cyprus, was embarking with all his retinue, about to set sail for Flanders. Fortunatus instantly thought of offering himself as his page. The earl, seeing he was a very smart-looking lad, and hearing the quick replies he made to the questions he asked him, was very willing to engage him. So, without delay, he went on board.

On their way the ship touched at Veruce, where Fortunatus had an opportunity of seeing many new and surprising things which both helped to raise his desire of traveling, and to improve his understanding.

Soon after they arrived in Flanders and had not been long on shore, the earl his master was married to the daughter of the Duke of Cleves: and the ceremony was accompanied by all sorts of public rejoicings, tilts, tournaments, and entertainments, which lasted several days: Among the events, the earl's bride gave two jewels as prizes to be tilted for, each at the value of one hundred crowns.

One of the tilts was won by Fortunatus, and the other by Timothy, an attendant serving the Duke of Burgundy; who afterward challenged Fortunatus to run another tilt with him, so that he who won would have both the jewels. Accordingly, they tilted: and at the fourth course, Fortunatus lifted Timothy a full spear's length from his horse, and thus won both the jewels; which pleased the earl and countess so much that they praised Fortunatus, and held him in greater esteem than ever.

Upon this occasion, also, Fortunatus received many rich presents from the nobility who were present; but the high favor he enjoyed made his fellow-servants jealous; and one among them, whose name was Robert, who had always pretended a great friendship for Fortunatus, persuaded him that, notwithstanding all the earl's kindness, he in secret envied Fortunatus. So, he lied and assured Fortunatus that he had heard the earl give private orders to one of his servants to find some means of killing him the next day, while they would be out hunting.

Fortunatus thanked the treacherous Robert for what he thought was a great kindness, and the next day at daybreak he took the swiftest horse in the earl's stables and left his dominions.

Upon hearing that Fortunatus had suddenly left his dominions, the earl was very surprised and questioned all his servants about what they knew about the affair; but they all denied knowing anything about it, or for what reasons Fortunatus had departed. Then the earl declared that he was a lad for whom he had a great esteem; and that some of them must have offended him, and that, whenever he discovered the truth, he would not fail to punish the people involved in a severe way.

In the meantime, Fortunatus had traveled beyond the earl's dominions and stopped at an inn for some refreshment. It was there that he began to consider what he was worth; and having taken out all his fine clothes and jewels to look at, he could not help putting them on and looking at himself in a mirror. After he admired his own appearance, he took out his purse and counted the money that had been given him by the lords and ladies at the tournament.

Finding that he was worth five hundred crowns in all, he bought a horse, taking care to send back that which he had taken from his master's stables. He then set off for Calais; crossed the Channel, landed safely at Dover, and proceeded to London, where he soon introduced himself into good society. However, his sort of life, as it may well be supposed, soon exhausted his little stock of money.

When Fortunatus found himself penniless, he began to think of returning to France, and soon afterward, he embarked on a ship bound for Picardy. Here he landed; but since he did not find a means to employ himself, he set off for Brittany. However, when he was crossing a forest, he lost his way and was obliged to stay in the forest the entire night.

The next morning he was but little better off than before. He couldn't find a path. So, he wandered about from one part of the forest to the other until evening arrived. Fortunately, he happened to find a spring where he drank very heartily; but still he had nothing to eat and was about to die of hunger,

When night finally arrived, and he heard the growling of the beasts, he climbed up a high tree for safety. No sooner did he seat himself on some branches than some wolves came to the spring to drink, and he was very frightened. Once the wolves disappeared, a bear came to drink also; and as the moon shone brightly, the bear looked up and saw Fortunatus and immediately began to climb up the tree to get him.

However, Fortunatus drew his sword, and sat quietly until the bear came within an arm's length. Then he pierced his body with the sword several times. This made the bear so furious that he made a great effort to grab Fortunatus. But the bough broke and down he fell, sprawling and yelling on the ground.

Fortunatus looked around on all sides, and seeing no more wild beasts, he thought this would be an excellent opportunity to get rid of the bear once and for all. So down he came and killed him at a single blow. Then since he was famished and needed some food, he stooped down and was going to suck the blood out of the bear, when he looked around once more to see if any wild beast was coming. To his amazement he caught sight of a beautiful lady standing by his side, with a bandage over her eyes, leaning upon a wheel, and looking as if she intended to speak.

Well, the lady did not make him wait long before she pronounced the following words: "Know, young man, that my name is Fortune. I have the power to bestow on mortals wisdom, strength, riches, health, beauty, and long life. One of these I am willing to bestow on you. Choose for yourself which it shall be."

Fortunatus did not take much time before he answered: "Gracious lady, I prefer to have riches in such abundance that I may never again know what it is to be so very hungry as I now find myself."

The lady then presented him with a purse, telling him that in whatever country he might happen to be, he had only to put his hand into the purse as often as he pleased, and he would be sure to find in it ten pieces of gold. The purse would never fail to produce the like sum as long as it remained in his possession and his children; but that when he and his children were dead, the purse would lose this extraordinary quality.

Fortunatus was wild with joy and began to thank the lady very eagerly, but she told him he had better think of taking the best way out of the forest and accordingly set him on the right path to take and then bade him farewell.

He walked by the light of the moon as fast as his weak condition would allow until he came near an inn. Before he went inside, however, he thought it would be prudent to see if the Lady Fortune had been as good as her word. So, he put his hand into his purse, and to his great joy, he counted ten pieces of gold.

Having nothing to fear, therefore, Fortunatus walked boldly into the inn and called for the best supper they could get ready in a minute: "I must wait until tomorrow," he said, "before I eat a nice meal. Given my present appetite, anything will do."

Fortunatus very soon satisfied his hunger and called for every sort of wine the house provided, and after supper he began to think what sort of life he should now lead. "For," he thought, "I shall now have money enough for everything I can desire."

He slept that night on the very best bed in the house; and the next day ordered the most sumptuous meals of every kind. If he rang his bell, all the waiters tried to see who could run fastest to inquire what he wanted, and the landlord himself, hearing what a princely guest had come to his house, took care to be standing at the door to bow to him whenever he left the inn.

Fortunatus inquired of the landlord if any fine horses were to be found in the neighborhood. Also, if he knew of some smart-looking, clever men-servants who wanted work. To his great liking the landlord fortunately was able to provide him with both.

After he had been furnished with everything he wanted, Fortunatus set out on the handsomest horse ever seen, attended by two servants. He headed for the nearest town where he bought some magnificent suits of clothes, put his two servants in liveries laced with gold, and then proceeded to Paris.

Once there he took the finest house that was to be had and lived in great splendor. He entertained the nobility, and gave the finest balls for all the most beautiful ladies of the court. He went to all public places of entertainment, and the first lords in the country constantly invited him to their houses.

Fortunatus had lived in this manner for about a year when he began to think of returning to Famagosta and to visit his parents, whom he had left in a very poor condition: "But," he thought, "Since I am young and inexperienced, I should like to meet with some person with more knowledge than I have. It would make my journey both useful and pleasing to me."

He hadn't wished for this very long before he encountered a venerable old gentleman called Loch Fitty, who was, he learned, a native of Scotland, and had left a wife and ten children a great many years ago in hopes to better his fortune. However, he was now poorer than ever due to different accidents and didn't have money enough even to take him back to his family.

After finding how much Fortunatus desired to obtain knowledge, Loch Fitty told him many of the strange adventures he had experienced and gave him an account of all the kingdoms he had visited, as well as of the customs, dress, and manners of the inhabitants.

Fortunatus thought to himself: "This is the very man I need." Therefore he made him a very generous proposal, which the old gentleman accepted on condition that he should be first permitted to go and visit his family.

Fortunatus assured him he did not have the least objection. "And," added he, "since I am a little tired of being always in the midst of such noisy pleasures as one finds at Paris, I shall, with your leave, go with you to Scotland and see your wife and children."

They set out the very next day and arrived at the house of Loch Fitty. Along the way Fortunatus did not think once about changing his opinion of his kind companion and returning to the splendid entertainments he had left behind him.

Loch Fitty embraced his wife and children, five of whom were daughters, and the most beautiful creatures he had ever beheld. When they had taken some refreshment, his wife said to him: "Ah, dear Lord Loch Fitty, how happy I am to see you once again! Now I trust we shall be together for the rest our lives! What does it matter if we are poor? We will be content if you will promise not to think again of leaving us and searching for money and wealth. We are happy with the little we have."

Fortunatus listened with great surprise and exclaimed: "If you are a nobleman, then you should be a rich nobleman as well. And so that you may not think you owe me any obligation for the fortune that I am about to give you, I shall put it in your power to make me your debtor. So, I would like you to bestow on me your youngest daughter, Cassandra; and let us have the pleasure of your company as far as Famagosta. Also take your whole family with you so that you may have pleasant companionship on your way back, when you have rested in that place from your fatigue."

Lord Loch Fitty shed tears of joy, to think he should at last see his family restored to all the honors it had once enjoyed. After accepting Fortunatus as a husband for his daughter Cassandra, he related to him the misfortunes that obliged him to live in poverty in Paris and to call himself by the plain name of Loch Fitty.

When Lord Loch Fitty had ended his story, they agreed that the Lady Cassandra should be asked to accept the hand of Fortunatus the very next morning and that, should she consent, they would embark in a few days for Famagosta.

The next morning the proposal was made, as was agreed on, and Fortunatus had the pleasure of hearing from the lips of the beautiful Cassandra that the very first time she cast her eyes on him, she thought him the most handsome and accomplished gentleman in all the world.

Everything was soon ready for their departure. Fortunatus, Lord Loch Fitty, his lady, and their ten children embarked in a large commodious ship. They had prosperous winds and soon landed happily in the port of Famagosta. Then they spent a few days making the necessary preparations, and the marriage was then celebrated with all the magnificence and rejoicing imaginable.

Since Fortunatus, on his arrival, found that his parents were both dead, he asked Lord Loch Fitty if he would be kind enough to allow him to remain with him and his wife. So, now they all lived together in the finest manor that was to be found in the city of Famago, where they held the most splendid entertainments.

By the end of the first year the Lady Cassandra had a little son, who was christened Ampedo; and the year following a boy who was christened Andolocia.

For twelve years Fortunatus lived the happiest life imaginable with his wife and children and his wife's relatives, and each of her sisters received a fortune from the bountiful purse of Fortunatus. Soon after they married to great advantage; but by this time his taste for traveling returned, and he thought, as he was now so much older and wiser than when he was in Paris, that he didn't want a companion, for Lord Loch Fitty was at this time too old to deal with fatigue.

After great difficulty in obtaining the consent of the Lady Cassandra, who, at last, insisted on his staying away only two years, he prepared everything for his departure, and taking his wife into one of his private rooms, he showed her three chests of gold, one of which he asked her to keep for herself, and to take charge of the other two for their sons in case he had an accident. He then led her back to the apartment where the whole family was sitting. After tenderly embracing them all one by one, he set sail with a fair wind for Alexandria.

Fortunatus, being told, on his arrival in this place, that it was customary to make a handsome present to the sultan, sent him a piece of plate that cost five thousand ducats. The sultan was so extremely pleased that he ordered a hundred casks of spices to be given to Fortunatus in return. Then Fortunatus sent them immediately to the Lady Cassandra with the tenderest letters imaginable by the very ship that brought him to Alexandria and was soon to go back to Famagosta.

Fortunatus took an early opportunity of telling the sultan he wished to travel through his dominions by land. So, the sultan immediately procured such passports and letters of recommendation that he might stand in need of foreign dominions. Then, Fortunatus purchased a camel, hired proper attendants, and set off on his travels.

He went through Turkey, Persia, and then Carthage. After that he proceeded to the country of Prester John, who rides on a white elephant and has kings to wait on him. Fortunatus gave him some rich presents, and went on to Calcutta; and, returning, took in Jerusalem on his way back to Alexandria, where he had the good fortune in finding the same ship which had brought him, and to learn from the captain of the ship that that his wife and family were all in perfect health.

The first thing he did in Alexandria was to pay a visit to his old friend the sultan. Once again gave a handsome present and was soon invited to dine at his palace.

After the repast, the sultan said: "It must be very amusing, Fortunatus, to hear an account of the different places you have seen. Please, favor me with a history of your travels."

Fortunatus did as he was asked and pleased the sultan extremely by relating the many curious adventures he had experienced, particularly the way he had made the acquaintance with Lord Loch Fitty, and the desire of that nobleman to maintain the honors of his ancestors.

When he had finished, the sultan said that he was very delighted by what he had heard; and added that he possessed a greater marvelous object than anything Fortunatus had told him about, and he immediately led him into a room nearly filled with jewels. Then he opened a large closet, and taking out a cap, told Fortunatus that it was of greater value than all the rest.

Fortunatus imagined the sultan was jesting and told him he had seen many a better cap than that.

"Ah," said the sultan, "that is because you do not know its value. Whoever puts this cap on his head, and wishes himself in any part of the world, he will be instantly conveyed there."

"Indeed!" said Fortunatus; "Please tell me whether the man who made it is still living."

"That I know nothing about," said the sultan.

"Really, one would scarcely have believed it," Fortunatus remarked. "Please, sir, tell me, is it very heavy?"

"Not at all," replied the sultan. "You may feel it."

Fortunatus picked up the cap, put it on his head, and could not help wishing himself on board the ship that was going back to Famagosta.

In less than a minute he was carried through the winds on board the ship, just as it was ready to set sail. And there being a brisk gale, they were out of sight in less than half an hour.

FORTUNATUƒ & THE WIƒHING CAP

The ship arrived in safety at Famagosta after an easy passage, and Fortunatus had the satisfaction to find his wife and children well. However, Lord Loch Fitty and his lady had died of old age, and were buried side by side.

Fortunatus now started to take great pleasure in educating his two boys; and taught them all sorts of manly exercises such as wrestling, tilts, and tournaments. Now and then he recollected the wonderful cap he had in his possession, and at such times would wish he could just take a peep at what was happening in different countries. Though his wish was always granted, he always contented himself with staying only an hour or two, and the Lady Cassandra never found him missing and had no further uneasiness about his love of traveling.

At last, Fortunatus began to get old, and the Lady Cassandra fell sick and died. Her loss caused him so much grief, that he soon fell sick. Believing that he did not have long to live, he called his two sons to his bedside, and told them the secret of the purse and cap, which he wished them not to disclose to anyone: "Follow my example," said Fortunatus. "I have had the purse some forty years, and no living creature knew how I obtained my riches."

He then recommended that they make use of the purse between themselves and to live together in harmony. Soon after he said all this, he died.

Fortunatus was buried in great pomp by the side of the Lady Cassandra, in his own chapel, and was for a long time mourned by the people of Famagosta. It was not long after the death of Fortunatus, that Andolocia went to his brother Ampedo, who, being the eldest, had the purse in his possession, and asked his brother whether he would let him have it for a certain time since he wished to set out on his travels for distant countries. To this Ampedo would by no means consent, and they came to hostile words concerning it. After some time had passed, however, Ampedo consented to let his brother have the purse for six years; and accordingly, after filling all his coffers, he put it into his hands with an agreement, however, that he was afterward to keep it for as long a time himself.

Since Andolocia possessed his father's love of traveling to distant countries, he was overjoyed to think he had obtained the purse and immediately began his preparations for setting out. The first place he visited was Paris.

In this place there was a famous wrestler called Strongfist, who had never yet been defeated by any man. Andolocia sent him a challenge, which Strongfist willingly accepted, and a day was appointed for the fight. In the meanwhile the news reached all the inhabitants of Paris who accordingly resolved to watch the match. The combatants met at the time and place appointed, and they began wrestling with great spirit. But it was soon apparent that Strongfist was not half as skillful as Andolocia, who after a few blows, made Strongfist cry out he would fight no longer.

No sooner, however, had Strongfist recovered from the blow he had received, than he became enraged to think he had been conquered by a stranger and had lost his reputation. So, he sent Andolocia another challenge; and they accordingly met as before. But Strongfist gained nothing in this second attempt; for Andolocia made him once more cry out "he was satisfied" so that the air resounded with the acclamations bestowed on Andolocia, while Strongfist was so maimed he could never after engage in wrestling.

After staying some time longer in Paris, where he was bestowed with every mark of distinction, the news of his great skill reached England, and he was invited by the king to the court of London. This was just the time that England was going to war with the King of Scotland, and he wished to have Andolocia's advice about how to conduct his army.

Andolocia accepted the proposal with joy; for it was the King of Scotland's father who had deprived his grandfather, the Lord Loch Fitty, of all his fortune and caused him to leave his wife and his home and live in poverty in Paris.

He lost no time in preparing for the journey, and reached London in safety, where he was received with the greatest kindness by the king and the whole court. Immediately, Andolocia informed his majesty of the ill-will he owed the King of Scotland. Indeed, they immediately agreed that Andolocia should head an army of the choicest troops in the English dominions and march against him.

They accordingly set out for Scotland, had a furious battle with the king, and defeated him and his whole army. Upon returning to London, Andolocia was awarded with the highest honors at the court of the King of England.

Thereafter, Andolocia took a magnificent house in the finest square in London, and frequently entertained the king and all his nobles, whom he treated in so sumptuous a manner that the king could not help wondering how a private gentleman could possibly have so much wealth.

One day Andolocia was at court, and he happened to see the king's daughter, Agrippina, with whom he fell passionately in love and made her such costly presents that surprised the king more than ever before, so that he could not help telling the queen he couldn't imagine how Andolocia had come by such a fortune.

The queen immediately began to try to discover his secret, and therefore, she told her daughter Agrippina, to help her find out if possible when she was alone with him what the secret of Andolocia's wealth was.

Soon after when Andolocia was sitting by the princess, he told her how very beautiful he thought she was and how much he wished for the honor of making her his wife. The princess thought this a very good opportunity for finding out the secret of his wealth, so she answered that she liked him very much but supposed he could not possibly have sufficient funds to maintain the daughter of a king.

Upon hearing this, Andolocia pulled out his purse and threw ten pieces of gold at a time into her lap; and after a while, he told her how his father had managed to possess this purse and every particular concerning it.

The Princess Agrippina hastened to tell the queen all she had heard, and pretending to be very fond of Andolocia, the queen took him into her chambers and presented him with a glass of the richest cordial, into which she had put a drug that soon threw him into a sound sleep. Then the queen put her hand into his pocket, took the purse, and had him immediately conveyed to his own house fast asleep.

Then the queen gave the purse to the young princess, saying that she had taken it for her sake and that it was but right that it should be in her possession.

When Andolocia awoke and found that the purse was missing, he became frantic. Indeed, he ran about the house for a long time, not knowing what to do. At last, he thought of what had happened to him at the palace, where he immediately went and asked to speak with the queen, but was told she could not be seen. He then inquired for the princess and obtained the same answer. All this convinced Andolocia that the queen had taken his purse and did not intend to return it. The first thing he did was to borrow a hundred crowns from his steward by means of which he got to Famagosta as fast as he could. Then with great difficulty, he prevailed on his brother to lend him the cap for a short time so that he might transport himself in a moment wherever he pleased.

Having obtained it, he put it on and instantly wished himself to be in Princess Agrippina's chamber, whom he intended to consult about getting back his purse from the queen. But no astonishment could be greater than his, when, looking at the princess, he saw his purse fastened to her girdle.

Once he perceived this, Andolocia asked the princess to restore it. However, she refused, and so he clasped her in his arms and wished himself to be in an orchard full of fruit trees in the neighborhood of Constantinople.

His wish was instantly accomplished, and they found themselves sitting under a large fig-tree; when the princess, seeing what fine figs there were on it, persuaded him to get her one to eat. Since Andolocia still loved Agrippina very much, notwithstanding she had used him so unkindly, he immediately threw his cap on the ground and began to climb the tree.

The princess, quite ignorant of the virtue in the cap, and feeling greatly fatigued with the scorching sun bearing down on her, wished she was in her cold bath of her father's palace. All at once she soared up into the air and was out of sight in a minute.

When Andolocia looked around and saw that both the princess and his cap were gone, his anger was so great that he didn't know what step to take. Yet, after walking about some time, and feeling thirsty, he began to eat some apples, when two large horns sprang directly out of his forehead.

He now ran like a madman all around the orchard, and his cries were heard by an aged hermit, who came up to him and inquired what the matter was. After Andolocia related the manner in which the accident had happened, the hermit assured him that, if he would eat some apples from another tree, he would soon find his horns would disappear.

Andolocia lost no time in doing as he was advised, and the horns immediately disappeared. Now that he was relaxed, he decided to fill his pockets with some of both sorts of these extraordinary apples. Then he set out on foot for the palace of Princess Agrippina's father, where he stood at the gate disguised as a poor man who had the finest apples to sell that ever were seen in England.

Just at this time, the princess left the palace and walked about. When she observed the apples, and saw that they were as fine as those she had seen in the orchard near Constantinople, she began to buy them with great eagerness. Then she returned to the palace where she began eating them.

Immediately two great horns sprang from her forehead and caused the princess to scream so loudly as to alarm everyone in the palace; and the king, among the rest, came running to her assistance. Upon seeing what had happened, he called in all the physicians to see if a cure were possible. However, not one doctor could be found who understood her case.

Finally, Andolocia disguised himself as a physician with a great false nose, went to the palace, and offered his services, which were willingly accepted.

Once he was shown into her room, he perceived his cap lying disregarded on a chair. So, pretending he must speak with his patient in private, he sent the nurse out of the room, and in the meanwhile found an opportunity to put the cap into his pocket.

Andolocia then produced some of the apples that were a cure for the horns that were produced by those he had sold her. He cut them very small and told her to eat them. Then the horns immediately began to grow less from that moment on.

The princess was so delighted by this that she thought she could not too handsomely reward her physician. However, as soon as she took out her purse, he snatched it from her, clapped on his cap, and wished himself to be at Famagosta, where he immediately landed. But since he was still in love with the princess, he took care not to give her enough of the apples to remove the horns entirely so that no other man might fall in love with her.

After relating his adventures to his brother Ampedo, the latter said he had no inclination to have either the cap or purse because they brought their possessor into so much danger. Therefore, he wanted to give them wholly to Andolocia, provided he consented to pay him a handsome allowance as long as he lived.

Thus, Andolocia kept the purse and cap for himself. Yet, though he had such immense treasures and power of conveying himself wherever he pleased in a moment, he was not quite happy.

Convinced that nothing but Agrippa could make him happy, he first set about building a magnificent palace, taking care every now and then to put on his cap to wish himself at the court of London where he sometimes had the good fortune to see the princess as she took an airing in her carriage, and found means to know if the horns still remained on her head as before.

When the palace was finished, Andolocia equipped himself with all the splendor imaginable; and taking with him some of the handsomest gentlemen of Famagosta, who looked like great lords, and in addition the most costly jewels that were to be offered as presents for the princess, he set out for England to demand her formally in marriage.

The King of England received him very courteously, while the queen, supposing it impossible that any prince would offer to marry a princess with horns on her head, and perceiving there was no other way of getting the purse, she gave her consent as well. Finally, the Princess Agrippina, who had always wished to wed him, said she really loved the prince, but that she would never bring such a great misfortune on him as to be his wife while she had horns on her head.

"Dear Princess Agrippina," replied Andolocia, "then all our wishes will be gratified, for I have the power to make them disappear immediately."

Saying this, he left the room, and returned in a few minutes with some of the apples he had given her once before, and which he had taken care to keep. When presenting them to the princess, he asked her if she did not remember the physician with the great nose, who some time before had made her horns grow less.

The princess at once began eating the apples given to her by Andolocia, and the horns immediately disappeared. All at once, she embraced Andolocia with tenderness, and they were married that very day, and shortly after were conducted in the greatest pomp to the palace built for her reception at Famagosta, where they lived a long and a happy life.

Andolocia kept his cap and purse in a cabinet set apart so that nobody could find them, and so that there would not be further trouble. Indeed, he never allowed the key to the closet to be touched by anyone but himself.

The Round Castle of the Red Sea

Charles Marius Barbeau

This story came originally from France. Many years ago, it went to French Canada, years before the United States of America or the Dominion of Canada were ever imagined. Father told it to son, and son to his son for generations, and at last somebody told it to Mr. Marius Barbeau, who wrote it down in French in the Journal of American Folk-Lore. *Mr. Barbeau allowed Mr. Gregory MacDonald to translate it into English and gave me permission to put it into this book. I don't think it has ever been read before by English-speaking children in English. I have had to add a few words here and there because the man who first told it was short in his speech.*

Once upon a time, I may as well tell you, there lived in these parts, a king with his wife, and their only child, who was a little boy. One day the king said to his wife: "I think I'll go now to visit my gardens in the forest. Will you come too?"

"Why, yes," answered the queen.

"Let's go in our carriage."

As they were driving along the forest road, what should they see but a little white napkin lying in their way, and no sooner had they seen it than the king said to the queen, "I'm going to get out of our carriage, and I'm going to pick up that little white napkin."

"My dear husband," said the queen, "you are going to do nothing of the sort. It is not right to pick up whatever one finds lying in the road."

"Have it your own way then, my dear," answered the king resignedly, "but I tell you what. If that little white napkin is still there when we return, I'm going to get out of our carriage, and I'm going to pick it up."

Sure enough, on the way home, the king saw the little white napkin lying in the road just where it had been before, and since he had promised, he got out of the carriage and picked it up.

But what do you suppose was underneath the napkin? A wicked old fairy, all dirty and covered with sores.

"Now," said the wicked old fairy, "I am going to scratch your wife's two eyes out of her head, and you will drive her into the forests forever, and marry me in her place."

And what the fairy said came to pass. Weeping as hard as ever a woman wept, the queen was driven into the forest with her little son. Never more was she to set foot in the royal palace.

And the poor king (who loved the queen very dearly, but he really had no choice in the matter) was married all too soon to the horrible fairy by whom he had been bewitched.

DOI: 10.4324/9781003297536-4

Well, the years passed, and when her son had become a good-sized lad, the poor blinded queen sent him to the king's castle.

"Good morning, papa," said the young man to his father.

"My own dear son!" cried the king, overcome with joy, "You must live with us from this hour! A fine likely-looking lad you are, and we shall all three be happy together."

It was just like the horrible fairy, his stepmother, that she should be in the room at the time, and of course she did not agree with this at all; but for the moment she only gave the lad a spiteful glance and said nothing.

Some days passed while she made her plans. Then she said to the king: "That boy of yours simply does nothing but boast. Why, he says that he can find the round castle at the bottom of the Red Sea, one hundred thousand fathoms deep beneath the waves."

"Oh ho!" said the king. "Is that so? My boy, have you been boasting that you can find the round castle at the bottom of the Red Sea, one hundred thousand fathoms deep beneath the waves? If that is the case, you had better go and find it."

"Father!" cried the young man in surprise. "I have never boasted any such thing, but I'll go and find it if I must."

So, off he went, the poor young fellow, with his sack of provisions on his shoulders.

After a time he came to a little log cabin in the woods.

Pan! Pan! Pan! he knocked at the door.

"Come in!" cried a voice. And then who should open the door for him but an amazingly ugly fairy, from whose mouth spread a long tongue of flame.

"My poor young man," said she, "you look as though you were frightened to death of me."

"Yes, I am very much afraid."

"And where are you going?" she asked.

"I am going to find the round castle at the bottom of the Red Sea, one hundred thousand fathoms deep beneath the waves. I wonder if you can tell me how to find it?"

"No," she answered, "I can't tell you myself. But I have two sisters who live in the depths of the forest. When you reach the first, ask her how to find the other."

The young man thanked her very politely and continued his journey for another day. In the evening he came to the log cabin of the second fairy who was even more hideous than her sister, and the flame that spread out of her mouth was as long as her arm. Why, the poor fellow did not even dare to approach her cabin. She watched him coming through the woods and saw him stop in terror at the edge of her clearing.

"What is this? What is this?" she asked, in a brisk and kindly way. "You appear to be afraid of something."

"Indeed, I am, madam, I am afraid of you. You are a terrible sight with all that fire coming out of your mouth."

"Oh, don't be afraid of that," she answered (and as she laughed in a friendly fashion a great cloud of fire and steam and smoke belched forth from her mouth and frightened the young man almost out of his senses). "But tell me, why are you wandering like this in the depths of the forest?" she asked.

"I am trying to find the round castle at the bottom of the Red Sea, one hundred thousand fathoms deep beneath the waves."

"Well, that's easy enough," said she. "One of my sisters lives some distance from here in the depths of the forest, and she will tell you where the castle is."

So, off he went again (after thanking her politely) and in the evening of the next day's march he came upon a little log cabin in which the third sister lived, the most unsightly of them all. The flame that spread out of her mouth was so long that it scorched the trees at the edge of the clearing, and he would come no nearer than shouting distance.

"My poor young man," she cried, "don't you have the courage to approach my cabin? Are you afraid?"

"Yes, indeed, I am very much afraid."

"Well, what do you want, anyhow?" she shouted, seeing he would not approach her hut.

"Can you tell me how to find the round castle at the bottom the Red Sea, one hundred thousand fathoms deep beneath the waves?"

"Oh, there's no difficulty about that," she replied. "The King of the Fishes ought to be here any time now, and I shall ask him where the castle is at the bottom of the Red Sea."

Then she went away to the Red Sea and bellowed, "King of the Fishes! King of the Fishes!"

When the King of the Fishes came, as he did very soon, she asked him, "Do you know where the round castle at the bottom of the Red Sea is, one hundred thousand fathoms deep beneath the waves? Have you ever seen it?"

"I know it very well," replied the King of the Fishes. "It is down there, straight down through yonder clear patch of water."

Then the fairy said to the young man; "Look now. Take my little two-oared boat, and you will find yourself there at once."

"Thank you very much, madam," said he.

The young man began to row down, down, down, through the clear patch of water which extended to the bottom of the sea. And so he got right to the castle, as close as he could, and saw three princesses at a window on the second floor.

"Poor young man!" said they, "where are you going?"

"I am searching for the round castle at the bottom of the Red Sea, one hundred thousand fathoms deep beneath the waves. Is it here?"

"Yes, this is it!" they said all together. "And we will help you to come up to us."

They threw him a rope, saying, "Tie your foot." Then, all three of them pulled at the other end of the rope and drew him up, head over heels. Once he was with them in the room on the second floor, they all said at once: "So there you are! Now which one of us are you going to marry?"

One of them was fifteen years old. Another was twenty-one, and the third was twenty-five. He married the youngest.

That evening, when he went to bed, what should he see at the side of the room but three lights! He asked his princess, "What are those three lights for?"

"Well, my dear husband, I can hardly afford to tell you."

"And why not?" he asked.

She answered, "I shall tell you because I love you, but you must take good care to keep it a secret. Those lights are wax candles. Two of them are the lives of my sisters. If you were to blow them out, my two sisters would fall down stiff and die."

"And the other light?"

"That is the life of the old fairy covered with sores, who has married the king, your father. In a plate on the table are the two eyes which she snatched from the queen, your mother. If you blew out the candle, the mangy old fairy would fall down stiff and die."

During the night, the young man rose and went to the side of the room where he blew out the two candles, those of the two sisters. Then he quietly went back to bed. And what did he find under his bed in the morning? A handle with ropes tied to it.

"Tell me, my wife, what is this for?"

"My dear husband, you have only to seize this handle to find yourself transported to the castle of the king, your father, and of the wicked fairy."

Rising up, the princess went to the candles and found her two sisters dead.

"Oh, my dear husband! Have you killed my two sisters?"

"Yes, wife, it would have been bad luck for me if I had not blown out the candles. As it is, I am relieved of a great worry."

The young man who was exceedingly prompt in his actions, lost no time in seizing hold of the handle under the bed and wishing himself carried with the around castle and all to his father's door.

Meanwhile at home the wicked fairy suddenly began to complain of illness to her husband the king.

"Oh, how unwell I feel!" she cried. "I have pains all up and down, and in and out! Oh! Oh!"

"For goodness' sake," said the king, "tell me what the matter is with you."

"Everything is the matter with me!" she answered, making all sorts of faces and running up and down the room. "Oh, I am terribly ill!"

At this point the young man walked into his father's palace carrying a lighted candle in one hand and a pair of eyes in the other.

"Ha! You old witch," he cried. "You snatched out my mother's eyes and sent her away to the forest! Today I have your life in my hands. Prepare to die!"

Thereupon he blew out the third candle, and the fairy fell down stiff and dead.

"My boy," said the king, aghast, "what have you done?"

"Father, do you love this old hag better than your wife, the queen? Come with me into the forest to find my poor blind mother, and we will lead her home."

Both of them went in the carriage into the forest, and at last they came to the place where the poor blind queen lived all alone in her little log-cabin. Her son put back the two eyes into her head that he had found in the round castle, and, wonderful to relate, after all those years, she recovered her sight. The first thing she saw was the king, who put his arms around her neck with great joy and kissed her. You can well imagine that she was much more attractive than the old fairy covered with sores.

So they returned together to the king's castle. The young man lived happily ever after with the princess of the around castle at the bottom of the Red Sea, one hundred thousand fathoms deep under the waves. And the king lived happily ever after with his dear wife, the queen. Take my word for it, never again would he think of picking up a napkin lying in the road.

And as for me, they sent me here to tell you this story.

The Wolf's Bride

Diamond Jenness

This is an Eskimo story taken down and translated by Mr. D. Jenness of Canada, a very famous man. He wrote it just as the Eskimo told it, short and sharp, but since you could never make heads or tails out of the Eskimo's words, they have been set out at greater length here. I promise you that this is a real Eskimo story, and a very queer one. If you do not like it, blame Wolf and not me, for it happened to him.

Once upon a time in the land of perpetual ice and snow, lived a man and his wife with their only daughter. They lived by the seashore and believed that they were the only folk in the world until their daughter grew up.

In that country there is only one night and one day in the whole year, and, during the night, which is winter, the sea is frozen over from horizon to horizon. Even in summer, snow lies everywhere, and it is only in places that the sun burns it off the land and discloses patches of moss, wild Arctic poppies, and flowers that we never see in our fields at home, can be seen. On this scanty herbage the caribou feed, which the Eskimo people hunt as we hunt the stag.

One winter's morning, the daughter of these lonely people got up as usual while her parents were still sleeping, and went outside the snow hut in which they lived, to see what she could see. The moon shone brightly, and the stars were out, and by the light of the moon she saw, in the distance, something black lying in the snow. She waited a little while to see if it would move, and then set out to discover what it was. To her surprise, she found a freshly killed caribou. Now caribou do not come down in winter out of the shelter of the forests, nor are they usually killed by ghosts, so she ran home and told her parents about her singular discovery. Immediately, they followed her out of the hut, and, having divided the caribou in pieces, took it home. They ate very well that day, and went to bed and slept heavily, for not only had they had an unexpected feast, but the larder was full for several days to come. In the middle of the night, the girl woke up with a palpitating heart; she felt that someone had entered the hut and saw around the corner of the door a wolf's tail disappearing. No doubt she thought it was a dream, for she turned over and slept until morning.

The following day, I call it day though it was still as dark as night, the girl saw nothing to explain what she had seen, but that night she was again wakened by a palpitating heart, and again she saw a wolf's tail disappearing around the door. However, she turned over on her side and slept till morning. In the morning she went outside and had a good look around while her parents still slept. Far away, out upon the frozen sea, she saw something black which, upon inspection, turned out to be a freshly killed seal. She ran home at once and wakened her parents. Her father told her to fetch

DOI: 10.4324/9781003297536-5

the seal, which she did, dragging it in with a harness made for that purpose over the ice. Then the family cut it up and had a great feast that day. In the night the girl was again wakened with a palpitating heart. She was quite sure this time that somebody was in the hut, but there was nothing to be seen but a wolverine's tail disappearing around the door. She got up, determined to get to the bottom of the matter, took a lamp-stick, and went out into the night, but there was not a sign of anything. So, in she went to sleep again.

In the morning there was not a sign of either wolf or wolverine.

When she and her parents were sitting around the blubber stove after their evening meal, they heard a crunch of footsteps in the snow. Someone opened the door, and in came a young man, whose clothes were decorated with wolf fur. Without more ado, he placed himself opposite the girl and said, "My father bid me come to you."

Before anyone had time to answer, footsteps were heard crunching in the snow, and another young man came into the hut. Around the hem of his sealskin tunic he had a border of wolverine fur. He sat down opposite the girl and said to Wolf, "You came first, but I shall marry the girl."

"I am the girl's husband," replied Wolf, and they began to quarrel. The old father said, "If you want to fight, get out of the hut."

So out they went. Then the girl and her parents heard them wrestling up and down, but they did not interfere, and at last the noise ceased. Without inquiring into the result of the fight, for these poor people believed there was something uncanny afoot in which it were best not to interfere. Then the girl and her father and mother went to bed. When she awoke next day, the girl went outside to have a look around and saw two tracks in the snow, a wolf's track, and a wolverine's track, and all along, wherever they led, the snow was red with blood.

She followed the tracks until she saw something black lying in the snow. It was a dead wolverine with its side cut open. So, she ran home and told her parents, and her father said she had better stay near the hut.

That night they determined to sit up and await results, for they felt they had not seen the last of Wolf, and at the hour when the two young men had come the night before, they did, indeed, hear footsteps crunching in the snow. A man came into the hut, and his tunic was fringed with wolf fur, but he was old. He said, without more ado, "Give me your daughter, for my son is mortally ill. He is probably at the point of death, so I can't stand on ceremony."

The girl's father and mother were too old to travel. However, they asked Wolf's father if he had a sledge, for the girl was not a great walker. He said he had no sledge but, nevertheless, they let the girl go, and Wolf's father took her by the hand and set off over the ice and snow. Soon they were well away from the house, and he said, "Get on my back but do not look around."

So up she got on the old man's shoulders, and he set off at a run, but the further he ran the more like a wolf he went. Toward morning he put her down and bade her follow him until they came to a hut. Then he made her crawl after him on her hands and knees down the long entrance passage. As she emerged into the hut, she saw a young man huddled over the fire.

"Are you dead?!" asked the father.

But the young man looked up and smiled. Wolf's mother said, "We are now giving our son into the bride's care," and Wolf's father told his wife to fetch new clothes which they gave to the girl.

Then they took off the girl's old clothes and dressed her up afresh. After that she set to work to nurse her husband. Young Wolf was as thin as a skeleton, but under the girl's care he recovered slowly and was even able to go hunting after some time had passed.

When he was healthy again, his father and mother ordered the young couple to pay a visit to the old folk down by the sea and attend to their wants. Accordingly, young Wolf prepared a sledge for the voyage. He piled it with caribou meat and deerskins, and amid the deerskins he made a tent for his wife. Then he put her into the sledge and said "Mind you don't look around."

They started off at a slow pace but soon they went at a surprising rate. Toward morning, he let the girl get down off the sledge, and she found, when they had walked a little way, that she was not far from home. They went in at once and told the old folk that they had brought them food. So, a great feast was held that day, and when night came they all slept contentedly.

In the morning, Wolf set off hunting, but he warned his wife and her parents to stay within doors at midday. They obeyed him, and toward evening he came in saying that he had had good hunting. So, he took them outside and showed them five caribou laid side by side. The evening was spent in cutting them up and filling the larder. Now, though young Wolf killed many caribou, he never caught a single seal. However, that is not surprising, for until this time he had never lived by the sea. So, his wife's father instructed him in the art of sealing and gave him a set of weapons. The young man soon learned sealing, under the old man's tuition, and after that caught many a great seal which he dragged home, like an old hand, in harness.

After a while the young man collected a considerable quantity of food, which was stored, in the Eskimo fashion, in two piles, much as wood is stored for the winter in other countries. And, indeed, the meat was not unlike wood, for it was frozen into solid logs. The girl's father and mother, having now no reason to detain the young people, sent them home.

Accordingly, young Wolf prepared a sledge for the voyage. He piled it with blubber and skins, and amid the skins, he made a tent for his wife. Then he put her on the sledge and started out, first at a slow pace, but gradually, they went at a surprising rate. After traveling a considerable distance, he let the girl get down off the sledge to rest, for the sledge was overladen and they were not yet home. Later in the day they resumed their journey and arrived safely at their destination.

So far, all had gone well with the girl and her wolf-husband, but misfortune is bound to come some time or other. They had not been settled at home for very long before some people invited young Wolf to a dance at a distant village. His father and mother advised him not to take his wife, or even to go himself, for they said, "Son, there is a great bird with malicious intentions toward you in that place."

Nevertheless, young Wolf was determined to go, and when the messengers who had invited him prepared to set off, young Wolf also made his preparations.

So, one day Wolf put his wife in the sledge and set out with the men, each one pulling his own sledge. The journey was by no means easy, even for Wolf, who had certainly miraculous powers of traveling. In time, the company came to a river that ran between banks which were so steep that the men, instead of pulling their sledges, went behind to hold them back. Consequently, Wolf and his wife were left to their own devices. The others crossed the river and went up the opposite bank, but when, after much difficulty, they gained the top, they looked around, and realized that Wolf needed help. So, they returned and fastened Wolf's wife down upon the sledge and with ropes, lowered her to the bottom of the cliff. Then they carried her, as one carries a corpse in a coffin, sledge and all, across the frozen river. When they were about to climb the other side, an amazing thing happened – the sledge flew up in the air. It hovered for a few minutes and then arose like a bird. Wolf and his companions sprang on to it, and the sledge carried them up the cliff in no time.

When they were all together with their goods and on the top, they sighed with relief and set out again on their travels. In time, they came to another river where precisely the same events occurred, although this time, Wolf's sledge showed a certain reluctance to proceed. However, all went well in the end, and they fastened Wolf's wife down on her sledge and went on until they came to a village where singing and dancing were already in full swing. Wolf and his wife went straight to the dance hall and gave the host the customary presents. Everyone was delighted, saying they had never seen such presents before and apologized for having nothing worthy in exchange. When the dancing was over, Wolf and his wife went to their host's home.

Nobody knows what was in Wolf's mind when he set out on this journey, nor whether he knew beforehand about the strange events that were to befall his wife. That very night, before going to bed, Wolf's wife went outside for a breath of fresh air. As she was in the open, a child came to her and said, "Come with me, Grandmamma wants you."

Wolf's wife felt that some misfortune was about to befall her, but the little girl urged her, and in spite of her feelings, Wolf's wife went. They walked down to the river and soon came to a little cave. No sooner were they at the entrance to the cave than Wolf's wife thought she smelt blood, and indeed, inside she saw a cauldron boiling with something like blood. The child's grandmother, who was attending to the cauldron, said, with many kindly glances, "Take off your clothes, and let me wash you."

The young wife's clothes were taken from her and put on a pile. Then, the old woman set about washing her with the horrid liquid from the pot. Next she washed her grandchild, and after that bade her to throw the water into the river. However, the child instead threw the water over Wolf's wife, and the poor young woman became as small as the child, and the child turned into a woman. The child-woman dressed herself in the poor girl's clothes and ran away. When the child-woman had gone, Wolf's wife was forced to dress in the little garments, which no sooner had she done, than she went to the house where her husband was. Alas, the false wife had already been let inside, and Wolf, when he came to the door, did not recognize his own wife. So, he kicked her and sent her away.

The poor girl was, therefore, homeless, for neither the witch nor her husband would have her. Next day, Wolf and his false wife again attended the dance, and the wicked woman danced like a demon and showed off with more than human art. That night she went home with him again, and the poor girl whose position she had usurped was forced to sleep out in the snow again.

In the middle of the night someone came to the true wife as she slept in the snow, took hold of her, and wakened her. It was another child, very like the first one who had guiled her away, and, sure enough, the child said, "Come with me. Grandmamma wants you. You may as well come, for your husband is going to desert you."

The child then left her, and the girl, who was now desperate, thought she might as well see where the child would lead her. She followed her down to the river where soon they came to a little cave. No sooner did they enter than Wolf's wife saw a cauldron boiling with water. The child's grandmother, who was attending the cauldron, said with many kindly glances, "Take off your clothes and let me wash you."

Then the old-woman washed her in the water from the pot. After washing her for a long time, the old woman said, "Do you recognize yourself?"

And the girl answered, "I am myself again."

The grandmother made her throw the water into the river. Then she took more water and washed the poor wife's outer garments, which had belonged to the wicked child, and gave her an under-garment of squirrel-skin and some shoes. When she was dressed the grandmother said to her, "Now take the water in which I have washed your tunic, and pour it into your rival's ear. Then, throw your shoes, the garment of squirrel-skin and the water-pot into the entrance and wish, at the same time, in these words – 'Go home pot! Go home shoes! Go home squirrel-skin,' and they will come back to me of their own accord."

The poor girl listened with great attention, for she now knew that this old woman intended to restore her happiness, though she at first had mistaken her for the other witch.

When Wolf's wife had committed to memory all that the old woman said, she went to her husband's house dressed in nothing but the squirrel-skin and the shoes. She crept inside without anyone seeing her and poured the water into her rival's ear. Then she threw the shoes, the pot and the squirrel-skin into the entrance, wishing in these words, "Go home pot! Go home shoes! Go home squirrel-skin!"

And then they all immediately vanished. She then hid herself behind a pile of clothes and wrapped herself in one of her own coats. Meantime, the wicked wife had become a little girl again, and upon discovering that she was a witch, he kicked her out of the house and told her to leave forever.

When he came back, he saw his own wife seated in the hut, and he tried to make friends with her and ask her pardon. But she said, "Don't come near me, you have a new wife now." Whereupon Wolf shouted out, "I've been tricked!"

So, he got ready to rush out and avenge himself for the trick that had been played upon him by killing every one within sight. He looked so fierce that those around him believed that he could, and would slay the whole village. So, they sent a deputation to his wife, begging her to forgive Wolf, for he had acted in ignorance. Thereupon, Wolf's wife, who was really very good-natured, forgave her husband, and persuaded Wolf to moderate his anger.

Now, after Wolf and his wife were reconciled, they decided that they had better set off for home because they hadn't had a very fortunate experience in the village. So, they took their sledge and went back to the river. They were accompanied on their journey by the companions who had originally set out with them. When they got to the river, they had some trouble to cross it, as before. It was easy enough to get down the river bank, but as for getting up the other side, they found it impossible, and the sledge this time didn't show the least inclination to fly. There was nothing they could do but to turn the sledge into a boat. This they did, and made a little house of skins upon it with a door, and a lamp inside to keep the girl warm. They put food in the boat and, in order to occupy the girl, and keep her thoughts from her harrowing situation, they gave her fine skins and materials for making garments out of them. The girl got into the boat, and the companions assured her that, in time, she would find herself at her old home.

Moreover, they said, "If ever you want to land from the boat and walk about a bit, just let us know and the boat will moor itself until you enter it again."

Then Wolf said, "Although I cannot accompany you" (for the boat was very small) "I shall know where you are, and my influence will protect you. Between this place and your home lie three villages. Have no fear of the people there. You will be quite safe."

And he promised that about the anniversary of their marriage, she would hear of him in much the same way she did when she had first heard of him. So the girl got into the boat and the companions sent it out into the middle of the river. The girl was happy enough in the boat. She slept, she ate, she sewed, and whenever she wished to stretch her legs, the boat landed her safely on the shore, and whenever she got on board again, it set off without any effort on her part. But out of curiosity when she tried to push it from the bank herself, it never would move an inch. It befell as her husband had said. As she sailed down the river, she passed three villages, but though she saw many people in each of them, she was herself invisible.

At last, one morning when she woke up, she felt that the boat was no longer proceeding, and looking out of the little door, she saw that she was near her old home. She disembarked, pulled the boat out of the water, and taking with her all the meat and skins that Wolf had given her, went home. When she got home, her mother said, "Where is Wolf?" and the girl said, "I have no idea," and told her parents about the circumstances of her lonely journey, but said nothing that would reflect upon her husband. She also told them that, some time around the anniversary of her marriage, she expected to hear from him in much the same way as she heard before. So the girl, and her father and mother, lived happily together, awaiting the messenger.

True enough, when the year came around again to midwinter, Wolf's father arrived. He said, "I have come for your daughter. My son is mortally ill. He is probably at the point of death, but if the girl will come back with me, I promise that my son will in future be a good husband to her, that is, if he survives his present illness."

Then Wolf's father took the girl by the hand and set off over the ice and snow. Soon they were well away from the house, and he said, "Get on my back and do not look around."

So, she got up on the old man's shoulders, and he set off at a run, but the further he ran the more like a wolf he went. Toward morning, he put her down and asked her to follow him until they came to a hut. Then, he made her crawl after him on her hands and knees down the long entrance passage. As she emerged into the hut, she saw Wolf lying asleep. He was thinner than can be imagined; his head alone was the usual size. The girl at once set to work to nurse him, and gave him weak broth until he began to revive. Then, she made him thick soup, until he slowly recovered and was even able to go hunting after some time had passed.

When he was well again, they returned to her parents and there they stayed until the old people died. After that, they went back to Wolf's old father and mother and supported them until they passed away also.

After many years Wolf divided all his belongings among his companions and said, "I and my wife are going today to the land where there is no more pain, and where people live happily forever," and immediately he and his wife transformed themselves into two real wolves, and loped away from the village together. Ever since that day, they have never been seen again.

The Musicians of Bremen

Jacob and Wilhelm Grimm

This little tale and the following one, "Rapunzel," are two German stories collected by Wilhelm and Jacob Grimm who lived in the time of Napoleon. They made a tremendous collection of all the children's tales of their country and published the first set of them in 1812, the year that Napoleon retreated from Moscow. "The Musicians of Bremen" is a very clever animal story, and "Rapunzel," of course, is famous all over the world.

Once upon a time an honest farmer had an ass that had been a faithful servant to him for a great many years, but was now growing old and every day more and more unfit for work. His master, therefore, was tired of keeping him and began to think of putting an end to him. However, the ass, who saw that some mischief was in the wind, slyly bid good bye to the farm and began his journey toward the great city, "for there," thought he, "I may turn musician."

After he had traveled a little way, he spied a dog lying by the roadside and panting as if he were very tired.

"What makes you pant so much, my friend?" asked the ass.

"Alas!" said the dog, "my master was going to knock me on the head, because I am old and weak and can no longer make myself useful to him in hunting. So, I ran away; but what can I do to earn my livelihood?"

"Hey, perk up your ears!!" said the ass, "I'm going to the great city to turn musician: Suppose you come with me, and try what you can do in the same way?"

The dog said he was willing, and they jogged on together. They had not gone far before they saw a cat sitting in the middle of the road and making a most rueful face.

"May I ask, my good lady," said the ass, "what's the matter with you? You look quite out of spirits!"

"Ah me!" said the cat, "how can one be in good spirits when one's life is in danger? Just because I am beginning to grow old, and had rather lie at my ease by the fire than run about the house after the mice, my mistress laid hold of me and was going to drown me. Though I have been lucky enough to get away from her, I don't know what I am to live on."

"Oh!" said the ass, "By all means, come with us to the great city. You are a good night singer and can make your fortune as a musician."

The cat was pleased with the thought and joined the party.

Soon afterward, as they were passing by a farmyard, they saw a cock perched on a gate, and screaming with all his might and strength.

DOI: 10.4324/9781003297536-6

"Bravo!" said the ass "Upon my word you make a famous noise. Please, tell me, what is all this about?"

"Why," said the cock, "I was just now saying that we should have fine weather for our washing-day, and yet, my mistress and the cook don't thank me for my pains, but threaten to cut off my head tomorrow and make a broth of me for the guests who are coming on Sunday!"

"Heaven forbid!" said the ass. "Come with us, Master Chanticleer. It will be better, at any rate, than staying here to have your head cut off! Besides, who knows? If we learn to sing in tune, we may create some kind of a concert. So, come along with us."

"With all my heart," said the cock.

So all four went on in a jolly mood.

They could not, however, reach the great city the first day. So, when night arrived, they went into a forest to sleep. The ass and the dog laid themselves down under a great tree, and the cat climbed up into the branches; while the cock, thought that the higher he sat, the safer he would be. So, the cock flew up to the very top of the tree, and then, according to his custom, before he went to sleep, looked out on all sides of him to see that everything was well. In doing this, he saw afar off something bright and shining. So, he called to his companions and said:

"There must be a house not far away, for I see a light."

"If that be the case," said the ass, "we had better change our quarters, for our lodging is not the best in the world!"

"Besides,"nadded the dog, "I would not be the worse for a bone or two, or a bit of meat."

So they walked together toward the spot where Chanticleer had seen the light; and as they came near, it became larger and brighter, until they, at last, came close to a house in which a gang of robbers lived.

Being the tallest of the company, the ass marched up to the window and peeped inside. "Well, Donkey," said Chanticleer. "What do you see?"

"What do I see?" replied the ass, "why I see a table spread with all kinds of good things and robbers sitting around it making merry."

"That would be a noble lodge for us," the cock said.

"Yes," said the ass, "if we could only get in there!"

So they consulted together how they might contrive to get the robbers out; and at last they hit upon a plan. The ass placed himself upright on his hind legs. With his forefeet resting against the widow, the dog got upon his back. Then the cat scrambled up to the dog's shoulders, and the cock flew up and sat upon the cat's head. When everyone was ready, a signal was given, and they began their music. The ass brayed, the dog barked, the cat mewed, and the cock screamed; and then they all broke through the window at once, and came tumbling into the room, among the broken glass, with a most hideous clatter!

The robbers, who had been not a little frightened by the opening concert, had now no doubt that some frightful hobgoblin had broken in upon them, and scampered away as fast as they could. The coast once clear, our travelers soon sat down, and dispatched what the robbers had left, with as much eagerness as if they had not expected to eat again for a month. As soon as they had satisfied themselves, they put out the lights, and each one sought out a resting-place to his own liking. The donkey laid himself down upon a heap of straw in the yard; the dog stretched himself upon a mat behind the door; the cat rolled herself up on the hearth before the warm ashes;

and the cock perched upon a beam on the top of the house; and, since they were all rather tired from their journey, they soon fell asleep.

But about midnight, when the robbers saw from afar that the lights were out and that all seemed quiet, they began to think that they had been in too great a hurry to run away; and one of them, who was bolder than the rest, went to see what was happening. Finding everything still, he marched into the kitchen and groped about until he found a match to light a candle, and then, espying the glittering fiery eyes of the cat, he mistook them for live coals, and held the match to them to light it. But the cat, not understanding this joke, sprang at his face and spit, and scratched at him. This frightened him dreadfully, and away he ran to the back door; but there the dog jumped up and bit him in the leg; and as he was crossing over the yard, the ass kicked him, and the cock, who had been awakened by the noise, crowed with all his might. Upon hearing this, the robber ran back as fast as he could to his comrades, and told the captain how a horrid witch had got into the house, had spit at him, and. scratched his face with her long bony fingers; how a man with a knife in his hand had hidden himself behind the door, and stabbed him in the leg; how a black monster stood in the yard and struck him with a club, and how the devil had sat upon the top of the house and cried out, "Throw the rascal up here!"

After hearing this, the robbers never dared to return to the house. On the other hand, the musicians were so pleased with their quarters that they made this house their home. And they are still living there, I dare say, to this very day.

THE MUSICIANS OF BREMEN

Rapunzel

Jacob and Wilhelm Grimm

Once upon a time there lived a man and his wife, who wished very much to have a child, but for a long time it was in vain. These people had a little window in the back part of their house, out of which one could see into a beautiful garden which was full of fine flowers and vegetables, but it was surrounded by a high wall, and no one dared to enter because it belonged to a witch who possessed great power, and who was feared by the whole world.

One day the woman stood at this window looking into the garden, and there she saw a bed filled with the most beautiful radishes, and which seemed so fresh and green that she felt quite happy. Consequently, she had a great desire to eat of some these radishes. This wish tormented her daily, and since she knew that she could not have them, she fell ill and became very pale and miserable.

This frightened her husband, who asked her, "What ails you, my dear wife?"

"Ah!" she replied, "If I cannot get any of those radishes from the garden behind the house I shall die!"

The husband, who loved her very much, thought, "Rather than let my wife die, I must fetch her some radishes, cost what they may."

DOI: 10.4324/9781003297536-7

So, in the gloom of the evening, he climbed the wall of the witch's garden, and, snatching a handful of radishes in great haste, he brought them to his wife, who made herself a salad, which she had extremely relished. However, they were so nice and so delicious that the next day she felt the same desire again and could not get any rest. Consequently, her husband was obliged to promise her some more.

THE WITCH

In the evening, therefore, he got ready and began clambering up the wall; but, oh! how terribly frightened he was, for there he saw the old witch standing before him.

"How dare you!" she began, looking at him with a frightful scowl, "How dare you climb over into my garden to take away my radishes like a thief? You will suffer evil for this!"

"Ah!" he replied. "Please let me live before you judge me. I have only done this from a great necessity. My wife saw your radishes from her window, and took such a fancy to them that she would have died if she had not eaten them."

Then the witch ran after him in a passion, saying, "If she's behaving as you say, I shall let you take away all the radishes you please, but I shall make one condition: you must give me the child which your wife will bring into the world. All will go well for the child, and I will care for it like a mother."

In his anxiety the man consented, and when the child was born, the witch appeared at the same time, gave the child the name "Rapunzel," and took the baby away with her.

Rapunzel grew to be the most beautiful child under the sun, but when she was twelve years old the witch locked her up in a tower, which stood in a forest, and had neither stairs nor door, nor window except for a little one right at the top. When the witch wished to enter, she stood beneath this window and called out:

> "Rapunzel, Rapunzel!
> Let down your hair,
> That I may climb
> Without a stair."

Rapunzel had long and beautiful hair, as fine as spun gold. Whenever she heard the witch's voice, she untied her tresses and opened the window. Then her hair fell down twenty feet, and the witch climbed up by it.

After a couple of years had passed, the king's son happened to be riding through the wood and came by the tower. There he heard a song so beautiful that he stood still and listened. It was Rapunzel, who, to pass the time of her loneliness away, was exercising her sweet voice. The king's son wished to climb the tower to see her, but when he looked for a door in the tower, he could find none. So, he rode home again. However, the song had touched his heart and drew him every day to the forest so that he might listen to it. One day, as he stood behind the tree enraptured by sweet music, he saw the witch come up and heard her call out:

> "Rapunzel! Rapunzel!
> Let down your hair,
> That I may climb
> Without a stair."

Rapunzel let down her tresses, and the witch mounted.

"So that is the ladder by which one must climb! Then I will try my luck, too," said the prince; and the following day, his heart overflowing with longing, he went to the tower, and cried,

THE WITCH SHUT RAPUNZEL UP IN THE TOWER

"Rapunzel! Rapunzel!
Let down your hair,
That I may climb
Without a stair."

Then the tresses dropped down, and he climbed up. Rapunzel was very frightened at first when a man entered, for she had never seen one before. However, the king's son talked in a loving way to her, and told her how his heart had been so moved by her singing that he couldn't have any peace until he had seen her himself.

Rapunzel gradually lost her fright, and soon, he asked her if she would have him for a husband. So, she began to see that he was young and handsome, and thought, "I'd rather have anyone than the old woman." So, she put her hand within his hand and said "Yes, I shall willingly go with you, but how am I to descend the tower?"

Then, they agreed that whenever he came, he would bring a skein of silk, out of which Rapunzel would weave a ladder, "and when it is ready" she said, "I shall climb down by it, and you must take me upon your horse."

They also decided that they should only meet in the evening because the witch only came during the day.

Time went on, and the woman noticed nothing, because Rapunzel hid the silk that the prince brought to her, but alas, one day, she said innocently: "Tell me, mother, how is it you find it more difficult to come up to me than the young king's son who arrives in a flash!"

"Oh, you wicked child!" exclaimed the witch, "What do I hear? I thought I had separated you from the entire world, and yet you have deceived me."

And, seizing Rapunzel's beautiful hair in a fury, she gave her a couple of blows with her left hand. Then she took a pair of scissors in her right, snip, snap, she cut off all her beautiful tresses, and they fell to the ground. After this, the hard-hearted woman took the poor maiden to a great desert and left her to die in great misery and grief. But the same day, in the evening, the witch took the tresses she had cut from the poor girl's head, fastened them above the window latch of the tower, and when the king's son came to see Rapunzel, he called out as usual:

"Rapunzel! Rapunzel! Let down your hair."

The old witch let down Rapunzel's golden locks, and the prince climbed up the tower. But when he got to the top, he found not his dear Rapunzel, but the witch, who looked at him with furious and wicked eyes.

"Aha!" she exclaimed scornfully, "you would like to fetch your dear wife; but the beautiful bird does not sit any longer in her nest, singing. The cat has taken her away and will now scratch out your eyes. To you Rapunzel is lost! You will never see her again!"

When he heard these words, the prince lost his senses with grief and jumped out of the window of the tower in his bewilderment. He escaped with his life, but the thorns into which he fell punctured his eyes. So, he wandered blind, in the forest, eating nothing but roots and berries, and he did nothing but weep and lament the loss of his beloved wife. He wandered about this way in great misery for a few years until he at last arrived at the desert where Rapunzel, with her twins, a boy and a girl, lived in great sorrow. Hearing a voice which he thought he knew, he followed in its direction;

RAPUNZEL IS LEFT IN THE DESERT

THE PRINCE MOUNTED & MET THE WITCH

and as he approached, Rapunzel recognized him and embraced him and wept. Two of her tears moistened his eyes, and they became clear again so that he could see as well as before.

Then he led her away to his kingdom, where he was received with joyous celebrations and where they lived long, content and happy. No one ever discovered what became of the old witch.

The Shirt Collar

Hans Christian Andersen

This story was written by Hans Christian Andersen, a Danish gentleman, who had the honor of reading his stories to the late Queen Alexandra of England, when she was a child at her father's palace in Denmark. In his day, people wore great top boots which they could only take off with a bootjack, a contrivance to wood that fit around the boot-heel. Shirt collars were more magnificent than they are now, and Garters were sometimes several yards long, and were often knitted and embroidered by hand.

There was once a rich gentleman whose entire possessions consisted of a bootjack and a hair-comb, but he also had the finest Shirt Collar in the world, and it is this Shirt Collar which is the subject of my story.

The collar was now old enough to think of marrying, and it happened that he was sent to the wash together with a garter.

"My word!" exclaimed the Shirt Collar. "I have never seen anything so slender and delicate, so charming and genteel. May I ask your name?"

"I shall not tell you that," said the Garter.

"Where is your home?" asked the Shirt Collar.

But the Garter was of rather a modest disposition, and it seemed such a strange question to answer.

"I presume you are a girdle?" said the Shirt Collar – "a sort of under girdle? I see that you are useful as well as ornamental, my little lady."

"You are not to speak to me," said the Garter. "I have not, I think, given you any occasion to do so."

"Oh! When one is as beautiful as you are," cried the Shirt Collar, "that is occasion enough."

"Go!" said the Garter. "Don't come so near me: you look to me quite like a man."

"I am a fine gentleman, too," said the Shirt Collar. "I possess a bootjack and a hair-comb."

And that was not true at all, for it was his master who owned these things, but he was boasting.

"Don't come too near me," said the Garter, "I'm not used to that."

"Affectation!" cried the Shirt Collar.

And then they were taken out of the wash and starched and hung over a chair in the sunshine. Afterward, they were laid on the iron board, and now came the hot ironing.

DOI: 10.4324/9781003297536-8

"Mrs. Widow!" said the Shirt Collar, "little Mrs. Widow, I'm getting quite warm. I'm being quite changed. I'm losing all my creases. You're burning a hole in me! Ugh! I propose to you."

"You old rag!" said the Iron, and rode proudly over the Shirt Collar, for it imagined that it was a steam boiler, and that it ought to be out on the railway, dragging carriages.

"You old rag!" said the Iron.

The Shirt Collar was a little frayed at the edges. Therefore, the paper scissors came to smooth away the frayed places.

"Ho, ho!" said the Shirt Collar; "I presume you are a first rate dancer. How you can point your toes! No one in the world can do that like you."

"I know that," said the Scissors.

"You deserve to be a countess," said the Shirt Collar. "All that I possess consists of a fine gentleman, a bootjack, and comb. If only I had an estate!"

"What! Do you want to marry?" cried the Scissors; and they were angry and gave such a deep cut that the Collar had to be cashiered. "I shall have to propose to the Hair-comb," thought the Shirt Collar. "It is wonderful how well you keep all your teeth, my little lady. Have you never thought of engaging yourself?"

"Yes, you can easily imagine that," replied the Hair-comb, "I am engaged to the Bootjack."

"Engaged!" cried the Shirt Collar.

Now there was no one left to whom he could offer himself, and so he despised love-making.

A long time passed, and the Shirt Collar was put into the sack of a paper miller. There was a terribly ragged company, and the fine ones kept to themselves, and the coarse ones to themselves as is right. They all had much to tell, but the Shirt Collar had most of all, for he was a terrible Jack Brag.

"I have had a tremendous number of sweethearts," said the Shirt Collar. "They would not leave me alone; but I was a fine gentleman, a starched one. I had a bootjack and a hair-comb that I never used. You should only have seen me then, when I was turned down. I shall never forget my first love. It was a girdle, and how delicate, how charming, how genteel it was! And my first love threw herself into a washing-tub, and all for me! There was also a widow who became quite glowing, but I let her stand alone until she turned quite black. Then there was a dancer who gave me the wound from which I still suffer. She was very hot tempered. My own hair-comb was in love with me, and lost all her teeth from neglected love. Yes, I've had many experiences of this kind; but I am most sorry for the garter – I mean for the girdle, that jumped into the wash-tub for love of me. I've a great deal on my conscience. It's time I was turned into white paper."

And to that the Shirt Collar came. All the rags were turned into white paper, but the Shirt Collar became the very piece of paper we see here, and upon which this story has been printed, and that was done because he boasted so dreadfully about things that were not at all true. And this we must remember so that we may on no account do the same, for we cannot know at all whether we shall not be put into the rag bag and manufactured into white paper on which our whole history, even the most secret, will be printed, so that we shall be obliged to run about and tell it, as the Shirt Collar did.

The Ut-Röst Cormorants

Peter Christen Asbjørnsen and Jørgen Moe

"Ut-Röst is one of the fabled islands in northern waters. There the hill-people live and carry on fanning and fishing. The island shows itself only to good people and only when they are in danger of their lives. It is noted for its fertile fields and green pastures."

That is what Mr. and Mrs. John Gade, who translated this story from the Norwegian, say.

They very kindly gave me permission to print this tale. So, I took permission to print what they have to tell about it, for if they do not know the rights of the matter, who does?

Once upon a time a poor fisherman named Isaac lived in Väro close to Röst. He owned nothing in the world but a boat and a couple of goats which his wife kept alive with scraps of fish and the few spears of grass which they could cut up on the mountain side. And yet, though Isaac's cabin was full of hungry youngsters, he was quite content with what the Lord had ordered for him and complained only because of a neighbor who gave him no peace. The neighbor was a rich man who thought that he ought to be much better off than such a beggar as Isaac, and he wanted to get rid of him so he could take possession of the landing place in front of Issac's hut.

One day Isaac was out fishing a couple of miles from shore when a thick fog came up, and then suddenly such a storm that he had to throw all his fish overboard to lighten the boat and keep it from capsizing. Even then it was not easy to keep her afloat, but he just managed to steer through and over the great waves which every minute threatened to sink him. He had been driving on in this way for five or six hours when he thought he must soon be nearing land. But just then the fog grew thicker, and the storm raged worse and worse, so as he sailed and sailed and never came in sight of land, it dawned on him that he must be driving straight out to sea, or else that the wind had veered. Suddenly, just beyond the bow, he heard a frightful shriek, and then he felt certain it was the water kelpy singing a dirge for him. So, he prayed to God for his wife and children, so sure was he that his last hour had come. As he sat praying with all his might, he caught a glimpse of something black. However, when he drew closer, he saw it was only three cormorants sitting on a piece of driftwood, and whisk! he had passed them by.

So he drove on for a long, long time, and he grew so hungry, thirsty, and tired that he didn't know, for the life of him, what to do, and almost fell asleep, still holding on to the tiller, when suddenly the keel scraped the bottom, and the boat ran aground! You may be sure Isaac was wide awake in jiffy, and as the sun broke through the

DOI: 10.4324/9781003297536-9

fog, he saw a beautiful countryside fresh after the storm. The slopes of the hills and mountains were covered with green fields and fertile meadows up to their very crests. He could smell the young grass and flowers, and it seemed to him, as he drew deep breaths of the fragrant air, that the whole countryside was lovelier than anything he had ever seen in all his lifelong days.

"God be praised. Now I'm saved," said Isaac to himself, "This is Ut-Röst!"

Right in front of him stretched a field of barley, the ears so big and full that he had never seen the like before. A little path led through the barley to a hut thatched with green turf, and on top a white goat with gilded horns and udders as big as a cow's was grazing. On a bench outside the hut sat a little man dressed in blue, puffing at his pipe. His beard was so long, it reached way down over his chest.

"Welcome to Ut-Röst, Isaac," said the old man.

"Well met, father!" answered Isaac. "But do you know me?"

"Yes, indeed I do!" replied the old man "I suppose you want lodgings here for the night."

"Yes, if I am lucky enough," said Isaac, "whatever you have is the best in the world for me."

"There might be trouble with my boys," said the old man. "They can't stand the smell of human flesh. Haven't you met them?"

"No, I've seen no one but three cormorants perched on a piece of driftwood. They were screaming," Isaac answered.

"Well," said the old man, knocking the ashes out of his pipe, "those were my boys. Now you had better go inside, for I'm sure you must be both hungry and thirsty."

"I'm much obliged to you," said Isaac.

But when the old man opened the door, what Isaac saw was so wonderful that his eyes almost popped out of his head. He had never seen anything like it before. The table was laden with bowls of milk and cream and haddock and reindeer steak and liver-cakes covered with syrup and cheese. There was pastry from Bergen, and whisky and beer and mead and everything else that is good.

Isaac ate and drank all he could, but somehow his plate was never empty, and his glass was always full. The old man did not eat much, nor did he say much either. All of a sudden, they heard a scream and a rumbling outside, and the old man went out. After a while he came back with his three sons. They were dark, stumpy fellows, and Isaac was startled a little as he saw them in the doorway, but the old man had probably calmed them down, for they seemed rather pleasant and good natured, though they said to Isaac, who had finished and got up to leave the table, that he must show some table manners, keep his seat, and drink with them. So, Isaac humored them and stayed, and they all drank dram after dram of whisky, with now and then a swallow of beer or mead. Finally, they became very good friends, and the boys said they would all have to go fishing together, so that Isaac would have something to take home with him.

The first day they were out, a terrible storm came up. One of the sons sat at the tiller, one in the bow, and one in the cockpit, while Isaac had to bail so hard that the sweat poured off him. They sailed as if they were stark raving mad; they never reefed the sail, and when the boat was full of water, they just sailed her up on the crest of the waves till she tilted over, and the sea poured like a waterfall out of the cockpit. After a while the storm abated, and they began to fish. Their catch piled up so high that they couldn't even find the iron ballast which was kept in the bottom of the boat. The

Ut-Röst boys hauled in one fish after another. Isaac used his own tackle and got many a good bite, but every time he hauled a fish just to the surface, it got away before he could pull it into the boat. When the boat was filled, they sailed home to Ut-Röst, and the boys cleaned the fish and hung them up to dry. Then Isaac complained of his own hard luck to the old father, who gave him a couple of hooks and promised him better luck with them.

The next time they went out, Isaac pulled in the fish as fast as the boys, and when they came back, he had as his share three big lines full.

But Isaac grew homesick and decided to leave. Then the old man gave him a new eight-oared boat, filled with flour and sail-cloth and many other useful things. Isaac thanked him many times over, and the old man invited him to come back when the fishing season was on again and promised to take him to Bergen so that he could sell his fish at a good price.

Isaac was very pleased with this offer and asked the old man what course he should steer when he wanted to come back to Ut-Röst.

"Straight after the cormorant when it flies out to sea," said the old man, "then you'll be on the right course. Good luck!"

When Isaac had pushed from shore and looked around, Ut-Röst had disappeared, and he saw nothing but the great, wide ocean.

When the fishing season came again, Isaac was on hand. He had never seen such a wonderful boat as the old man's. It was so long that when the mate on watch in the bow shouted to the sailor at the oars, his voice could not carry so far, and another fellow had to stand between them by the mast and shout back at the top of his lungs. They put Isaac's share of the catch in the bow, but he could not understand how it was that, though he himself took the fish off the lines, there were always new ones there, and when he stopped working, there were just as many as ever.

When he came to Bergen, he sold his fish at such a high price that he was able to follow the old man's advice and buy a fine new boat, all fitted out complete. Late one night, just as Isaac was about to leave, the old man came aboard and begged him not to forget his neighbor's children.

"He has been drowned," said the old man.

Thereupon he wished Isaac all kinds of luck with his new boat.

"Everything will come out all right in the end," he said which really meant that there was one on board whom no one saw, but who would steady the mast with his back when it came to a pinch.

Ever afterward Isaac had good luck in everything he undertook, but he knew where it came from, and when he put up his boat in the autumn, he never forgot the fellows who would be out on watch all winter. Every Christmas Eve his boat was all ablaze with lights, and one could hear the sound of fiddling and laughter and dancing in the cabin.

THEY FOUND A POOR LITTLE GIRL

The Nightingale

Hans Christian Andersen

"The Nightingale" is one of the most famous of all Hans Christian Andersen's Tales. It has been set to music and turned into a ballet by Mr. Stravinsky and Mr. Diagheleff. As for the mechanical nightingale in this story, my uncle has one made to the same pattern. Press a button of the little gold box, up flies the lid, out hops a nightingale sparkling with blue and silver, it flutters its wings, shakes its head and trills like a real bird, and will do it a hundred times a day if you like, until the works wear out. So you see this tale must be true.

In China, as you know, the Emperor is Chinese, and all the people around him are Chinese, too. It is many years since the story I am going to tell you happened, but that is all the more reason for telling it, lest it should be forgotten.

The Emperor's palace was the most beautiful thing in the world; it was made entirely of the finest porcelain, very costly, but at the same time so fragile that it could only be touched with the very greatest care. There were the most extraordinary flowers to be seen in the garden; the most beautiful ones had little silver bells tied to them, which tinkled perpetually, so that one could not pass the flowers without looking at them. Every little detail in the garden had been most carefully thought out, and it was so big that even the gardener himself did not know where it ended.

If one went on walking, one came to beautiful woods with lofty trees and deep lakes. The forest extended to the sea, which was deep and blue, deep enough for large ships to sail right up under the branches of the trees. Among these trees lived a nightingale, which sang so sweetly, that even the poor fisherman who had plenty of other things to do, lay still to listen to it, when he was out at night drawing in his nets.

"Heavens, how beautiful it is!" he said, but then he had to attend to his business and forgot it. The next night when he heard it again, he would again exclaim, "Heavens, how beautiful it is!"

Travellers came to the Emperor's capital, from every country in the world. They admired everything very much, especially the palace and the gardens, but when they heard the nightingale, they all said, "This is better than anything!"

When they got home, they described it, and the learned ones wrote many books about the town, the palace, and the garden, but nobody forgot the nightingale, for it was always put above everything else. Those among them who were poets wrote the most beautiful poems, all about the nightingale in the woods by the deep blue sea. These books went all over the world, and in course of time, some of them reached the Emperor. He sat in his golden chair reading and reading, and nodding his head, well

DOI: 10.4324/9781003297536-10

pleased to hear such beautiful descriptions of the town, the palace, and the garden. "But the nightingale is the best of all," he read.

"What is this?" said the Emperor. "The nightingale? Why, I know nothing about it. Is there such a bird in my kingdom, and in my own garden into the bargain, and I have never heard of it? Imagine my having to discover this from a book."

Then he called his gentleman-in-waiting, who was so grand that when anyone of a lower rank dared to speak to him, or to ask him a question, he would only answer "P" which means nothing at all.

"There is supposed to be a very wonderful bird called a nightingale here," said the Emperor. "They say that it is better than anything else in all my great kingdom! Why have I never been told anything about it?"

"I have never heard it mentioned," said the gentleman-in-waiting. "It has never been presented at court."

"I wish it to appear here this evening to sing to me," said the Emperor. "The whole world knows what I possess and I know nothing about it!"

"I have never heard it mentioned before," said the gentleman-in-waiting. "I will seek it, and I will find it!"

But where was it to be found? The gentleman-in-waiting ran upstairs and downstairs and in and out of all the rooms and corridors. No one of all those he met had ever heard anything about the nightingale; so the gentleman-in-waiting ran back to the Emperor, and said that it must be a myth, invented by the writers of the books.

"Your imperial majesty must not believe everything that is written; books are often mere inventions, even if they do not belong to what we call the black art!"

"But the book in which I read it was sent to me by the powerful Emperor of Japan, so it can't be untrue. I will hear this nightingale! I insist upon its being here tonight. I extend my most gracious protection to it, and if it is not forthcoming, I will have the whole court trampled upon after supper!"

"Tsing-pe!" said the gentleman-in-waiting, and away he ran again, up and down all the stairs and in and out of all the rooms and corridors. Half the court ran with him, for none of them wished to be trampled on. There was much questioning about this nightingale, which was known to all the outside world, but not to anyone at court.

At last they found a poor little maid in the kitchen. She said, "Oh heavens, the nightingale? I know it very well. Yes, indeed it can sing. Every evening I am allowed to take some meat to my poor sick mother. She lives down by the shore. On my way back when I am tired, I rest awhile in the forest, and then I hear the nightingale. Its song brings the tears into my eyes, I feel as if my mother were kissing me!"

"Little kitchen-maid," said the gentleman-in-waiting, "I will procure you a permanent position in the kitchen and permission to see the Emperor dining, if you will take us to the nightingale. It is commanded to appear at court tonight."

Then they all went out into the wood where the nightingale usually sang. Half the court was there. As they were moving along at their best, a cow began to bellow.

"Oh!" said a young courtier, "there we have it. What wonderful power for such a little creature. I have certainly heard it before."

"No, those are the cows bellowing. We must go a long way yet from the place."

Then the frogs began to croak in the marsh.

"Beautiful!" said the Chinese chaplain, "it is just like the tinkling of church bells."

"No, those are the frogs!" said the little kitchen-maid. "But I think we shall soon hear it now!"

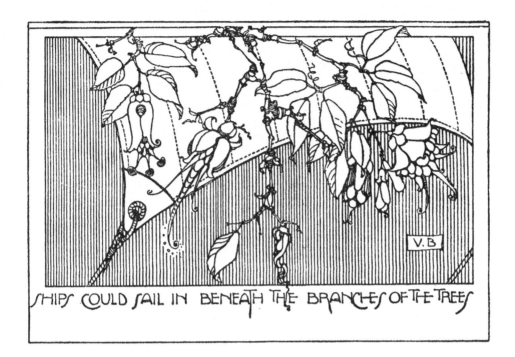

SHIPS COULD SAIL IN BENEATH THE BRANCHES OF THE TREES

Then the nightingale began to sing.

"There it is!" said the little girl. "Listen, listen, there it sits!" and she pointed to a little gray bird up among the branches.

"Is it possible?" said the gentleman-in-waiting. "I would never have thought it was like that. How common it looks. Seeing so many grand people must have frightened all its colors away."

"Little nightingale!" called the kitchen-maid quite loud, "our gracious Emperor wishes you to sing to him!"

"With the greatest pleasure!" said the nightingale, warbling away in the most delightful fashion.

"It is just like crystal bells," said the gentleman-in-waiting.

"Look at its little throat, how active it is. It is extraordinary that we have never heard it before! I am sure it will be a great success at court!"

"Shall I sing again to the Emperor?" said the nightingale, who thought he was present.

"My precious little nightingale," said the gentleman-in-waiting, "I have the honor to command your attendance at a court festival tonight, where you will charm his gracious Majesty, the Emperor, with your fascinating singing."

"But it sounds best among the trees," said the nightingale.

Nevertheless, it went with them willingly when it heard that the Emperor wished to hear it.

The palace had been brightened up for the occasion. The walls and the floors, which were made all of china, shone by the light of many thousand and olden lamps. The most beautiful flowers, all of the tinkling kind, were arranged in the corridors.

There was hurrying to and fro, and a great draught, but this was just what made the bells ring. Indeed, one's ears were full of the tinkling. In the middle of the large reception room where the Emperor sat, a golden rod had been fixed, on which the nightingale was to perch. The whole court was assembled, and the little kitchen maid had been permitted to stand behind the door, as she now had the actual title of cook. They were all dressed in their best, and everybody's eyes were turned toward the little gray bird at which the Emperor was nodding.

The nightingale sang delightfully, and tears came into the Emperor's eyes, nay, they rolled down his cheeks, and then the nightingale sang more beautifully than ever; its notes touched all hearts.

The Emperor was charmed, and said the nightingale should have his gold slipper to wear around its neck. But the nightingale declined with thanks, and said it had already been sufficiently rewarded.

"I have seen tears in the eyes of the Emperor. That is my richest reward. The tears of an Emperor have a wonderful power! God knows I am sufficiently recompensed!" and then it again burst into its sweet heavenly song.

"That is the most delightful coqueting I have ever seen!" said the ladies, and they took some water into their mouths to try and make the same gurgling, whenever anyone spoke to them, thinking so to equal the nightingale. Even the lackeys and the chambermaids announced that they were satisfied, and that is saying a great deal, for they are always the most difficult people to please. Yes, indeed, the nightingale had made a sensation. It was to stay at court now, and to have its own cage, as well as liberty to walk out twice a day, and once in the night. It always had twelve footmen with each one holding a ribbon which was tied around its leg. There was not much pleasure in an outing of that sort.

The whole town talked about the marvelous bird, and if two people met, one said to the other "Night," and the other answered "Gale," and then they sighed, perfectly understanding each other. Eleven cheese mongers' children were named after it, but they didn't have a voice among them.

One day a large parcel came for the Emperor. The word "Nightingale" was written on the outside.

"Here we have another new book about this celebrated bird," said the Emperor. But it was not a book, it was a little work of art in a box, an artificial nightingale, exactly like the living one, but it was studded all over with diamonds, rubies, and sapphires. When the bird was wound up, it could sing one of the songs the real one sang, and it wagged its tail which glittered with silver and gold. A ribbon was tied around its neck on which was written, "The Emperor of Japan's nightingale is very poor, compared to the Emperor of China's."

Everybody said, "Oh, how beautiful!" And the person who brought the artificial bird immediately received the title of Imperial Nightingale-Carrier-in-Chief.

"Now, they must sing together," said the Emperor. "What a duet that will be!"

Then they had to sing together, but they did not get on very well, for the real nightingale sang in his own way, and the artificial one could only sing waltzes.

"There is no fault in that," said the music master; "It is perfectly in time and correct in every way!"

Then the artificial bird had to sing alone. It was just as great a success as the real one, and then it was so much prettier to look at, for it glittered like bracelets and

TWELVE SERVANTS WERE APPOINTED TO THE NIGHTINGALE

THE ARTIFICIAL NIGHTINGALE

breast-pins. It sang the same tune three and thirty times over, and yet, it was not tired. People would willingly have heard it from the beginning again, but the Emperor said that the real one must have a turn now – but where was it? No one had noticed that it had flown out of the open window, back to its own green forest. "But what is the meaning of this?" said the Emperor.

All the courtiers railed at it, and said it was a most ungrateful bird.

"We have got the best bird though," said they, and the artificial bird had to sing again, and this was the thirty-fourth time that they heard the same tune, but they did not know it thoroughly even yet, because it was so difficult.

The music master praised the bird tremendously, and insisted that it was much better than the real nightingale, not only with regard to the outside with all the diamonds, but the inside, too.

"Because you see, my ladies and gentlemen, and the Emperor before all, in the real nightingale you never know what you will hear, but in the artificial one everything is decided beforehand! So it is, and so it must remain; it can't be otherwise. You can account for things, you can open it and show the human ingenuity in arranging the waltzes, how they go and how one note follows upon another!"

"Those are exactly my opinions," they all said, and the music master was permitted to show the bird to the public next Sunday. They were also to hear it sing, said the Emperor. So they heard it, and all became as enthusiastic over it, as if they had drunk themselves merry on tea, because that is a thoroughly Chinese habit.

Then they all said "Oh," and stuck their forefingers in the air and nodded their heads; but the poor fishermen who had heard the real nightingale said, "It sounds very nice, and it is very like the real one, but there is something wanting, we don't know what."

The real nightingale was banished from the kingdom. The artificial bird had its place on a silken cushion, close to the Emperor's bed. All the presents it had received of gold and precious jewels were scattered around it. Its title had risen to be "Chief Imperial Singer of the Bed-Chamber," in rank number one, on the left side; for the emperor reckoned that side the important one, where the heart was seated. And even an emperor's heart is on the left side. The music master wrote five-and-twenty volumes about the artificial bird. The treatise was very long, and written in all the most difficult Chinese characters. Everybody said they had read and understood it, for otherwise they would have been reckoned stupid, and then their bodies would have been trampled upon.

Things went on in this way for a whole year. The emperor, the court, and all the other Chinese knew every little gurgle in the song of the artificial bird by heart; but they liked it all the better for this, and they could all join in the song themselves. Even the street boys sang "zizizi" and "cluck, cluck cluck," and the emperor sang it too.

But one evening, when the bird was singing its best, and the emperor was lying in bed listening to it, something gave way inside the bird with a "whizz." Then a spring burst, "whirr" went all the wheels, and the music stopped. The emperor jumped out of bed and sent for his private physicians, but what good could they do? Then they sent for the watchmaker, and after a good deal of talk and examination, he got the works to go again somehow; but he said it would have to be saved as much as possible, because it was so worn out, and he could not renew the works so as to be sure of the tune.

This was a great blow! They only dared to let the artificial bird sing once a year, and hardly. Meanwhile, the music master made a little speech using all the most difficult words. He said it was just as good as ever, and his saying it made it so.

Five years now passed, and then a great grief came upon the nation, for they were all very fond of their emperor, and he was ill and could not live, it was said. A new emperor was already chosen, and people stood about in the street and asked the gentleman-in-waiting how their emperor was doing.

"Poorly," he answered, shaking his head.

The emperor lay pale and cold in his gorgeous bed, the courtiers thought he was dead, and they all went off to pay their respects to the new emperor. The lackeys ran off to talk matters over, and the chambermaids gave a great coffee party. Cloth had been laid down in all the rooms and corridors so as to deaden the sound of footsteps, so it was very, very quiet. But the emperor was not dead yet. He lay stiff and pale in the gorgeous bed with its velvet hangings and heavy golden tassels. There was an open window high above him, and the moon streamed in upon the emperor, and the artificial bird beside him.

The poor emperor could hardly breathe, and he seemed to have a weight on his chest. He opened his eyes, and then he saw that it was Death sitting upon his chest, wearing his golden crown. In one hand he held the emperor's golden sword, and in the other his imperial banner. From among the folds of the velvet hangings peered many curious faces; some were hideous, others gentle and pleasant. They were all the emperor's good and bad deeds, which now looked him in the face when Death was weighing him down.

"Do you remember that?" whispered one after the other.

"Do you remember this?" and they told him so many things that the perspiration poured down his face.

"I never knew that," said the emperor. "Music, music, sound the great Chinese drums!" he cried, "that I may not hear what they are saying."

But they went on and on, and Death sat nodding his head, just like a Chinaman, at everything that was said.

"Music, music!" shrieked the emperor. "You precious little golden bird, sing, sing! I have loaded you with precious stones, and even hung my own golden slipper around your neck, sing, I tell you, sing!"

But the bird stood silent. There was nobody to wind it up, so of course it could not go. Death continued to fix the great empty sockets of its eyes upon him, and all was silent, so terribly silent.

Suddenly, close to the window, there was a burst of lovely song. It was the living nightingale, perched on a branch outside. It had heard of the emperor's need and had come to bring comfort and hope to him. As it sang, the faces around the emperor became fainter and fainter, and the blood coursed with fresh vigor in the emperor's veins and through his feeble limbs. Even Death himself listened to the song and said, "Go on, little nightingale, go on!"

"Yes, if you give me the gorgeous golden sword; yes, if you give me the imperial banner; yes, if you give me the emperor's crown."

And Death returned each of these treasures for a song, and the nightingale went on singing. It sang about the quiet churchyard, when the roses bloom, where the elder flower scents the air, and where the fresh grass is ever moistened anew by the tears of

DEATH SAT ON HIS CHEST

the mourner. This song brought to Death a longing for his own garden, and like a cold gray mist, he flew out of the window.

"Thanks, thanks!" said the emperor; "you heavenly little bird, I know you! I banished you from my kingdom, and yet, you have charmed the evil visions away from my bed by your song, and even Death went away from my heart! How can I ever repay you?"

"You have rewarded me," said the nightingale. "I brought the tears to your eyes, the very first time I ever sang to you, and I shall never forget it! Those are the jewels which gladden the heart of a singer – but sleep now, and wake up fresh and strong! I will sing to you!"

Then the nightingale sang again, and the emperor fell into a sweet refreshing sleep. The sun shone through his window, when he woke refreshed and well. None of his attendants had yet come back to him, for they thought he was dead, but the nightingale still sat there singing.

"You must always stay with me!" said the emperor. "You shall only sing when you like, and I will break the artificial bird into a thousand pieces!"

"Don't do that!" said the nightingale. "It did all the good it could! Keep it as you have always done! I can't build my nest and live in this palace, but let me come whenever I like. Then I shall sit on the branch in the evening, and sing to you. I will sing to cheer you and to make you thoughtful too; I will sing to you about the happy ones, and of those that suffer, too. I will sing about the good and the evil, which are kept hidden from you. The little singing bird flies far and wide, to the poor fisherman, and the peasant's home, to numbers who are far from you and your court. I love your heart more than your crown, and there is an odor of sanctity around the crown too! I shall come and I sing to you! But you must promise me one thing!"

"Everything!" said the emperor, who stood there in his imperial robes which he had just put on, and he held the sword heavy with gold upon his heart.

"One thing I ask you! Tell no one that you have a little bird who tells you everything. It will be better so!"

Then the nightingale flew away. The attendants came in to his room to see after their dead emperor, and there he stood, bidding them "Good-morning!"

The Lake Princess

Herbert Giles and Pu Singling

This story is also about China. It was written by a Chinese man of high education, and since Chinese poets use very long words, if there is anything in it you don't understand, I suggest that you have recourse to your lexicon.

Once upon a time there was a poor man of good birth who, being a gentleman, had, at considerable sacrifice upon his father's part, obtained high honors in literature in his final examination in Peking. In China, if one can write an ode in the manner of the best poets, and if one knows all the old classic literature from beginning to end, one can usually obtain at least a minor post in the Civil Service.

This poor man, whose name, for all useful purposes, was Cheng, obtained the post of Secretary to a General called Chia. He accompanied General Chia wherever he went. It happened that General Chia made an excursion into the interior of China and, in the course of his journey, came to a great lake. Now, Chia had with him not only his Secretary, but also a whole company of bowmen and sailors. The lake was a pleasant place, and the General, from all accounts, spent a considerable time there and amused himself with fishing. One day a large fish was seen swimming around the boat, and the General called for his bow and arrows and tried to shoot it, but only succeeded in wounding it. When they hauled the fish out of the water, they found a little fish hanging on to its tail. The sailors strung up the big fish to the mainmast, and the poor creature, which was not yet dead, gasped as any fish out of water will, but Cheng thought that it was begging for its life and said to the General, "Please, let that fish go, my lord."

General Chia laughed and said, "Since you have fallen in love with the mermaid, do as you like with her."

So, Cheng, who was in a cheerful mood, healed his mermaid's wound with court plaster and, with the help of the sailors, threw her, with the little fish still hanging on to her tail, back into the lake, and the ugly fish, for she was indeed not beautiful, disported herself in the water near the ship as if to express her thanks to Cheng.

Some time afterward, Cheng had occasion to visit this lake, but while he was thinking of his former amusing experience there, a squall came down and upset his boat, and he was almost drowned. If he had not had the good luck to seize hold of a great bamboo cage full of unsinkable goods, he would certainly have been drowned. As it was, he was in the water all night.

In the morning, the crate drifted under a bank, and with the assistance of a tree, Cheng was able to climb on shore. After a while, a corpse drifted alongside the crate. Cheng dragged it out and discovered it was the dead body of his servant. Cheng felt

DOI: 10.4324/9781003297536-11

AN ORNAMENTAL BARGE FLOATED OVER THE WATER.

very melancholy. He was worn out with fatigue and would have given all the beautiful landscape before him for the sake of a human voice.

He stayed some hours wondering what would become of him and was beginning to despair, when he saw the corpse beside him twitch, and whether it was the sun, or whatnot, his servant presently revived and became as live as Cheng himself, which is not saying much. However, when two are together in the same plight, things do not look so bad, and Cheng was prevailed upon to attempt to dry his clothes. So he and his servant undressed and dried their clothes on some willows. When they were dry, they dressed, and feeling very hungry, decided to cross the hills behind them in search of food.

They had not walked very far before they were almost killed by an arrow that seemed to come from nowhere, and before they had time to recover from this fright, two beautiful girls rushed past them on white horses. As for the dresses of the girls, they were the most amazing riding habits that have ever been seen. They wore red head-dresses, trimmed with pheasant feathers, purple satin riding-jackets and emerald-green sashes embroidered with butterflies, and all manner of flowers. The elder maiden carried a cross-bow, and the younger a quiver full of arrows. Cheng and his servant, in spite of this encounter, pursued their way to the top of the hill, and from there they saw a whole army of Amazons engaged in hunting. At last Cheng was really frightened, not knowing into what country they had strayed. Soon, they encountered a young man who seemed to be either a page or superior slave. The young man gave them some food from a hunting bag that he carried, and warned them to make their way out of the country.

"If the Amazons should see you again," he said, "they will certainly put an end to you."

So Cheng and his servant departed with great haste. They went down the hill and found themselves in a forest. In the midst of the forest stood a building, in shape and proportions much like a temple. It was surrounded by a high wall, and the wall was protected by a moat. Across the moat stood a bridge. Cheng, who was at the end of his tether, decided to cross the bridge. He did so and peered in at the door in the temple wall that had not been properly shut. To his amazement, instead of a temple within the wall, he saw a floating palace with pleasure grounds, parks, willow trees, pavilions, flowers, winding walks and ornamental ponds, exactly like those in the summer palace of Peking, with this difference that the whole of this magnificent estate was lazily drifting about in the air like a cloud. By some means, Cheng and his servant discovered themselves in the midst of this aerial garden where the song of a bird made the flowers dance, and the breeze caused showers of delight from the huge trees. No one has ever seen or heard anything to compare with the beauty of this curious place, either before or since.

So, Cheng came to a pavilion and found a swing nearby – it hung down from heaven. In order to make his presence known, Cheng coughed and said: "I believe we must be near the Private Apartments."

And since he would not for the world have intruded upon the ladies' quarters, being a man of very polite manners, he prepared to depart, but suddenly sounds of girlish laughter and the tramping of horses' feet broke the stillness of the air. There was nothing for Cheng and his servant to do if they wanted to avoid the insult of the ladies with their presence. No sooner had they hidden themselves behind a flowering shrub than the girls came to the pavilion. One of them cried out: "What a wretched day!"

Another said, "Yes, all this fuss and only a goose."

They continued to discuss the day's hunting until a maiden of amazing loveliness entered the pavilion, attended by several companions in scarlet uniform. Nothing more lovely than this maiden ever lived. If it might be said without offence, she would have put a goddess to shame. She was so delicately made, that one feared a breeze might blow her in half, and her hair looked like the morning mist upon the mountains. After she had seated herself in the pavilion, slaves offered her a cup of the most exquisite tea, and then posed themselves around her, looking like a flower-bed in their glorious uniforms, for everyone in that palace wore costumes befitting their rank, embroidered all over with every imaginable flower.

After tea, one of her companions suggested that she might care to amuse herself with the swing. A dozen attendants immediately lifted her from the ground, and having shod her feet with swing slippers, stood there in the swing and then, as if by magic, she swung far away out of sight and in again, out of sight and in, until she was tired of it. Immediately the twelve attendants assisted her to the ground, complimenting her with these words: "One would think, your highness, that you were an angel from Heaven."

Poor Cheng, who had hidden in the flower bush with his servant, practically fainted with love and amazement. Fortunately for his recovery, the swinging party went away, and Cheng and his servant came from behind the bush. Full of sentimental longings, he paraded near the swing, dreaming impossible dreams and soon almost overcome by joy at the sight, he saw a scarlet handkerchief lying upon the ground. With a thousand raptures he entered the summer-house, and discovering everything that he needed there for writing, he sat down right away and composed the following lines, which he wrote upon the handkerchief:

"With sighs I ask, who is this angel
Who not only puts to shame all worldly beauty,
But with her loveliness dims the very stars?
I have seen her walk on earth and fly in heaven."

Cheng's excellent education stood him in good stead. He at once set this poem to music and wandered away thinking to leave the palace without further intrusion, but to his embarrassment, the door by which he had come in was shut, and he could not open it. There was nothing he could do but return to the summer-house, and if he was challenged by anyone there, to make a polite and modest answer. In time, one of the princess's companions did come to the summer-house and said in amazement, "What are you doing here?"

"Madam," said Cheng, "I came here not knowing my destination. Please direct me to some place suitable for my accommodation."

The young lady, instead of answering him directly, said, "I have lost a scarlet handkerchief."

Cheng replied, "I have had the honor to find it but, alas, I had the temerity to soil it." Thereupon, he handed the handkerchief to the young lady.

"Alas," cried the girl, "this is your death warrant. It is the princess's own handkerchief, and you have ruined it."

Cheng trembled all over and begged the girl to help him.

"What can I do?" she asked. "You have introduced yourself here without permission. Seeing that you are highly educated and of distinguished manners, I might have obtained an excuse for you, but now you have ruined the princess's favorite handkerchief, what is to be done?"

Cheng sighed, and the girl took the handkerchief and ran away. The poor man feared his immediate death and wished, with all his heart that he could turn into a bird and fly away. When he was in the very depths of despair, the girl came back and said, "Sir, you are very lucky. The princess has actually condescended to read your poem. I believe that, ultimately you will be set free. However, until the princess has spoken on the subject, you must stay here. Make no attempt, however, to climb the walls or trees, for if you try to escape without permission, it will certainly end in your death."

Cheng had now been given his parole, and the girl went away. He again resigned himself to the misery of an uncertain fate, aggravated by hunger. He was so desperately in need of food that he thought death would be preferable to life.

After dark, the girl who had befriended him brought him a lamp. She was attended by a female slave carrying an excellent meal upon a tray, which was set out before Cheng. The unhappy man asked the girl if the princess had yet condescended to arrange his fate. The young lady answered, "I have had the boldness to speak of you to the princess, but owing to the lateness of the hour, she has not come to any conclusion about you, except to order that you should not die of starvation."

Cheng thanked her, and after she had gone, supped, but though he was not now starving, he could not sleep and spent the whole night walking up, and down, worrying about the future.

When the young lady brought him food in the morning, he begged her to urge the princess to consider his case, but the young lady said, "It would ill become me to urge the princess continually about such a trifle."

So, Cheng passed another day in despair. Toward nightfall, his friend ran wildly into the pavilion, crying, "The princess's mother, the queen herself has heard of your presence. She used the most dreadful language. I am afraid, sir, that you are done for."

Cheng prostrated himself at the young lady's feet, but as he was about to beg for interest on his behalf, she ran away, and immediately a number of people came into the pavilion ready to bind poor Cheng and drag him off to execution. At the last moment, a young female slave suddenly exclaimed, "It is Mr. Cheng," and, bidding the executioner's pause, ran to the queen. She reappeared very quickly and said that the queen invited his presence. So, he followed her out of the pavilion and through the vast halls of the palace. As may be assumed, he was shivering with fear. At last, he entered an apartment of more than common loveliness and a beautiful girl, parting a curtain, said in a loud voice, "Mr. Cheng requests admittance!"

Cheng hurried forward and threw himself at the feet of the queen, who was enthroned in the inner apartment, crying, "Have mercy on this wretched life, your slave is a foreigner."

To his surprise, the queen became exceedingly gracious and herself raised him from the ground.

"Sir," she said, "it is I who owe you my life. Have the goodness to overlook my maid's discourtesy."

A feast was at once ordered, of which Cheng was invited to partake. The queen said, as they sat at table, "It is quite beyond my power to reward you for saving my life, but since you have deigned to notice the princess, my daughter, it is quite clear that Heaven has destined you to be her husband. Take her and do with her as you will."

Cheng had not the slightest idea what prompted this special honor, or why he was paid the priceless compliment of marriage with the princess. However, the wedding took place immediately. Wedding music sounded throughout the palace; wedding carpets were laid down, and the vast gardens were illuminated with fairy lights.

Cheng said to his wife, "Madam, I am amazed that a vagabond, who had the temerity to soil your handkerchief, should have escaped execution: I deserved no kindness of Fate. That you should have had the extraordinary condescension to become my wife, is an almost incredible piece of good fortune."

The princess answered, "The queen, who is married to the Lake King, is descended from the River Prince. It happened that once, while making a journey to her old home incognito, she was severely wounded, but owing to your kindness, she was saved from death, and a piece of court-plaster was placed upon her wound. We, therefore, owe you all imaginable service. Do not fear that you have married a creature of another world, for I have obtained the elixir of life of which you must also drink."

Now Cheng was aware that he had married a fairy. Later on, they held another conversation in which he begged her to tell him how it was that the slave girl had recognized him. She said, "Do you remember the little fish that was hanging on the great fish's tail? That girl was the little fish who was accompanying my mother on her journey."

Cheng asked how it was that his fate had hung so long in the balance.

"I was trying," said the princess, "to make up my mind how to inform my mother of the interest your poem had awakened in me. I am sure that I could rest neither day nor night."

Then Cheng asked her a number of other questions of much less interest, and finally said, "I owe you a debt which I never can repay."

The princess replied that there was always plenty of time for the repayment of debts. After Cheng had enjoyed his happiness for a certain time, he began to wonder how his family fared, and received permission to dispatch a servant with the news of his good fortune. His father and mother, who, when they had heard of the disaster to his boat, believed him to have drowned, were beside themselves with joy. After a while, Cheng himself obtained permission to visit his parents and appeared at home splendidly dressed and splendidly equipped. He set up a magnificent palace, entertained his friends lavishly and was quite open about his adventures.

It happened that an old school friend of his by chance crossed the lake that had brought Cheng so much good luck, on his way home from a distant province where he had been acting as proconsul. When he was crossing the lake he encountered a magnificent house-boat from which sounds of merriment and music could be heard. As the house-boat passed his small craft, one of the windows opened, and he saw within a lovely lady. A young man was lying at the feet of the lady, and two lovely slaves were massaging him. The proconsul saw, to his surprise, that the young man was his school friend, Cheng. So, he called out to him, and when Cheng heard himself hailed, he stood up and, attended by his servants, went on deck and asked his friend to come aboard. The proconsul accepted the invitation and was at once led into the saloon and was entertained with a very handsome feast. During dinner the proconsul began to talk of old times. "You've done very well for yourself," he said.

"What's odd in that?" said Cheng, "Though I must confess, I was poor enough the last time we met."

His friend then asked who the lady at the window was, and Cheng said, "She is my honored wife."

"Where are you off to?" asked the proconsul.

"Oh," Cheng replied rather carelessly. "We are going west."

And in order to stop this friend from questioning him, he called for music. Soon, however, the proconsul began to get very talkative in spite of the music, for Cheng's wine was very strong. He said to Cheng: "Give me one of your female slaves as a memento of this happy occasion."

"You have had too much wine, old friend," said Cheng. "Here instead is a very expensive pearl for you. I don't want you to think me mean, but I have no time to waste in further gossip and must bid you good-bye."

Thus he got rid of the proconsul, who was becoming a nuisance, and the house-boat sailed on its way.

When the proconsul returned home, to his amazement he found Cheng, looking considerable older, sitting among his friends. So, he cried out: "Why, Cheng, I saw you in a house-boat on the Great Lake only yesterday. You've got home in amazing time."

Cheng said he knew of no house-boat, and the proconsul, who was a regular gossip, like many small government officials, told the whole tale of the party on the lake. But Cheng said, "You've let your imagination run away with you. How could I be here and there at the same time?"

His friends were inclined half to believe the story they had heard, but though it was discussed by all the town tattlers, nobody could make head nor tail about it.

Many years later, when Cheng died and was put in a coffin, the mutes at the funeral declared that the coffin was empty. It was opened, and sure enough, there was no body inside.

Now the truth of this story is that Cheng had indeed married the Lake Princess and had become immortal, but in order that his parents were to have the happiness of his company through their lifetime, and that he might pay them the customary ceremonies after their death, he was allowed to send his double back to his home.

And thus he was able to enjoy eternal happiness with his beautiful princess, and to honor his ancestors as a Chinaman of respectability and decent upbringing should.

The History of Ali Baba and the Forty Robbers Who Were Killed by One Slave

Antoine Galland

This very famous story is here set out at length with every particular of the cleverness of Morgiana, who, though a slave, was as brave as a lioness. The tale is one of those told by the Sultaness Scheherazade to the Sultan Schahriar, who threatened every night to cut off her head next morning for a crime she had not committed. However, he was so fascinated by her stories, which she took care never to finish, that he postponed her execution for one thousand and one nights. In the end he forgave her.

In a certain town of Persia, Oh great monarch, situated on the very confines of your majesty's dominions, there lived two brothers, one of whom was named Cassim, and the other Ali Baba. Upon the death of their father, he left them a very moderate fortune, which they divided equally. It might, therefore, be naturally conjectured that their situations in life would turn out to be the same. Chance, however, ordered it otherwise.

Cassim married a woman, who very soon after her nuptials, inherited a well-furnished shop, a warehouse filled with good merchandise, and some considerable property in land. Her husband thus found himself suddenly quite a prosperous man and became one of the richest merchants in the whole town. On the other hand, Ali Baba, who had taken to wife a woman no better off for worldly goods than himself, lived in a very poor house, and had no other means of gaining his livelihood, and supporting his wife and children, than by going to cut wood in a neighboring forest, and carrying it about the town to sell, on three asses, which were his only possession.

One day, Ali Baba went to the forest and had very nearly finished cutting as much wood as his asses could carry, when he perceived a thick cloud of dust, which rose very high into the air, and appeared to come from a point to the right of the spot where he stood. It was advancing toward him. As he looked at it very attentively, he was soon able to distinguish a numerous group of men on horseback, who were approaching at a quick pace.

Although that part of the country had never been spoken of as being infested with robbers, Ali Baba nevertheless conjectured that these horsemen might belong to such a group of dangerous thieves. Therefore, without considering what might become of his asses, his first and only care was to save himself. So, he instantly climbed a large tree, the branches of which, at a very little height from the ground, spread out so close and thick that only one small opening was left. He hid himself among the thick branches, with great hope of safety, as he could see everything that occurred without being observed. The tree itself also grew at the foot of a sort of isolated rock, considerably higher than the tree, and so steep that it could not be easily ascended. The men, who

DOI: 10.4324/9781003297536-12

appeared stout, powerful, and well mounted, rode up to this very rock, and stopped at its foot. Once they got off their horses, Ali Baba counted forty of them and was very sure, from their appearance and mode of equipment, that they were robbers. Nor was he wrong in his conjecture. They were, in fact, a band of robbers, who abstained from committing any depredations in the neighborhood, but carried on their system of plunder at a considerable distance, and only had their place of rendezvous at that spot. Soon each thief took the bridle off his horse and hung over its head a bag filled with barley, which he had brought with him; and when all had fastened their horses to bushes and trees, they took off their traveling bags, which appeared so heavy that Ali Baba thought they must be filled with gold and silver.

The robber who was nearest to him, and whom Ali Baba took for the captain of the band, came with his bag on his shoulder close to the rock, beside the very tree in which Ali Baba had concealed himself. After making his way among some bushes and shrubs that grew there, the robber very deliberately pronounced these words "OPEN SESAME!" which Ali Baba distinctly heard.

The captain of the band had no sooner spoken, than a door immediately opened; and after making all his men pass before him, and go in through the door, the chief also entered and the door closed. The robbers continued within the rock for a considerable time, and Ali Baba was compelled to remain in the tree and wait with patience for their departure since he was afraid to leave his place of refuge and endeavor to save himself by flight, lest some of the horsemen should come out and discover him. He was, nevertheless, strongly tempted to creep down, seize two of their horses, mount one and lead the other by the bridle, and thus, driving his three asses before him, to attempt his escape. But the peril of the undertaking made him follow the safer method of delay.

After a while, the door opened, and the forty robbers came out. The captain, contrary to his former proceeding, made his appearance first. After he had seen all his troops pass out before him, Ali Baba heard him pronounce these words: "SHUT, SESAME!" Each man then returned to his horse, put on its bridle, fastened his bag, and mounted. When the captain saw that they were all ready to proceed, he took the lead, and they departed on the road by which they had come.

Ali Baba did not immediately climb down from the tree, because he thought that the robbers might have forgotten something and be obliged to come back, and that he should thus thrust himself into danger. He followed them with his eyes until he could see them no longer, and, in order to be more secure, delayed his descent a considerable time after he had lost sight of them. As he recollected the words the captain of the robbers had used to open and shut the door, he had the curiosity to try if the same effect would be produced by his pronouncing them. Therefore, he made his way through the bushes until he came to the door which they concealed. He went up to it, and called out, "Open, sesame!" and the door instantly flew wide open.

Ali Baba expected to find only a dark and gloomy cave and was very astonished at seeing a large, spacious, brightly lit and vaulted room, dug out of the rock, and so high that he could not touch the roof with his hand. It received its light from an opening at the top of the rock. He observed in it a large quantity of provisions, numerous bales of rich merchandise, a store of silk stuffs and brocades, rich and valuable carpets, and besides all this, great quantities of money, both silver and gold, partly piled up in heaps, and partly stored in large leather bags, placed on one another. At the sight of all these things, it seemed to him that this cave must have been used, not only for years, but for centuries, as a retreat for successive generations of robbers.

Ali Baba did not hesitate long to make a plan he would pursue and went into the cave, and as soon as he was there, the door shut. But since he knew the secret by which to open it, this circumstance gave him no sort of concern. He paid no attention to the silver, but went straight for the gold coins, and particularly that portion which was in the bags. He had to take several trips to carry the coins, and when he had got together what he thought sufficient for loading his three asses, he went and gathered them together, as they had strayed away some distance. He then brought them as close as he could to the rock and loaded them; and in order to conceal the sacks, he covered them over with wood so that no one could perceive that his beasts had any other load. When he had finished his task, he went up to the door and pronounced the words, "Shut, sesame!" The portal instantly closed. Although it shut by itself every time he went in, it remained open on his coming out until he commanded it to close.

Ali Baba now took the road to town; and when he got to his own house, he drove his asses into a small courtyard and shut the gate with great care. He threw down the branches of brushwood that covered the bags, and carried the latter into his house, where he laid them down in a row before his wife who was sitting on a sofa. His wife felt the sacks to find out what might be inside, and when she found them to be full of money, she suspected her husband of having stolen them and when he laid them all before her, she could not help saying "Ali Baba is it possible that you should—?"

He immediately interrupted her. "Peace, my dear wife!" he exclaimed. "Do not alarm yourself: I am not a thief, unless it be robbery to deprive thieves of their plunder. You will change your opinion of me when I have told you about my good fortune."

Thereupon, he emptied the sacks in one great heap of gold that quite dazzled his wife's eyes; and as he did this, he related his whole adventure from beginning to end. In conclusion he begged her above all things to keep it secret. Recovering from her alarm, his wife began to rejoice with Ali Baba on the good fortune which had befallen them, and was about to count the money that lay before her piece by piece.

"What are you going to do?" he asked. "You are very foolish, Oh wife! You will never be done counting this mass. I will immediately dig a pit to bury it in. We have no time to lose!"

"But, it is only right," replied his wife, "that we should know how much there may be. I will go and borrow a small measuring cup from one of our neighbors, and while you are digging the pit, I will ascertain how much we have."

"What you want to do, wife," replied Ali Baba, "is senseless, and if you will take my advice, you should give up this plan. However, you can have your own way; only remember not to betray the secret."

Persisting in her plan, Ali Baba's wife set off and went to her brother-in-law, Cassim, who lived a short distance from her house. Cassim was away from home. So, she addressed herself to his wife, whom she asked to lend her a measuring cup for a few minutes. Cassim's wife inquired if she wanted a large or a small one, to which Ali Baba's wife replied that a small one would suit her.

"That I will lend you with pleasure," said the sister-in-law. "Wait a moment, and I will bring it you."

She went to find a measuring cup, but, knowing the poverty of Ali Baba, she was curious to know what sort of grain his wife wanted to measure. Therefore, she put some tallow under the measure, in such a way that it could not be observed. She returned with the vessel, and, giving it to the wife of Ali Baba, apologized for having made her wait so long, with the excuse that she had some difficulty in finding what she wanted.

Ali Baba's wife returned home, and placing the measure on the heap of gold, filled and emptied it at a little distance on the sofa, until she had measured the whole mass. Since her husband had by this time dug the pit for its reception, she informed him how many measures there were, and both rejoiced at the magnitude of the treasure. While Ali Baba was burying the gold, his wife, to prove her exactness and punctuality, carried back the measuring cup to her sister-in-law, without observing that a piece of gold had stuck to the bottom of it

"Here, sister," said she, on returning it, "You see I have not kept your measure very long. I am much obliged to you for lending it to me."

So, soon as the wife of Ali Baba had taken her departure, Cassim's wife looked at the bottom of the measure, and was inexpressibly astonished to see a piece of gold sticking to it.

Envy instantly took possession of her heart.

"What!" said she to herself. "Has Ali Baba such an abundance of gold that he measures, instead of counting it? Where can that miserable wretch have got it?"

Her husband Cassim was not home. He had gone as usual to his shop and would not return until the evening. The time of his absence appeared a year to her, for she was burning with impatience to acquaint him with a circumstance which, she concluded, would surprise him as much as it had astonished her.

On Cassim's return home, his wife said to him, "Cassim, you think you are rich, but you are deceived. Ali Baba has infinitely more wealth than you can boast. He does not count his money as you do; he measures it."

Cassim demanded an explanation of this enigma, and his wife unraveled it by acquainting him with the expedient she had used to make this discovery, and showing him the piece of money she had found adhering to the bottom of the measure. The coin was so ancient that the name engraved on it was unknown to her. Far from feeling any pleasure at the good fortune which had rescued his brother from poverty, Cassim developed an implacable jealousy on this occasion. He could scarcely close his eyes the whole night long. The next morning, before sunrise, he went to Ali Baba. He did not call upon him as a brother, mainly because that endearing appellation had not passed his lips since his marriage with the rich widow.

"Oh, Ali Baba," said he addressing him. "You are very reserved in your affairs. You pretend to be poor and wretched, and a beggar, and yet you have so much money that you must measure it."

"Oh, my brother," replied Ali Baba, "I don't understand your meaning. Please, explain yourself."

"Don't pretend ignorance," resumed Cassim. And showing Ali Baba the piece of gold his wife had given him, he continued: "How many pieces have you like this that my wife found sticking to the bottom of the measure which your wife borrowed from her yesterday?"

From this talk Ali Baba at once understood that, in consequence of his own wife's obstinacy, Cassim and his wife were already acquainted with the fact that he was anxious to conceal his treasure from them; but the discovery was made, and nothing could be done to remedy the evil. Without showing the slightest sign of surprise or vexation, he frankly confessed the whole affair to his brother and told him how he had accidentally discovered the cave used by the thieves, and where it was situated. In fact, he even offered to give him directions if Cassim would agree to keep the secret and share the treasure with him.

"Well, I certainly expect you will do so," replied Cassim in a haughty tone; and he added, "but I demand to know also the precise spot where this treasure lies concealed, and the marks and signs which may enable me to visit the place myself, should I feel inclined to do so. If you refuse this information I will go and inform the officer of the police about the whole transaction, and if I take this step, you will not only be deprived of all hope of obtaining any more money, but you will even lose what you have already taken. In contrast, I shall receive my portion for having informed against you."

Moved more by his natural goodness of heart, than intimidated by the insolent menaces of this cruel brother, Ali Baba gave him all the information he demanded, and even told him the words he had to pronounce both on entering the cave and on leaving it. Cassim made no further inquiries of Al Baba. He simply left him with the demand that he be informed of any further news he might have about the treasure. Full of the hope of gaining possession of the whole mass, he set off the next morning, before break of day with ten mules furnished with large hampers, which he intended to fill. Moreover, he indulged himself in the prospect of taking a much larger number of animals in a second expedition, according to the sums he might find in the cave.

He took the road which Ali Baba had pointed out and arrived at the rock and the tree which, from the description, he knew to be the one that had concealed his brother. So, now he looked for the door, and soon discovered it. Using the special words, "Open, sesame!" he opened the door and entered, and it immediately closed behind him. On examining the cave, he felt the utmost astonishment on seeing so much more wealth than the description of Ali Baba had led him to expect. Indeed, his admiration increased as he examined each department separately. Avaricious and fond of money as he was, he could have passed the whole day in feasting his eyes with the sight of so much gold, but he reflected that he had come to load his ten mules with as much treasure as he could collect.

So, he picked up a number of sacks, and approaching the door, his mind was distracted by a multitude of ideas, and he found that he had forgotten the important words. Instead of pronouncing "sesame," he said "Open, barley." He was thunder-struck on perceiving that the door, instead of flying open, remained closed. He named various other kinds of grain, all but the right description. However, the door did not budge.

Cassim was not prepared for an adventure of this kind. Fear took entire possession of his mind. The more he endeavored to recollect the word "sesame," the more his memory became confused, and he remained as far from any recollection of it as if he had never heard the word mentioned. He threw to the ground the sacks he had collected and paced with hasty steps backward and forward in the cave. The riches which surrounded him had no longer any charms for his imagination.

Toward noon the robbers returned to their cave, and when they were within a short distance of it and saw the mules belonging to Cassim standing all around the rock laden with hampers, they were greatly surprised. They immediately advanced at full speed, and drove away the ten mules, which Cassim had neglected to fasten. Therefore, they soon fled all over the forest. The robbers did not bother to run after the mules, for their chief object was to discover the owner of the beasts. While some were employed in searching the exterior recesses of the rock, the captain arrived with the rest of the men and drawing their sabers, the party went toward the door, pronounced the magic words, and it opened.

Cassim, who had heard the noise of horses trampling on the ground from the inside of the cave, felt certain that the robbers had arrived, and that his death was inevitable. Resolved, however, to make an effort to escape and reach some place of safety, he posted himself near the door, ready to run out as soon as it should open. The word "sesame," which he had in vain endeavored to recall to his memory, was scarcely pronounced when the portal opened, and he rushed out with such violence that he threw the captain to the ground. He could not, however, avoid the other thieves, who, having their sabers drawn, cut him to pieces on the spot.

After this execution the robbers entered the cave and found, near the door, the bags which Cassim, after filling them with gold, had moved there for the convenience of loading his mules; and they put them in their places again without observing the absence of those which Ali Baba had previously carried away. Conjecturing and consulting upon this event, they could easily account for Cassim's inability to make his escape, but they could not in any way imagine how he had been able to enter the cave. They supposed that he might have descended from the top of the cave, but the opening which admitted the light was so high, and the summit of the rock so inaccessible on the outside, besides the absence of any traces of his having adopted this mode, that they all agreed such a feat was impossible. They could not suppose he had entered by the door, unless he had discovered the password which caused it to open; but they felt quite secure that they alone knew this secret, for they had no knowledge of having been overheard by Ali Baba.

But since the manner in which someone had entered the cave remained a mystery, and since their treasure was no longer in safety, they agreed to cut the corpse of Cassim into four quarters, and place them in the cave near the door, two quarters on one side and two on the other, to frighten away anyone who might be bold enough to hazard a similar enterprise. Then they decided not to return to the cave for some time. This decision they put into immediate execution, and since they had nothing further to detain them, they left their place of retreat well secured. Then they mounted their horses to scour the country, and, as before, to infest the roads used most frequently by caravans that afforded them favorable opportunities for exercising their accustomed dexterity in plundering.

In the meantime, Cassim's wife began to feel uneasy when she observed night approach, and yet her husband did not return. In the utmost alarm she went to Ali Baba and said to him, "Oh, Brother, I believe you are well aware that Cassim went to the forest, and he has not returned yet, and night is already approaching. I fear that some accident may have happened to him."

Ali Baba suspected his brother's intention after the conversation he had held with him, and for this reason he had abstained from visiting the forest on that day so that he might not offend Cassim. However, without uttering any reproaches that could have given the slightest offence either to her or her husband, he replied that she need not yet feel any uneasiness because Cassim most probably thought it prudent not to return to the city until daylight had entirely vanished. The wife of Cassim felt satisfied with this reply and was the more easily persuaded of its truth when she considered how important it was that her husband should use the greatest secrecy for the accomplishment of his purpose. She returned to her house and waited patiently until midnight;

but after that hour her fears returned with twofold strength, and her grief was the greater, since she could not proclaim it, nor even relieve it by cries, which might have caused suspicion and inquiry in the neighborhood. She then began to repent of the silly curiosity which, heightened by the most bitter envy, had induced her to endeavor to pry into the private affairs of her brother and sister-in-law. She spent the night in weeping, and at break of day she ran to Ali Baba, and announced the cause of her early visit less by her words than by her tears.

Ali Baba did not wait until his sister entreated him to go and look for Cassim. After advising the disconsolate wife to restrain her grief, he immediately set off with his three mules and went to the forest. As he drew near the rock, he was astonished to observe that blood had been shed near the door. Not having encountered his brother or the ten mules, on his way, he looked upon this as an unfavorable omen. When he reached the door and pronounced the proper words, it opened. Immediately, he was struck with horror when he discovered the body of his brother cut into four quarters. Yet, despite the small share of fraternal affection he had received from Cassim during his life, he did not hesitate on the course he was to pursue in rendering the last act of duty to his brother's remains. He found materials in the cave that enabled him to wrap up the body and to make two packages of the four quarters. Then he placed them on one of his mules and covered them with sticks to conceal them. The other two mules were then loaded expeditiously with sacks of gold, putting wood over them as on the preceding occasion; and after he finished all he had to do, he commanded the door to close. Then he took the road to the city and waited at the entrance of the forest until night had fallen so that he might return without being observed. When he got home, he left the two asses that were laden with gold and asked his wife to unload them. After telling her in a few words what had happened to Cassim, he led the third ass away to his sister-in-law, where Ali Baba knocked at the door. It was opened to him by a female slave named Morgiana. This Morgiana was crafty, cunning, and fruitful in inventing successful plans that guaranteed the success of the most difficult enterprises, and Ali Baba knew her abilities well. After he had entered the courtyard, he unloaded the wood and the two packages from the ass. Then he took the slave aside and said: "Morgiana, the first thing I have to request of you is inviolable secrecy. You will soon see how necessary this is, not only for me, but for your mistress. These two packets contain the body of your master, and we must endeavor to bury him as if he had died a natural death. Let me speak to your mistress, and take good heed of what I shall say to her."

Morgiana went to tell her mistress that Ali Baba had returned, and soon he followed her to his sister-in-law's apartment.

"Well, brother," she inquired in an impatient tone, "what news do you bring about my husband? Alas! I perceive no hope of consolation in your countenance."

"Oh, my sister," replied Ali Baba, "I cannot answer you unless you first promise to listen to me from the beginning to the end of my story without interruption. It is of no less importance to you than to me, under the present circumstances to preserve the greatest secrecy. Discretion is absolutely necessary for your repose and security."

"Ah," cried the sister, in a mournful voice, "this preamble convinces me that my husband is no more; but at the same time, I feel the necessity of the secrecy you require. I must do violence to my feelings. Speak, I hear you."

Ali Baba then related to her all that had happened during his journey, until he had brought away the body of Cassim.

"Sister," he added, "here is a great and sudden affliction for you, the more distressing as it was unexpected. The evil is without remedy, but nevertheless, if my good offices can afford you consolation, I offer to join the small property Heaven has granted me to yours, by marrying you. I can assure you my wife will not be jealous, and we will live comfortably together. If this proposal meets your approbation, we must contrive to bury my brother as if he had died a natural death; and this is an office which I think you may safely entrust to Morgiana, and I will, on my part, contribute all in my power to assist her."

The widow of Cassim reflected that she could not do better than consent to this offer, for Ali Baba now possessed greater riches than she could boast, and besides, due to his discovery of the treasure, he might increase them considerably. She did not, therefore, refuse his proposal, but, on the contrary, regarded it as a reasonable source of consolation. She wiped away her tears, which had begun to flow abundantly, and suppressed those mournful cries which women are accustomed to utter on the death of their husbands. By these signs she sufficiently testified to Ali Baba that she accepted his offer.

Ali Baba left Cassim's widow in this disposition of mind, and having strongly recommended to Morgiana to use the utmost discretion in the difficult part she was to perform, he returned home with his ass.

Morgiana did not belie her character for cunning. She went out with Ali Baba and walked to an apothecary who lived in the neighborhood. When she knocked at the shop door, she asked for a particular kind of lozenge, supposed to possess great efficacy in dangerous disorders. The apothecary gave her as much as the money she offered would buy and asked who was ill in her master's family.

"Alas!" she exclaimed with a deep sigh, "It is my worthy master Cassim himself. No one can understand his complaint. He can neither speak nor eat."

Upon saying this, she took the lozenges which Cassim would never need anymore. Then, on the following day, Morgiana went to the apothecary once again, and with tears in her eyes. inquired for an essence which was only to be administered when the patient was reduced to the last extremity, and when no other remedy had been left untried.

"Alas!" cried she, as she received it from the hands of the apothecary, and she aptly pretended to have the deepest affliction, "I fear this remedy will not be of more use than the lozenges. I shall lose my beloved master!"

Moreover, as Ali Baba and his wife were seen going backward and forward to and from the house of Cassim in the course of the day, no one was surprised when, toward evening, the piercing cries of the widow and Morgiana announced the death of Cassim. At a very early hour the next morning, when day began to appear, Morgiana, knowing that a good old cobbler lived some distance away from them and was one of the first to open his shop, went out to visit him. As she approached, she wished him a good day and put a piece of gold into his hand.

Baba Mustapha, a man well known throughout all the city, was naturally light-hearted and had always something laughable to say. He examined the coin, and seeing that it was gold, he said, "This is a good payment, What is to be done? I am ready to do your bidding."

"Baba Mustapha," said Morgiana to him, "take your materials for sewing, and come with me right away. But I must insist on this condition that you let me put a bandage over your eyes when we have reached a certain place."

Upon hearing these words, Baba Mustapha began to make objections.

"Oh, ho!" said he. "You want me to do something against my conscience or my honor." But Morgiana interrupted him by putting another gold coin into his hand.

"Allah forbid," she said, "that I should require you to do anything that would stain your honor. Just come with me, and fear nothing."

Baba Mustapha allowed himself to be led by the slave, who when she had reached the place she had mentioned, tied a handkerchief over his eyes, and brought him to her deceased master's home; nor did she remove the bandage until he was in the chamber where the body was deposited, the severed quarters having been put together.

When she took off the handkerchief from his eyes, she said, "Baba Mustapha, I have brought you here so that you might sew these pieces together. Lose no time; and when you have done it, I shall give you another piece of gold."

After Baba Mustapha had finished his work, Morgiana covered his eyes again before he left the chamber, and after giving him the third piece of money, according to her promise, and earnestly warning him to keep her secret, she led him to the place where she had first put the handkerchief over his eyes. Here she took the bandage from his eyes, and left him to return to his house, watching him, however, until he was out of sight, lest he should have the curiosity to return and follow her.

Morgiana had heated some water to wash the body of Cassim; and Ali Baba, who entered just as she returned, washed it, perfumed it with incense, and wrapped it in the burying clothes with the customary ceremonies. The joiner also brought the coffin which Ali Baba had requested. In order that he might not observe anything particular, Morgiana received the coffin at the door, and having paid the man and sent him away, she assisted Ali Baba in putting the body into it. After he had nailed down the lid of the coffin, she went to the mosque to notify the Iman that everything was ready for the funeral.

The people who belonged to the mosque and were responsible for washing the bodies of the dead, offered to come and perform their office, but she told them that all was done and ready.

Morgiana had scarcely returned before the Iman and the other ministers of the mosque arrived. Four of the neighbors took the coffin on their shoulders and carried it to the cemetery, following the Iman, who repeated prayers as he walked along. Morgiana, as slave to the deceased, walked next, with her head uncovered. She was bathed in tears and uttered the most piteous cries from time to time, beating her breast and tearing her hair.

Ali Baba closed the procession, accompanied by some of the neighbors, who occasionally took the place of the bearers, to relieve them in carrying the coffin, until they reached the cemetery. As for Cassim's widow, she remained at home to lament and weep with the women of the neighborhood, who, according to the usual custom, had returned to her house during the ceremony of the burial. Joining their cries to hers, they filled the air with sounds of woe. It was in this manner the fatal end of Cassim was so well disguised and concealed by Ali Baba and the rest, that no one in the city had the least suspicion of the manner in which he had come by his death.

Three or four days after Cassim's interment, Ali Baba removed the few goods he possessed, together with the money that he had taken from the robbers' store, which he conveyed by night into the house of Cassim's widow to establish himself there and thus announce his marriage with his sister-in-law; and since such matches are by no means extraordinary in our religion, no one showed any marks of surprise on the occasion.

Ali Baba had a son who had passed a certain time with a merchant of considerable repute, who had always bestowed the highest commendations on his conduct. To this son he gave Cassim's shop with a further promise that, if the young man continued to behave with prudence, he would before long, marry him advantageously.

Leaving Ali Baba to enjoy his newly acquired fortune, we shall now return to the forty thieves. They returned to their retreat in the forest when the time they had agreed to be absent had expired, but their astonishment was indescribable when they found the body of Cassim gone, and it was greatly increased on perceiving a visible diminution of their treasure.

"We have been discovered," said the captain, "and we shall be entirely ruined if we are not very careful, or neglect to take immediate measures to remedy the evil. Indeed, we shall by insensible degrees lose all these riches which our ancestors as well as we have amassed with so much trouble and fatigue. All that we can at present judge concerning the loss we have sustained is that the thief whom we surprised at the fortunate moment, when he was going to make his escape, knew the secret of opening the door. But he was not the only one who possesses that secret. Yes, another person has the same knowledge. The removal of his body and the diminution of our treasure are incontestable proofs of the fact. Since we have no reason to suppose that more than two people are acquainted with the secret, having destroyed one, we must not allow the other to escape. What say you, my brave comrades?"

This proposal of the captain was thought so reasonable and right by the whole troop that they all approved it, and agreed that it would be advisable to relinquish every other enterprise, and occupy themselves solely with this affair, which they would not abandon until they had succeeded in detecting the thief.

"I expected this decision because of your known courage and bravery," resumed the captain, "but the first thing to be done is that one of you who is bold, courageous, and cunning must go to the city unarmed and dressed as a traveler and stranger. He must employ all his art to discover if the singular death we inflicted on the culprit whom we destroyed as he deserved is the common topic of conversation. Then he must find out who this man was and where he lived. It is absolutely necessary we should be acquainted with all this so that we may not do anything of which we may have to repent by making ourselves known in a country where we have been so long forgotten, and where it is so much in our interest to remain undisturbed. But in order to inspire the man whom I choose to undertake this commission and to prevent his bringing us a false report, which might cause our total ruin, I propose that he consent to submit to the penalty of death in case of failure."

Without waiting until his companions could speak, one of the robbers said: "I shall willingly agree to these terms and glory, and shall expose my life in the execution of such a commission. If I should fail, you will at least remember that I have displayed both courage and readiness in my offer to serve the whole troop."

Amid the commendations of the captain and his companions, the robber disguised himself in such a way that no one could have suspected him of belonging to the nefarious trade he followed and practiced. He set off at night and managed matters so well that he entered the city just as day was beginning to appear. He went toward the public bazaar, where he saw only one shop open, and that was the shop of Baba

Mustapha. The jovial cobbler was seated on his stool with his awl in his hand, ready to begin work. The robber went up to him, and wished him a good morning, and perceiving that Mustapha was advanced in years, he said, "My good man, you rise early to do your work. How is it possible that an old man like you can see clearly at this early hour? Even if it were broad day, I doubt whether your eyes are good enough to see the stitches you make."

"Whoever you are," replied Baba Mustapha, "you don't know much about me. Despite my age, I have excellent eyes, and you would have realized as much had you known that not long ago since I sewed up a dead body in a place where there was not more light than we have here."

The robber felt greatly elated at having on his arrival addressed himself to a man who of his own accord entered upon the very subject on which he ardently wished to gain information.

"A dead body!" he replied with feigned astonishment, to induce the other to proceed. Why should you want to sew up a dead body? I suppose you mean that you sewed the shroud in which he was buried."

"No, no," said Baba Mustapha. "I know what I mean. You want me to tell you more about it, but you shall not hear another syllable."

The robber required no further proof to be fully convinced that he was on the right road to discover what he wished to know. He produced a piece of gold, and putting it into Baba Mustapha's hand, he said, "I have no desire to cheat you of your secret, although I can assure you I should not divulge it even if you entrusted me with it. The only favor I beg at your hands is that you will have the goodness to direct me to the house where you sewed up the dead body, or that you will come with me, and show me the way."

"Should I even feel inclined to grant your request," replied Baba Mustapha, holding the piece of money in his hand as if ready to return it, "I assure you that I could not do it, and this you may take my word for. And I will tell you why I must refuse. My employers took me to a particular place, and there they bound my eyes, and from there I allowed myself to be led to the house, and when I had finished what I had to do I was brought back to my own house in the same manner. You see, therefore, how impossible it is that I should serve you in this matter."

"But at least," resumed the robber, "you must certainly remember the way you went after your eyes were bound. Please come with me: I will put a bandage over your eyes at the place where you were blindfolded, and we will walk together along the same streets, and follow the same turnings, which you will probably recollect to have taken. And since all labor deserves a reward, here is another piece of gold. Come, grant me this favor."

And as he spoke, he put another piece of money into the cobbler's hand.

"The two pieces of gold were a sore temptation to Baba Mustapha. He looked at them in his hand some time without saying a word, pondering within himself what he should do. At last he drew his purse from his bosom, and putting the gold into it, replied, "I cannot positively assure you that I remember exactly the way they took me, but since you will have it so, come along. I will do my best to satisfy you."

To the great satisfaction of the robber, Baba Mustapha got up to go with him, and without staying to shut up his shop, where there was nothing of consequence to worry about, he led the robber to the spot where Morgiana had put the handkerchief over his eyes.

"This is the place," said he, "where my eyes were covered, and then my face was turned in this direction."

The robber, who had his handkerchief ready, tied it over Mustapha eyes and walked alongside, partly leading him and partly led by him, until Baba Mustapha stopped.

"I think," he said, "I didn't go any farther than this."

Indeed, he was exactly in front of the house which had once belonged to Cassim, and where Ali Baba now resided. Before taking the handkerchief from the cobbler's eyes, the robber quickly made a mark on the door with some chalk he had brought for the purpose; and when he had taken the handkerchief off, he asked Baba Mustapha if he knew to whom the house belonged. The merry cobbler replied that he didn't live in that quarter of the town, and therefore could not tell. When the robber found that he could gain no further information from Baba Mustapha, he thanked him for the trouble he had taken; and after he had seen the cobbler turn away to go to his shop, he took the road to the forest, where he felt certain he would be well received.

Soon after the robber and Baba Mustapha had separated, Morgiana had occasion to go out on some errand; and when she returned, she observed the mark which the robber had made on the door of Ali Baba's house. She stopped to examine it. "What can this mark signify?" thought she. "Has anyone a spite against my master, or has it been made only for diversion? Whatever it may be, I may as well use precautions against the worst that may happen. Therefore, she took some chalk; and since several of the doors on the houses near her master's home were of the same appearance, she marked them in the same manner, and then went home, without saying anything of what she had done either to her master or mistress.

In the meantime the thief had taken the best way back into the forest, where he rejoined his companions at an early hour. He related the success of his journey, dwelling a good deal on the good fortune by befriending immediately the very man who could give him the best information on the subject he needed to know, and which only he possessed. They all listened to him with great satisfaction; and the captain, after praising his diligence, addressed the rest of the robbers: "Comrades," said he, "we have no time to lose. Let us arm ourselves and depart; and after we have entered the city (where we had best go separately so as not to create suspicion), let us all assemble in the great square, some on one side of it and some on the other, and I will go and find the house with our companion who has brought us this good news. Then I shall be able to judge what method will be most advantageous to pursue."

The robbers all applauded their captain's proposal, and they equipped themselves very soon for their departure. Once they did this, they went in small parties of two or three together; and, walking at a certain distance from each other, they entered the city without causing any suspicion. The captain and the robber, who had been there in the morning, were the last to enter, and the latter conducted the captain to the street in which he had marked the house of Ali Baba. When they reached the first door that had been marked by Morgiana, the thief pointed it out, saying that was the one he had marked. But as they continued walking on without stopping so that they might not raise suspicion, the captain perceived that the next door was marked in the same manner, and pointed out this circumstance to his guide, inquiring whether this was the house, or the one they had passed.

His guide was quite confused and didn't know what to answer; and his embarrassment increased, when, on proceeding with the captain he found that four or five doors successively had the same mark. He assured the captain with an oath that he had marked just one house.

"I cannot conceive," he added, "who might have imitated my mark with so much exactness; but I confess that I cannot now distinguish my mark from the others."

The captain, who found that his design was frustrated, returned to the large square, where he told the first of his people whom he met to inform the rest that all their good work had been for nothing and was a fruitless expedition. Now that there was nothing to be done but to return to their place of retreat, he set the example, and they all followed in the order in which they had come.

When the troop had reassembled in the forest, the captain explained to them the reason why he had ordered them to return. The spy was unanimously declared deserving of death, and he acquiesced to his condemnation, owning that he should have been more cautious in taking his measures. Advancing with a serene countenance, he submitted to the stroke of a companion who was ordered to cut off his head from his body since it was necessary for the safety of the entire band. The great setback they had suffered was not to pass unavenged. Now another robber, who flattered himself with hopes of better success than the first thief presented himself and requested preference, for he was confident he could catch their enemy. It was granted, and he went to the city where he used the same trick on Baba Mustapha that the first robber had used, and the cobbler led him to the house of Ali Baba with his eyes covered.

The thief marked the door with red chalk in a place where it would be less noticed, thinking that would be a sure method of distinguishing it from those that were marked with white. But a short time afterward Morgiana went out as on the preceding day, and on her return, the red mark did not escape her piercing eye. She understood what was happening and immediately made a similar mark on the neighboring doors.

When the thief returned to his companions in the forest, he boasted about the precautions he had taken, which he declared to be infallible, to distinguish the house of Ali Baba from the others. The captain and the rest agreed with him, and everyone thought they would certainly be successful this time. So, they returned to the city in the same order and with as much care as before, armed also in the same way, ready to execute the blow they anticipated. The captain and the robber went immediately to the street where Ali Baba resided, but they experienced the same difficulty as on the former occasion. The captain was irritated, and the thief was utterly just as confounded as the robber who had preceded him in the same business. Therefore, the captain was obliged to return a second time with his comrades, as little satisfied with his expedition as he had been on the preceding day. The robber who had caused the disappointment underwent the punishment which he had agreed to suffer as the penalty of failure. Now, the captain saw his troop diminished by two brave associates, and he feared it might decrease still more if he continued to trust to others to find the house where Ali Baba resided. Experience convinced him that his companions did not excel in affairs that depended on cunning, as in those in which strength of arm only was required. As a result he undertook the business himself.

The captain now went to the city, and with the assistance of Baba Mustapha, who was ready to perform the same service for him which he had rendered to the other two, he found the house of Ali Baba. However, he did not trust the strategy of making marks on it, which had hitherto proved so fallacious, so he imprinted it so thoroughly on his memory by looking attentively, and by passing before it several times so that, at last, he was certain he could not mistake it.

Satisfied that he had accomplished the object of his journey by obtaining the information he desired, he returned to the forest, and when he had reached the cave where the rest of the robbers were waiting his return, he addressed them as follows: "Comrades, nothing now can prevent our taking full revenge for the injury that has been done us. I know with certainty the house of the culprit who is to experience our wrath, and while on the road, I have thought of a way to equal scores with him so privately that no one will be able to discover the place of our retreat any more than the refuge where our treasure is deposited; for this must be carefully considered in our enterprise; otherwise, instead of being serviceable, it will only prove fatal to us all. I have hit upon a plan to obtain this end, and when I have explained the plan to you, if anyone can propose a better expedient, let him speak."

He then told them how he intended to conduct the affair, and since they all gave their approval, he ordered them to divide into small parties, and go into the neighboring towns and villages, and to buy nineteen mules and thirty-eight large barrels for carrying oil, one of which had to be full, and all the others empty. In the course of two or three days, the thieves had completed their purchases, and since the empty barrels were rather too narrow at the mouth for the purpose to which he intended to apply them, the captain had them enlarged. Then he made one of the men, thoroughly armed and dressed, enter each barrel. After that, he closed the barrels so that they appeared full of oil, leaving, however, a part open so that each robber would have air to breathe and could be able to carry on the deception. Then he rubbed the outside of each barrel with oil which he took from the full one.

Things being thus prepared, the mules were loaded with thirty-seven robbers, each concealed in a barrel, and with the barrel that was filled with oil. Then the captain as their leader took the road to the city at the hour that had been agreed on and arrived about an hour after sunset just as he had planned. Then he went straight to the house of Ali Baba intending to knock and request shelter for the night for himself and his mules. He was, however, spared the trouble of knocking, because he found Ali Baba at the door, enjoying the fresh air after supper. He stopped his mules and, addressing himself to Ali Baba, said, "My good friend, I have brought the oil which you see here from a great distance to sell tomorrow in the market, and at this late hour I don't know where to obtain shelter for the night. If it would not cause you much inconvenience, could you please let me spend the night here, and you will confer a great obligation on me."

Although Ali Baba had seen the man who now spoke to him in the forest and had even heard his voice, he had no idea that this was the captain of the forty robbers, disguised as an oil merchant.

"You are welcome," he said and immediately made room for the visitor and his mules to enter his grounds. At the same time, Ali Baba called a slave and ordered him, when the barrels were unloaded from the mules, not only to put them under cover in the stable, but to give them some hay and corn. He also took the trouble of going into the kitchen to ask Morgiana to get supper ready quickly for a guest who had just arrived and to prepare a chamber and bed for him.

Ali Baba went still further in his desire to honor his guest with all possible civility. Observing that, after the merchant had unloaded his mules, and they had been taken into the stables as he had wished, the newcomer seemed to be making preparations to spend the night with them, he went to him to invite him to come into the room where he received company, saying that he could not bear to think of him passing the night in the courtyard. The captain of the robbers endeavored to excuse himself from accepting the invitation by alleging that he was loath to be troublesome, but in reality he needed to have an opportunity to execute his meditated project with more ease. Indeed, it was not until Ali Baba had used the most urgent persuasions that the captain complied with his request.

Ali Baba not only remained with his perfidious guest, who sought his life in return for his hospitality, until Morgiana had served the supper, but he conversed with him on various subjects which he thought might amuse him and did not leave him until the guest had finished the repast provided for him. He then said: "You are at liberty to do as you please. You only have to ask whatever you may want, and all I have is at your service."

The captain of the robbers rose at the same time with Ali Baba and accompanied him to the door; and while Ali Baba went into the kitchen to speak to Morgiana, the robber went into the court, under the pretext of going to the stable to see after his mules. Ali Baba again enjoined Morgiana to be attentive to his guest and to make sure that he had everything he wanted, and then he added, "I want you to know that tomorrow before daybreak I shall go to the bath. Make sure that my bathing linen is ready, and give it to Abdalla – this was the name of his slave – and make me some good broth to take when I return."

After giving these orders he went to bed.

In the meantime the captain of the robbers left the stable and went to give his people the necessary orders for what they were to do. Beginning at the first barrel and going through the whole number, he said to the man in each: "When I throw some pebbles from the chamber where I am to be lodged tonight, do not fail to rip open the barrel from top to bottom with the knife you are furnished with and come out: I shall be with you immediately afterward."

The knife he spoke of was pointed and sharpened for the purpose of cutting the tops of the barrels. After giving these directions, he returned, and when he went to the kitchen door, Morgiana took a light and conducted him to the chamber she had prepared for him, and left him there. Right before she departed, she asked whether he needed anything more. Not to create any suspicion, he put out the light a short time after and lay down in his clothes, ready to rise as soon as he had taken his first sleep.

Morgiana did not forget Ali Baba's orders. She prepared her master's linen for the bath and gave it to Abdalla, who had not yet gone to bed. Then she put the pot on the fire to make the broth. However, while she was skimming it, the lamp went out. Since there was no more oil in the house, and she didn't have a candle, she didn't know what to do. She wanted a light to see so she could skim the pot and mentioned her dilemma to Abdalla.

"Why are you so disturbed by this?" said he. "Go and take some oil out of one of the barrels in the court. Morgiana thanked Abdalla for the advice, and while he retired to bed in the room next to Ali Baba so that he might be ready to go with his master to the bath, Morgiana took the oil-can and went into the court. As she drew near to the barrel that stood first in the row, the thief who was concealed within said in a low voice, "Is it time?"

Although he spoke softly, Morgiana was nevertheless struck by the sound, which she heard the more distinctly, since the captain, when he unloaded his mules, opened all the barrels to give a little air to his men, who, though not absolutely deprived of breathing-room, were nevertheless in an uneasy position. Any other slave but Morgiana would have made a great uproar at the first moment of surprise when finding a man in the barrel instead of the oil she expected, and this would have produced terrible consequences. But Morgiana was superior to the position she held as slave. She was instantly aware of the importance of secrecy and caution, and understood the extreme danger in which Ali Baba and his family, as well as herself, were placed. She also saw the urgent necessity of devising a speedy remedy that had to be silently executed. Her quick invention soon conceived the means.

She collected her thoughts, and without showing any emotion, assumed the manner of the captain and answered, "Not yet, but soon."

She approached the next barrel, and she was asked the same question. Then she went on to all the barrels in succession, giving the same answer to the same question, until she came to the last barrel, which was full of oil. By this means she discovered that her master, who had thought he was providing a night's lodging to an oil merchant, had given shelter to thirty-eight robbers, and that the pretended merchant was their captain. She quickly filled her oil can from the last barrel and returned into the kitchen. After having put some oil in her lamp and lighted it, she took a large kettle and went again into the court to fill it with oil from the barrel. Then she immediately put the kettle on the fire and used a large quantity of wood to make a great blaze. The sooner the oil boiled, she thought, the sooner her plan for the preservation of the whole family would be executed, and it required the utmost haste. At last, the oil boiled. So, she took the kettle, and from the first to the last barrel, she poured sufficient boiling oil to scald the robbers to death. Indeed, her goal was effectually carried out.

After Morgiana had thus silently, and without disturbing anyone, performed this intrepid act exactly as she had conceived it, she returned to the kitchen with the empty kettle and shut the door. Then she put out the large fire she had prepared for this purpose, and only left enough to finish boiling the broth for Ali Baba. She then blew out the lamp and remained perfectly silent, determined not to go to bed until, from a window of the kitchen which overlooked the court, she had observed what would ensue. Morgiana had scarcely waited a quarter of an hour, when the captain of the robbers awoke. He got up, opened the window, and looked out. All was dark, and a profound silence reigned all around. So, he gave the signal by throwing the pebbles, many of which struck the barrels, as the sound plainly proved. He listened, but heard nothing that could lead him to suppose his men obeyed the summons. He became uneasy at this delay and threw some pebbles a second, and even a third time. They all struck the jars, yet nothing appeared to indicate that the signal had been answered. He was at a loss to account for this mystery. Consequently, in the utmost alarm, he descended into the courtyard, with as little noise as possible, and approaching the first barrel he intended to ask if the robber – contained in it, and whom he supposed was still living – was asleep. Instead of the robber, he smelled a strong scent of hot and burning oil rising from the barrel. Then he began to suspect that his enterprise against Ali Baba, to destroy him, pillage his house, and carry off, if possible, all the money which he had taken from him and the community, had failed. He proceeded to the next barrels all in succession, and discovered that all his men had shared the same fate; and by the diminution of the oil in the vessel which he had brought full, he guessed the means that had been used to deprive him of the assistance he expected. Mortified at having missed his goal, he jumped over the garden gate, which led out of the courtyard. Then he raced from one garden to the next, and by jumping over the walls, he made his escape.

When Morgiana perceived that everything was silent and still, and that the captain of the thieves did not return, she suspected the truth: namely, that he had decamped by the gardens, instead of attempting to escape by the house door, which was fastened with double bolts. Fully satisfied he was gone, and overjoyed at having succeeded in securing the safety of the whole family, she finally retired to bed, and soon fell asleep.

Ali Baba went out before daybreak and headed to the bath, followed by his slave, totally unaware of the surprising event which had taken place in the house during the night. In fact, Morgiana had not thought it necessary to wake him, particularly since she had no time to lose while she was engaged in her perilous enterprise, and it was useless to interrupt his repose after she had averted the danger. When he returned from the bath, the sun had risen. Ali Baba was surprised to see the barrels of oil still in their places and to find that the merchant had not taken them to the market, with his mules. He asked Morgiana, who let him in, and who had left everything in its original state. She wanted to show him the so-called merchant's deceit and to impress him with the effort she had made for his preservation.

"My good master," said Morgiana to Ali Baba, "may heaven preserve you and all your family. You will be better informed of what you wish to know when you have seen what I am going to show you, if you will take the trouble to come with me."

Ali Baba followed Morgiana, and when she had shut the door, she took him to the first barrel and asked him to look into it and see if it contained oil. He did as she desired, and perceiving a man in the barrel, he hastily drew back and uttered a cry of surprise.

"Do not be afraid," she said. "The man you see there will not do you any harm. He attempted mischief, but he will never hurt either you or anyone else again. He is now a lifeless corpse!"

"Morgiana!" exclaimed Ali Baba. "What does this mean? I order you to explain this mystery."

"I shall explain it," replied Morgiana, "but please quiet down and don't awaken the curiosity of your neighbors or let them hear what is of the utmost importance – things that you should keep secret and concealed. Look first in all the other barrels."

So, Ali Baba examined the barrels, one after the other, from the first till he came to the last, which contained the oil. Then he remarked that its contents were considerably diminished.

When his survey was completed, he stood motionless with astonishment, sometimes casting his eyes on Morgiana, then looking at the barrels, but without speaking a word, so great was his surprise. At last, as if speech were suddenly restored to him, he said: "And what has become of the merchant?"

"The merchant," replied Morgiana, "is no more a merchant than I am. I can tell you who he is and what has become of him. But I shall tell you the whole story more conveniently in your own chamber, and moreover, it is now time that, for the sake of your health, you should take your broth, after coming out of the bath."

While Ali Baba went into his room, Morgiana returned to the kitchen to get the broth, and when she brought it, before Ali Baba would take it, he said, "Begin to relate this wonderful story and satisfy my extreme impatience, for I want I know all the circumstances."

In obedience to Ali Baba's request, Morgiana thus began: "Last night, Oh my master, when you had retired to bed, I prepared your linen for the bath, as you had desired, and put Abdalla in charge. After that, I put the pot on the fire, to make your broth, and as I was skimming it, the lamp went out suddenly due to a lack of oil. There was not a drop, and in the darkness, I searched for a light of any kind, but could not find any. Seeing myself in a dilemma, Abdalla reminded me of the barrels of oil which were in the court. At the very least, we suspected them to be oil barrels, and so, no doubt, did you. I took my can and went to the first barrel, but as I approached it, I heard a voice coming out of it, saying, 'Is it time?' I did not feel terrified, but instantly understanding the treachery intended by the feigned merchant, I replied without hesitation, 'Not yet, but soon.'

"I passed on to the next barrel, and another voice asked me the same question, to which I made the same answer. I went to all the barrels, one after the other, making the same reply to the same inquiry and did not find any oil till I came to the last, from which I filled my can. When I reflected that there were thirty-seven thieves in your court, intent, perhaps, on murdering you and only waiting for the signal of their chief, to whom, supposing him to be a merchant, you had given so hospitable a reception, and on whose account you set the whole household to work, I lost no time, but brought in the can and lighted my lamp. Then taking the largest kettle in the kitchen, I went and filled it with oil. After I placed it on the fire, it boiled, and I poured some oil into each of the barrels which contained the thieves – as much as I thought necessary to prevent them putting their pernicious plan into action that had brought them here. Once I finished the affair in the way I had proposed, I returned into the the kitchen, and extinguished my lamp. Before I went to bed, I placed myself at the window to watch quietly what steps the pretended oil merchant would take. After some time, I heard him throw some little pebbles from his window. They fell on the barrels without a response. The he threw pebbles a second time, and also a third, and since he neither heard nor saw anything stirring, he came down, and I observed him go to every barrel until he came to the last, after which the darkness of the night prevented me from distinguishing his movements.

"I still continued, however, to be on the watch, but since I found he did not return, I concluded that, mortified at his bad success, he had escaped by way of the garden. Convinced, therefore, that the family was now safe, I went to bed."

When she had finished this narrative, Morgiana added, "This is the detail you required of me, and I am convinced that it is the conclusion of a scheme of which I observed the beginning two or three days ago, but with the particulars of which I did not think it necessary to trouble you. One morning, as I returned from the city, at an early hour, I perceived the street door marked with white, and on the following day there was a red mark near the white one; each time, without knowing for what purpose these marks were made, I made the same kind of mark, and in the same part, on the doors of three or four of our neighbors on each side of this house. If you connect that fact with what has happened, you will find that the whole is a scheme, contrived by the thieves of the forest, whose troop, I know not why, seems to be diminished by two. But, be that as it may, the band is now reduced to three at most. This proves that the robbers had determined to kill you, and you will be smart to be on your guard against them so long as you are certain that one still remains. On my part, I will do all in my power to keep you safe. Indeed, I consider it my duty to do so.

When Morgiana ceased speaking, Ali Baba, filled with gratitude for the great obligation he owed her, replied, "I shall recompense you as you deserve before I die. I owe my life to you, and to give you an immediate proof of my feelings on the occasion, I give you your liberty from this moment and shall soon reward you in a more ample manner. I am as thoroughly convinced as you are, that the forty robbers laid this snare for me. Through your means Allah has delivered me from the danger. I hope He will continue to protect me from the malice of these my foes, and that in averting destruction from my head, He will make it recoil with greater certainty on them, and thus deliver the world from so dangerous and accursed a persecution. What we have to do now is to use the utmost dispatch in burying the bodies of this pest of the human race. Yet, we must do so with so much secrecy, that no one can entertain the slightest suspicion of their fate. For this purpose I will instantly go to work with Abdalla."

Ali Baba's garden was of considerable size and ended in a clump of large trees. He went, without delay with his slave Abdalla to dig a ditch or grave, of sufficient length and breadth under these trees to contain the bodies he had to inter. The ground was soft and easy to remove, so that they were not long in completing their work. They took the bodies out of the barrels and removed the weapons with which the robbers had furnished themselves. They carried the bodies to the bottom of the garden and placed them in the grave. After having covered them with the earth they had previously removed, they spread about what remained to make the surface of the ground appear even, as it was before. Ali Baba carefully concealed the oil barrels and the arms. As for the mules, which he did not then require, he sent them to the market at different times and disposed of them with the help of his slave.

While Ali Baba was taking these precautions to prevent its being publicly known by what means he had become rich in so short a space of time, the captain of the forty thieves had returned to the forest mortified beyond measure. In the agitation and confusion which he experienced at having met with such a disaster, so contrary to what he had promised himself, he reached the cave without coming to any resolution on what he should or should not do respecting Ali Baba.

The dismal solitude of this gloomy habitation appeared to him insupportable.

"Oh, ye brave companions!" he cried. "Ye partners of my work and my pains, where are you? What can I accomplish without your assistance? Did I select and assemble you only to see you perish altogether by a fate so cruel and so unworthy of your courage? My regret for your loss would not have been so great had you died with your sabers in your hands, like valiant men. When shall I be able to gather together another troop of intrepid men like you? And even should I wish to assemble a new troop, how could I undertake it, without exposing all our treasures of gold and silver to the mercy of him who has already enriched himself with a part of our possessions? I cannot, I must not, think of such an enterprise until I have put a period to his existence. What I have not been able to accomplish with your assistance, I am determined to perform alone; and when I have secured this immense property from the danger of pillage, I will endeavor to provide owners and heirs for it after my decease so that it may not only be preserved, but augmented, to the latest posterity."

Having formed this resolution, he postponed the consideration of means for its accomplishment, and, filled with the most pleasing hopes, he fell asleep and passed the rest of the night very quietly.

The next morning the captain of the robbers awoke at an early hour, and putting on clothes suitable to the design he meditated, he returned to the city, where he took a lodging in a khan. Since he supposed that the events which had happened in the house of Ali Baba might have become generally known, he asked the host if there were any news stirring. In his reply, the host talked about a variety of subjects, but he never mentioned the subject the captain had nearest at heart. By this the latter concluded that the reason why Ali Baba kept the transaction so profoundly secret was that he did not wish to divulge the fact of his having access to such an immense treasure, and also that he was apprehensive of his life being in danger on this account. This idea excited the captain to neglect nothing that could hasten his enemy's destruction, which he intended to accomplish by means as secret as those Ali Baba had adopted toward the robbers.

The captain provided himself with a horse, which he made use of to convey several kinds of rich stuffs and fine linens to his lodging, bringing them from the forest at various times, with all necessary precautions for keeping the place from where he brought them profoundly concealed. In order to dispose of this merchandise, when he had collected together as much as he thought proper, he looked for a shop. After he found one that suited him, he rented it from the proprietor, stocked it with his goods, and established himself in it. The shop that was exactly opposite to his had belonged to Cassim and was now occupied by the son of Ali Baba.

The captain of the robbers, who had assumed the name of Cogia Houssain, took an early opportunity of offering those civilities to the neighboring merchants, as a gesture that newcomers were expected to show. The son of Ali Baba was young and had a pleasant nature, and the captain had more frequent occasions to converse than with the others, and so the two men soon formed an intimacy. This friendship the robber soon resolved to cultivate with greater assiduity and care.

Three or four days after he had opened his shop, he recognized Ali Baba, who came to see his son, as he was in the constant habit of doing. After Ali Baba's departure, Cogia Houssain inquired and discovered that his foe was the young man's father. He now increased his attentions and friendship with the son. He made him several little presents and also often invited him to his table, where he regaled him very handsomely.

The son of Ali Baba did not choose to receive so much attention from Cogia Houssain without returning them, but his lodging was small, and he had no special place for regaling a guest as he wished. He mentioned his intention to his father, adding that it was not proper that he should delay any longer to return the favors he had received from Cogia Houssain. Ali Baba very willingly agreed to provide an entertainment at his home.

"My son," he said, "tomorrow is Friday, and since it is a day on which the most considerable merchants, such as Cogia Houssain and yourself, close their shops, invite him to take a walk with you after dinner. On your return contrive matters so that you may pass my house and then ask him to come in. It will be better to manage this way than to invite him in a formal way. I will give orders to Morgiana to prepare a supper and have it ready by the time you come."

On Friday, Cogia Houssain and the son of Ali Baba met in the afternoon to take their walk together, as had been agreed. On their return, Ali Baba's son led Cogia Houssain, as if by accident, through the street in which his father lived, and after they had reached the house, he stopped him and knocked at the door.

"This," said he, "is my father's house. He has asked me to procure the honor of your acquaintance, when I told him of your friendship for me. I entreat you to add this favor to the many I have received from you."

Cogia Houssain had now reached the object of his desires by gaining admission into the house of Ali Baba and had the possibility to take his life without hazarding his own or creating any suspicion. Yet, he now endeavored to excuse himself, and pretended to take leave of the son. However, since the slave of Ali Baba opened the door at that moment, the son took him by the hand in a very obliging manner, and going in first, drew him forward, and forced him to enter the house, though seemingly against his wishes.

Ali Baba received Cogia Houssain in a friendly manner and gave him as hearty a welcome as he could desire. He thanked him for his kindness to his son, saying, "The obligation he is under to you, and under which you have placed me also, is much the more considerable, since he is a young man who has not yet been in the world very much. So, it is very kind of you to consent to teach him manners."

Cogia Houssain profusely complimented Ali Baba's son in reply to his speech, assuring him that, although his son had not acquired the experience of older men, he nevertheless possessed a fund of good sense, which was of more service to him than experience was to many others. After a short conversation on other topics of an indifferent nature. Cogia Houssain was going to take his leave, but Ali Baba stopped him.

"Where are you going?" he asked. "Oh my friend, I beg you to do me the honor of staying to sup with me. The humble meal you will partake of is little worthy of the honor you will confer on it, but such as it is, I hope you will accept the offer as frankly as it is made."

"Oh, my master," replied Cogia Houssain, "I am fully sensible of your kindness, although I beg you to excuse me if I take my leave without accepting your obliging invitation. However, I must tell you that I am refusing you, not from incivility or pride, but because I have a very strong reason, and one which I am sure you would approve, were it known to you."

"What can this reason be?" resumed Ali Baba. "Might I take the liberty of asking you?"

"I do not refuse to tell it," said Cogia Houssain. "It is this: I never eat of any dish that has salt in it. Judge then what a strange figure I should make at your table."

"If this is your only reason," replied Ali Baba, "it need not deprive me of the honor of your company at supper, unless you have absolutely determined to refuse me. In the first place the bread which is eaten in my house does not contain salt, and as for the meat and other dishes, I promise you there will be none in those which are placed before you. I will go and give orders to that effect. Therefore, do me the favor to remain, and I shall be with you again in an instant."

Ali Baba went into the kitchen and asked Morgiana not to put any salt on the meat she was going to serve for supper. He also told her to prepare, without any salt, two or three of those dishes he had ordered.

Morgiana, who was just going to serve the supper, could not refrain from expressing some disapprobation at this new order.

"Who," said she, "is this fastidious man, who cannot eat salt? Your supper will be entirely spoiled if I delay it any longer."

"Do not be angry," replied Ali Baba, "he is a good man. Please do as I have wished."

Morgiana obeyed, though much against her will. She felt some curiosity to see this man who did not eat salt. After she had finished her preparations, and Abdalla had prepared the table, she assisted him in carrying in the dishes. On looking at Cogia Houssain, she instantly recognized who he was, notwithstanding his disguise, as the captain of the robbers, and, after examining him with great attention, she perceived that he had a dagger concealed under his clothes.

"I am no longer surprised," said she to herself, "that this villain will not eat salt with my master. He is his bitterest enemy and intends to murder him, but I will for sure prevent him from accomplishing his purpose."

When Morgiana had finished bringing out the dishes and assisting Abdalla, she availed herself of the time while her masters and their guest were at supper, to make the necessary preparations for carrying out an enterprise of the boldest and most intrepid nature. She had just completed them, when Abdalla came to tell her that it was time to serve the fruit. So, she carried the dessert out, and when Abdalla had taken away the supper, she placed it on the table. Then she put a small table near Ali Baba, with the wine and three cups, and left the room with Abdalla, as if to leave Ali Baba, according to custom, at liberty to converse and enjoy himself with his guest while they drank their wine.

Cogia Houssain, or rather the captain of the forty thieves, now thought he had gained a favorable opportunity for revenging himself on Ali Baba by taking his life. "I will make them both drunk," thought he, "and then the son against whom I bear no malice, will be unable to prevent me from plunging my dagger into the heart of his father, and I shall escape by way of the garden, as I did before, while the cook and the slave are at their supper, or perhaps asleep in the kitchen."

But instead of going to supper, Morgiana, who had a good idea of the pretended Cogia Houssain's intentions, did not allow him time to put his wicked plan into execution. She dressed herself like a dancing girl, put on a head-dress suitable to the character she assumed, and wore around her waist a girdle of silver gilt, to which she fastened a dagger made of the same metal. Her face was covered by a very handsome mask. After she had thus disguised herself, she said to Abdalla, "Take your tabor, and let's go and entertain our master's guest, and the friend of his son, by the music and dance we sometimes practice together."

Abdalla took his tabor, and began to play as he entered the room, walking before Morgiana. The wily slave followed him, making a low curtsy, with a deliberate air to attract notice, as if to request permission to show her skill in dancing to amuse the company. Abdalla sensed that Ali Baba was going to speak and stopped playing his tabor.

"Come in, Morgiana," cried Ali Baba: "Cogia Houssain will judge your skill and tell us his opinion. Do not think, however, oh my friend," he continued addressing Cogia Houssain, "that I have gone to any expense to procure this entertainment. We have all this skill in my house, and it is only my slave and my cook whom you see. I hope you will find their efforts amusing."

Cogia Houssain did not expect Ali Baba to add this entertainment to the supper he had given him; and this new circumstance made him apprehensive that he might not be able to avail himself of the opportunity he thought that now presented itself. But he still consoled himself with the hopes that there would be another chance if he continued the acquaintance with Ali Baba and his son. Therefore, although he would have gladly dispensed with this addition to the entertainment, he nevertheless pretended to be obliged to his host, and added that whatever gave Ali Baba pleasure could not fail of being agreeable to him.

When Abdalla perceived that Ali Baba and Cogia Houssain had stopped speaking, he again began to play on his tabor, singing a tune that would allow Morgiana to dance to it. She was equal in skill to any professional dancer and performed her part so admirably that even a critical spectator who had seen her would have been delighted. However, in the present company, perhaps Cogia Houssain was the least attentive to her excellence. After she had performed several dances with equal grace and agility, Morgiana at last drew out the dagger, and dancing with it in her hand, she surpassed all she had yet done. In her light and graceful movements, and in the wonderful attitudes which she interspersed in the figure, sometimes presenting the dagger as if ready to strike, and at others holding it to her own bosom, pretending to stab herself. At last, apparently out of breath, she took the tabor from Abdalla with her left hand, and holding the dagger in her right, she presented the tabor with the hollow part upward to Ali Baba, in imitation of the professional dancers, who are accustomed to go around in this way appealing to the liberality of the spectators, Ali Baba threw a piece of gold into the tabor. Morgiana then presented it to his son, who followed his father's example. Cogia Houssain, who saw that she was advancing toward him for the same purpose, had already taken his purse from his bosom to contribute his present and was taking out a piece of money, when Morgiana, with a courage and skill equal to the resolution she had displayed, plunged the dagger into his heart, so deeply that the life-blood streamed from the wound when she withdrew the weapon.

Ali Baba and his son were terrified by her action and uttered aloud, "Wretch! What have you done? You have ruined me and my family forever."

"What I have done," replied Morgiana, "is not for your ruin, but for your safety." Then, opening Cogia Houssain's robe to show Ali Baba the poniard, which was concealed under it, she continued: "Behold the cruel enemy you had to deal with! Examine his countenance attentively, and you will recognize the pretended oil merchant and the captain of the forty robbers. Don't you remember that he refused to eat salt with you? Before I even saw him, from the moment you told me of this peculiarity in your guest, I suspected his design, and was convinced that my suspicions were not unfounded."

Ali Baba, who now understood the new obligation he owed to Morgiana for having thus saved his life a second time, embraced her and said, "Morgiana, I gave you your liberty, and at the same time promised to show you stronger proofs of my gratitude at some future period. This period has now arrived. I present you to my son as his wife."

Then addressing his son, he continued, "I believe you to be too dutiful a son to take it amiss if I bestow Morgiana upon you without previously consulting your inclinations. Your obligation to her is not less than mine. You plainly see that Cogia Houssain only sought your acquaintance so that he might gain an opportunity to carry out his diabolical treachery. Had he sacrificed me to his vengeance, you cannot suppose that you would have been spared. You must further consider that, in marrying Morgiana, you connect yourself with the preserver of my family and the support of yours."

Far from showing any symptoms of discontent, Ali Baba's son replied that he willingly consented to the marriage, not only because he was desirous of proving his ready obedience to his father's wishes, but also because his own inclination strongly urged him to the union. They then decided to bury the captain of the robbers by the side of his former companions, and this duty was performed with such secrecy that the circumstance was not known until many years had expired, and no one was any longer interested to keep this memorable history concealed.

A few days after, Ali Baba celebrated the nuptials of his son and Morgiana with great solemnity. He organized a sumptuous feast, accompanied by dances, exhibitions, and other customary diversions; and he had the satisfaction of observing that the friends and neighbors whom he had invited did not know the true reason for the marriage, but were well acquainted with the good qualities of Morgiana and liked his generosity and applauded his discrimination.

Ali Baba, who had not revisited the cave since he had brought away the body of his brother Cassim, together with the gold which that unfortunate man had loaded onto his asses lest he should meet with any of the thieves and be slain by them, still refrained from going there, even after the death of the thirty-seven robbers and their captain. He didn't go there because he did not know anything about the fate of the other two thieves and supposed them to be still alive.

At the expiration of a year, however, finding that no attempt had been made to disturb or assassinate him, he became curious and decided to make a journey to the cave, taking all necessary precautions for his safety. He mounted his horse and rode there, and when he approached the cave, seeing no traces of either men or horses, he conceived this to be a favorable omen. So, he dismounted, and fastening his horse so that it might not stray, he went to the door and repeated the words, "Open Sesame," which he had not forgotten. The door opened, and he entered. The state in which everything appeared in the cave led him to judge that no one had been in it from the time that the pretended Cogia Houssain had opened his shop in the city and, therefore, he concluded that the whole troop of robbers was totally dispersed or exterminated and that he himself was now the only person in the world who was acquainted with the secret of entering the cave, and that consequently the immense treasure that it contained was entirely at his disposal. He had provided himself with a bag, and he filled it with as much gold as his horse could carry. Then he returned to the city.

From that time Ali Baba and his son, whom he took to the cave and taught the secret of entering it, and after them their posterity, who were also entrusted with the important secret, lived in great splendor, enjoying their riches with moderation and honored with the most dignified situations in the city.

The Man Who Understood Animals' Conversation

Charles Fillingham Coxwell

This story was told by a strange people of Turkish descent, who live in the middle of Asia – the Tarantchi-Tatars. It reminds one of the old saying, "Curiosity killed the cat."

Once a friend came to a man who was acquainted with the languages of all animals and expressed a wish to have the knowledge imparted to him. The man said: "I will teach you the languages, but if you afterward communicate your knowledge to anyone, even your wife, you will die."

The friend replied, "I will not tell anybody, not even my wife."

The instruction was given, and in time the friend had learned the language of all the animals. He owned a cat, a dog, an ass, and two oxen.

One day he went home and discovered his dog and cat in conversation. The dog asked the cat, "What do you desire most?"

The answer came, "I desire most that my master and his wife should be blind and that his household be made of meat and cream, so that I could feast on it all. That is my wish."

Next the cat in turn put the same question to the dog, who answered thus: "If my master were rich, then I would keep awake at night time and only guard his goods. My master would be pleased with me and feed me well. That is my wish."

The master laughed at the words of the cat and dog and, moreover, he struck the cat and drove her forth. His wife said to him, "You have been away a long time. Then, on your return, you sat and laughed by yourself. Then, you struck the cat and expelled her. You are certainly evil-minded to behave so. Tell me the truth. Do you have some wicked intention?"

The woman scolded her husband, and he was left in perplexity, for he knew that if he told her the secret, he would die, and if he did not tell her, she would be disagreeable. At last, he decided to say nothing, and only struck his wife with a whip, after which she asked no further questions.

One day this man had to plow. So, he yoked the oxen and plowed until evening, at which time the ass approached the oxen and said, "Where have you been today?"

The oxen answered "Our master has cared for us well during the winter because he intended to plow in the spring. Plowing-time has come, and today he harnessed us."

When the ass heard these words, He laughed and said: "You are very stupid! Plowing will last a long while, and he will torment you until the entire land is plowed."

"What are we to do?" cried the oxen.

DOI: 10.4324/9781003297536-13

I WILL TEACH YOU THE LANGUAGE OF ALL THE ANIMALS

The ass answered, "When our master has plowed several days, one of you must become ill! If he gives you grass, do not eat it; and mind that you refuse water. If you act this way, you will escape the plow."

The oxen asked the ass how it went with him. The ass replied, "I have nothing to do; I sometimes visit a mare, and I often roll about among the flowers."

Now, the master understood what passed between the ass and the oxen. Next morning he harnessed the oxen to the plow and returned home before nightfall. But one of the pair pretended to be sick. It didn't eat any grass and wouldn't drink. Next day the man not only yoked both oxen but harnessed the ass. Moreover, he rode the ass without stopping until evening and plowed. And when the ass did not get well, the master struck him with the stick, and by evening had thoroughly worn out the ass.

When they returned home at night, one of the oxen noticed that the ass said nothing and that his ears were hanging down.

The ox said, "What's the matter, ass?" and the ass replied, "I am your well-wisher and the protector of your souls. Our master said today, 'One of the oxen has become sick,' and he has sold you to a butcher who will kill you tomorrow. For this reason I am sad, don't speak, and let my ears droop."

The ox inquired, "In that case, what shall I do?"

The ass answered, "Appear healthy, eat grass, and drink water. Then he will say that you are sound and will not let the butcher kill you."

The man laughed heartily at the ass's words and his wife said, "Why are you amused?"

He replied, "Without cause!"

Thereupon she remarked, "You don't ever laugh without a reason. You have something stirring in your mind. You laughed before, and, when I questioned you as to the cause of your laughter, you struck me; and now you laugh again! If I don't ask you the reason you won't tell me. I shall leave you; let me go!"

So, she startled a quarrel with her husband, and since she became very violent, there was nothing left for him but to tell the truth. He said to her, "You have questioned me persistently, and since I have not answered, you have chided me. But if I tell you the truth I shall die."

His wife said, "Tell me the truth, even if it costs you your life!"

So he related how he had learned the language of animals and how the ass had advised the ox to appear ill. He communicated everything just as it had occurred, and then he died. Consequently, his wife became very sorry that she had extracted the truth from him, and wept bitterly.

The Brotherless Girl

Charles Fillingham Coxwell

Which shows that even Kalmucks are snobs.

A story told by the Kalmucks, the Russian tribe, which dwells in the district of Astrachan. The Kalmucks are an ugly dark people who live in tents made of felt and derive their living from breeding cattle. They wandered into Russia about 300 years ago, when their own country was conquered by the Chinese and might have wandered even further west but were stopped by the Volga, which, as you know, is an immense river. If you look at the map of Asia for the Thian Shan mountains, you will find where these people came from. If you look at the map of Russia, you will find Astrachan, where they now dwell. I am afraid they are not very nice people, but you must judge that for yourself when you have read what happened to The Brotherless Girl, who was a Kalmuck girl.

Here it begins:

Long ago, so I am told, an old temple stood in the middle of a great kingdom, and in the middle of the temple was a clay image of the god Chongshimboddisatva. He was a heathen god, so he had a very long name. The temple was a day's journey from anywhere. In the temple beside god Chongshimboddisatva, dwelt a number of monks, but they cannot have been very lively or this story would never have happened.

THERE STOOD IN THE MIDDLE OF A GREAT KINGDOM AN OLD MONASTERY TEMPLE

DOI: 10.4324/9781003297536-14

Nearby, in a broken-down hut, lived an old man and his wife, and their only daughter, who was perfectly beautiful. One night a poor man who had business at the temple happened to pass the cottage and, as he went past, he happened to hear voices inside. Well, since he was neither good nor content to mind his own business, he crept up to the door and listened.

"We are both old," he heard the old mother say, "and it is time our daughter was married."

Then, he heard the old man answer, "Yes indeed, she and some jewels are all we have in the world. However, we are on good terms with god Chongshimboddisatva, and since tomorrow is the eighth day of the new moon" (which was a very holy day in that country) "let us go to the temple tomorrow and ask God Chongshimboddisatva where we shall look for a husband for her and whether he should be a priest or an ordinary man. If we take him a fine offering, he is sure to tell us."

The poor man who was listening outside the door said to himself, "I know a trick that will get me the jewels and the girl! Ha, ha, old folks, you shouldn't tell family secrets."

So saying, he ran off to the temple, and when nobody was about, he made a hole in the back of Chongshimboddisatva's clay image and crept inside. Next morning, early, the old couple came with their daughter to the temple and, having made their offering to the clay image, bowed low before it.

"Divine Chongshimboddisatva," said the old father, "shall we marry our daughter to a priest, or to a common man, and if he is to be a common man, pray indicate the person. If you don't care to answer us now, have the goodness tell us in a dream tonight."

The poor cheat, who had been inside the god's image for several hours, felt that his patience was well rewarded. He reared his head up inside the head of god Chongshimboddisatva, and roared: "Marry your daughter to an ordinary man! Give her to whosoever comes first to your door tomorrow morning. That will put an end to your dilemma."

The old couple thought a miracle had happened. They thought the clay image had really spoken and were so beside themselves with joy, that they prostrated themselves and gave thanks a number of times before it, crying, "The image hath spoken."

Then, they went home to await events. Early the next morning, the man who had tricked them hastened as fast as his legs could carry him to the old folks' hut, and knocked on the door. The old woman opened it, and as soon as she saw him, stepped back into the room crying, "God Chongshimboddisatva has sent a husband for our Suvarna!"

"That is good news, mother," said the old man, and got up and invited the stranger to come in with great politeness. The cheat entered and soon made himself at home, and though he had to listen half a dozen times to the story of the miracle, in which he had not played a very creditable part, he managed to be amazed whenever the old couple recited the words of the clay image. He acted the ignorant stranger so well, that after a feast of several kinds of food and drink, the father and mother gave him their daughter for a wife, and handed over to him some surprisingly fine jewels. Before nightfall the cheat gathered up his jewels and took the girl by the hand, and they set off for his home at the mouth of the river. The wicked man did not care for the girl in the least and had no intention of marrying her since he had a wife already: but he did care for the jewels, for he loved nothing in the world as much as wealth.

When he was but a mile or two from home, he said to himself, "Well, I have got these jewels from the old folks by trickery, but if I turn up with them at home, my old game of begging will come to an end, for nobody gives anything to a man when it is known that he has a bag of diamonds and rubies in the house. I'll hide my jewels and pretend nothing has happened. As for the girl, I'll hide her too, until I make up my mind what to do with her, since she is of no use to me."

Now the man had carried the jewels in a wooden case, whether it was large or small I cannot tell, but whatever size it was, he pushed the girl into it along with the jewels, and buried it in the sand dunes down by the river. Then he went home.

As soon as he entered the village he humped up his back, bent his head, and started to whine, "I work hard but I earn nothing. So I am starving. I pray, have pity, kind friends, and I will summon blessings on your heads."

When anybody put a coin into his shaking hand he thought, "I shall soon be rich at this rate. I would have been a fool to show off the jewels."

While the cheat continued to collect money from his begging, the girl and the jewels lay in the case under the sand. Why she was not suffocated, no one knows, but many surprising things happen to people who are on good terms with god Chongshimboddisatva, as she and her parents certainly were. It happened one day that a prince came down to the river with two companies of warriors. They had been tiger hunting with bows and arrows, and they sought water for themselves and their horses. Now the prince saw a heap of dark sand that stimulated his curiosity, and he said to one of his warriors, "Shoot into that heap of sand."

The man did so, and the arrow, instead of scattering the loose sand and falling on its side, stuck upright where it struck. At once the prince ordered his men to discover the cause, and the hunters very quickly found that the arrow had rooted itself in a wooden chest. They soon took the lid off and saw, to their surprise, that the chest contained jewels, and a beautiful girl.

"Who are you?" they asked at once. Now Suvarna was terrified to see so many fierce men, but she had her wits about her and answered, in order to make them treat her respectfully:

"I am the Demon Serpent's Daughter."

The prince, who was overcome by her beauty, asked her to be his wife.

"I cannot marry you," said Suvarna, "unless you put someone into the chest to take my place," because the girl felt she owed the cheat something at least.

"We will put someone into the chest," answered the warriors, and she accordingly agreed to marry the prince. However, when they had taken the jewels out of the chest, the hunters put in a live tiger and buried the box as before. Subsequently, they all went away to attend the nuptials of the prince and the girl.

Meanwhile, the cheat had ended his praying, satisfied that he was well on the road to riches, and determined to dig up his jewels and the maiden. So, with this intent he went to the river saying, "I'll now kill the girl and sell the precious stones. With the money they will fetch, and with what I have begged, I shall be well off."

When he came to the river, he pulled the case from the sand, hoisted it on his back, and tramped home, where he set it down in an unused room, for he meant to open it at night in order to do away with the girl privately. Then he warned his wife that she might hear a great noise in the unused room that night, but on no account was she to enter it, for he said, "It will be me at my prayers, the prayers that are to bring us wealth."

THE MAIDEN SAID SHE WAS THE DAUGHTER OF THE
SERPENT KING

In this way, he hoped to account for the sudden arrival of the jewels, and also any noise the poor girl might make as he killed her.

After dark, accordingly, he shut himself up with the box and lifted the lid, saying to the girl who he thought was still inside, "And how have you fared, my dear?"

But, by way of answer a fierce tiger sprang out of the box and attacked him. Now he shrieked, "Come wife! Come children!"

But nobody came, although the noise he and the tiger made as they rolled and wrestled about the floor was frightful. His family listened and laughed, for none of them were particularly fond of him, and they cried out, "Your prayers for wealth seem rather painful, father!"

In the morning, when they went into the inner room to learn what success he had with his prayers, they found nothing but a bright and black tiger lying among some bones, and there was blood on the tiger's mouth and paws.

But although the adventures of the cheat were over for good, those of the girl he had meant to kill had only just begun. She was a princess now, and the mother of three children. The prince loved her, and she was treated with every respect by the court. But the people who liked ostentatious ceremonies and preferred princesses of high birth with rich relations and expensive possessions, began to grumble among themselves. They knew how the prince had found her, and thought there was something odd and uncanny about it. In short, they decided she was either nobody, or a demon.

"She has sons," they said, "and that is all very well, but who is she? She comes from the underground and has no brother."

These rumors came to the ears of the prince, and the princess saw that her husband was beginning to look doubtfully and reproachfully at her. She decided, therefore, to go away.

"I will go home," she said. "At least, my father and mother will be glad to see me once more before they die."

Accordingly on the fifteenth day of the next moon, when it was at its fullest, the princess left the town at night and set off to the hut of her old parents without either companion or friend.

After traveling a considerable distance she came to the district where she was born, but instead of the miserable wilderness that existed there in her time, she found the fields well cultivated and full of laborers working hard. Among them was a handsome young man who seemed to have prepared a feast for someone.

"Where are you from?" he asked the princess.

"From many miles away," she said. "Once upon a time this country was my country, and I have come home to see my parents before they die."

"You are the child of the old people who are chiefs here?"

"Yes, I am the daughter of an old couple who in former times, lived in a hut near the temple."

Now the young man surprised her and said, "I am their son, and I have been told that I had a sister. You must be she. Let us feast together, and afterward we will seek our father and mother."

So they ate and drank together, and then went over the mountains to seek her old home. But to her astonishment, when they got within view of the old cottage, she saw a group of wonderful palaces, finer than those of any pence. Flags, tapestries, and silk banners decorated them gaily, and as for the temple of god Chongshimboddisatva, it sparkled with gold and diamonds and displayed the finest brocades, and beautiful golden bells chimed from its belfry.

"How wonderful it is, my brother," she said. "Who owns it?"

"It is ours," replied the brother. "We have become rich ever since you went away. All is well at home."

After a while, the brother and sister came home, and the princess was astonished by the wealth of horses and mules and cattle which she saw everywhere. Her parents reposed on luxurious divans. When they saw their daughter, they cried out, "How are you? We are glad you have come to us before we pass away."

Then the girl told her parents everything that had happened since the cheat had stolen her, and they related everything that had happened to them. Finally, the daughter told her mother and father why she had left her husband, and how she was despised by her people because she could make no claim to have a brother, or great possessions, or high birth.

General feasting and rejoicing took place in the palace of her father and mother and, in order to make the joy perfect, her parents sent a deputation to the prince and invited him and his whole court to pay them a visit.

In due course, the prince, attended by a magnificent cavalcade, arrived, and was entertained in the most splendid fashion for three days until, at length, overwhelmed with the gifts of his wife's relations, the prince cried: "Behold! the kindred of our princess! We are to blame for considering her of no importance."

Then the prince and his royal court returned home, leaving the princess yet a little while to comfort her parents who commended her upon the choice that she had made, and thanked the god Chongshimboddisatva for his protection.

On the morning of the day after the prince's departure Princess Suvarna awoke at dawn. To her astonishment, her silken bed had disappeared, and she was lying on the poor hard couch that she had used in her youth,

"Where am I?" she cried. "Yesterday, I was with my parents. I went to sleep on a princely divan, but this morning I find myself in a little broken-down cottage!"

She walked out of doors and looked around her. Her parents' bones lay white and unburied in the dust. She wept bitterly. In her misery she thought she would go to the temple and pray for comfort to the statue of god Chongshimboddisatva, but she found the temple fallen down and the image destroyed.

However, as she gazed at the ruined temple, this thought entered her mind: "I must have lived through divine grace these last days in a vision. The gods themselves must have sent my parents to assist me, but the prince and his court will never know that this dream has not been real. I will go home."

Thereupon, she set out for her husband's palace. When she was near the prince's city, she was perceived from afar off by the prince and all his court, who hurried to receive her with respect and admiration, crying, "Welcome to our princess, a daughter of noble parents, sister of a noble brother, mother of noble sons. Welcome to our glorious princess, who is more beautiful and worthy of respect than any other."

OUR PRINCESS HAS DISTINGUISHED RELATIONS

THE TZAR MOUNTED ON THE BACK OF THE EAGLE

The Water King and Vasilissa the Wise

William Ralston

A famous Russian story told by the Man whom Nobody Knows, as all Folk Tales are. Baba Yaga, the old woman in the forest, who helps the prince in this tale, is an old Russian witch. Sometimes she is good, and sometimes bad, just as the mood takes her. There are many stories about her. It is as well to be on her right side, to ask her to all weddings and christenings, and show her every respect. It you say "Baba Yaga" to a Russian child, she will say "Bogey-man" back to you, for those two are much of a muchness.

Once upon a time there lived a king and queen, and the king was very fond of hunting and shooting. Well, one day he went out hunting, and he saw an Eaglet sitting on an oak. But just as he was going to shoot, the eaglet began to entreat him, crying "Don't shoot me, my lord king! It is better for you to take me home with you. Some time or other I shall be of service to you."

The king reflected awhile and said, "How can you be of use to me?" and again he was going to shoot, when the Eaglet said to him a second time: "Don't shoot me, my lord king! It's better to take me home with you. Some time or other I shall be of use to you."

The king thought and thought, but he couldn't imagine a bit what use the Eaglet could be to him, and so he decided to shoot it. Then a third time the Eaglet exclaimed: "Don't shoot me, my lord king! It's better take me home with you and feed me for three years. Some time or other I shall be of service to you!"

The king relented, took the Eaglet home with him, and fed it for a year, for two years. But it ate so much that it devoured all his cattle. The king had neither a cow nor a sheep left. Finally, the Eagle (for it had grown nearly to adulthood) said: "Now let me go free!"

The king set it at liberty; and the Eagle began trying its wings. But no, it could not fly yet! So it said: "Well, my lord king! You have fed me two years. Now, whether you like it or not, you must feed me for one year more. Even if you have to borrow money, you must feed me. You won't lose anything by doing this."

Well, this is what the king did. He borrowed cattle from everywhere around his realm, and he fed the Eagle for a space of a whole year. Afterward he set it free. The Eagle rose ever so high, flew and flew, then soared down again to the earth and said: "Now then, my lord king! Take a seat on my back! We'll take a fly together!"

DOI: 10.4324/9781003297536-15

THE WATER-KING PURSUED THEM

So, the king got on the Eagle's back. Away they went flying. Before very long they reached the blue sea. Then the Eagle shook off the king, who fell into the sea, and sank up to his knees. But the Eagle didn't let him drown! It jerked him on to its wing, and asked: "How now, my lord king! Were you frightened, perchance?"

"I was," said the king; "I thought I was going to drown!"

Again they flew and flew until they reached another sea. The Eagle shook off the king right in the middle of the sea, and the king sank up to his stomach. The Eagle jerked him on to its wing again, and asked: "Well, my lord King! were you frightened, perchance?"

"I was," he replied, "but all the time I thought, 'Perhaps, please God, the creature will pull me out.'"

Away they flew again, flew, and arrived at a third sea. The Eagle dropped the king into a great gulf, so that he sank right up to his neck. And the third time the Eagle jerked him on to its wing, and asked: "Well, my lord king! Were you frightened, perchance?"

"I was," the king, replied," but still I said to myself, 'Perhaps the bird will pull me out!'"

"Well, my lord king! Now you have felt what the fear of death is like! What I have done was in payment of an old score: Do you remember my sitting on an oak, and your wanting to shoot me? Three times you were going to shoot, but I kept on entreating you not to shoot, saying to myself all the time, 'Perhaps he won't kill me. Perhaps he'll relent and take me home with him!'"

Afterward they flew beyond thrice nine lands. Long, long did they fly.

"Look, my lord king!" cried the Eagle. "What is above us and what below us?"

The king looked.

"Above us," he said, "is the sky, below us the earth."

"Look again! What is on the right hand and on the left?"

"On the right hand is an open plain, on the left stands a house."

"We will fly there," said the Eagle; "my youngest sister lives there."

They went straight into the courtyard. The sister came out to greet them. She received her brother cordially and seated him at the oaken table. But she would not so much look at the king. Instead, she left him outside and set some greyhounds loose to attack him. The Eagle was exceedingly angry with her, and he jumped up from the table, seized the king, and flew away with him again. Well, they flew and flew. Soon the Eagle said to the king, "Look around; what is behind us?"

The king turned his head, looked, and said, "Behind us is a red house."

"That is the house of my youngest sister on fire, because she did not receive you, but set greyhounds on you!"

They flew and flew. Again the Eagle asked: "Look again, my lord king: what is above us, and what below us?"

"Above us is the sky, below us the earth."

"Look and see what is on the right hand and on the left."

"On the right is the open plain; on the left there is a house."

"There lives my second sister. We'll go and pay her a visit."

They stopped in a wide courtyard. The second sister received her brother cordially and seated him at the oak table. But the king was left outside. Then she set the greyhounds on him.

The Eagle was enraged. He jumped up from the table, seized the king, and flew away further with him. They flew and flew until the Eagle said: "My lord king, look around! What is behind us?"

The king looked back.

"A red house is standing behind us."

That's my second sister's house burning," said the Eagle. "Now we'll fly to where my mother and eldest sister live."

Well, they flew there. The Eagle's mother and eldest sister were delighted to see them, and received the king with cordiality and respect.

"Now, my lord king," said the Eagle, "stay awhile with us, and afterward I will give you a ship and will repay you for all I ate in your house, and then – God speed you home again!"

So the Eagle gave the king a ship and two coffers – the one red, the other green – and said: "Mind now! Don't open the coffers until you get home. Then open the red coffer in the back court, and the green coffer in the front court."

The king took the coffers, parted with the Eagle, and sailed along the blue sea. Soon he came to a certain island, and there his ship stopped. He landed on the shore and began thinking about the coffers, and wondering whatever there could be in them, and why the Eagle had told him not to open them. He thought and thought, and at last, he couldn't hold out any more. Indeed, he longed so awfully to know all about it. So he took the red coffer, set it on the ground, and opened it. Suddenly, out came such a quantity of different kinds of cattle that there was no counting them. In fact, the island had barely room enough for them.

When the king saw that, he became exceedingly sorrowful, and began to weep and said, "What is there now left for me to do? How shall I get all this cattle back into such a little coffer?"

All at once, a man came out of the water and asked: "Why are you weeping so bitterly, O Lord King?"

"How can I help weeping!" answers the king. "How shall I be able to get all this great herd into such a small a coffer?"

"If you like, I will set your mind at rest. I will pack up all your cattle for you. But on one condition only. You must give me whatever you have at home that you don't know of."

The king reflected and then said: "Whatever is there at home that I don't know of? I fancy I know about everything that's there."

He reflected, and consented. "Pack them up," he said. I shall give you whatever I have at home."

So that man packed away all his cattle for him. Then the king went on board the ship and sailed away toward his home. When he reached his destination, he learned only then that a son had been born to him. Immediately he began kissing the child, caressing it, and at the same time bursting into a flood of tears.

"My lord king," his wife said to him, "tell me why you are weeping so much."

"For joy," he replied, for he was afraid to tell her the truth. The prince would have to be given up. Afterward he went into the back court and opened the red coffer. Then out popped oxen and cows, sheep and rams. There were all sorts of cattle and so many that the sheds and pastures were crammed full. He then went into the front court, opened the green coffer, and there appeared a large and glorious garden. Indeed, there

A YOUNG EAGLE SAT ON A TREE

were amazing trees in it! The king was so delighted that he forgot all about giving up his son.

Many years went by. One day the king decided to go for a stroll, and he came to a river. At that moment the same man he had seen before came out of the water, and said: "You've certainly become forgetful, Lord King! Think a little! Surely, you're in my debt!"

The king returned home full of grief and told the complete truth to the queen and the prince. They all mourned and wept together, but they decided that there was nothing they could do – the prince had to be surrendered. So, they took him to the mouth of the river, and there they left him alone.

The prince looked around, saw a footpath, and followed it, trusting God would lead him somewhere. He walked and walked and soon came to a dense forest. In this forest stood a hut, and in this hut lived Baba Yaga.

"Perhaps, I should enter it?" the prince said to himself and went in.

"Good day, prince!" said Baba Yaga. "Are you seeking work or shunning work?"

"Eh, granny! First give me something to eat and drink, and then ask me questions."

So she gave him food and drink, and the prince told her where he was going and with what purpose. Then Baba Yaga said: "Go, my child, to the seashore. Twelve spoonbills will turn into fair maidens and begin bathing there. You are to sneak quietly and grab hold of the eldest maiden's shift. When you have come to terms with her, go to the Water King. On the way there you will meet Obedalo and Opivalo, and also Moroz Treskun – take all of them with you. They will serve you well."

The prince bid Baba Yaga farewell, went to the appointed spot on the seashore, and hid behind the bushes. Soon, twelve spoonbills came flying there, and once they struck the moist earth, they turned into fair maidens and began to bathe. The prince stole the shift from the eldest princess and sat down behind a bush – he didn't budge an inch. The girls finished bathing and came out on the shore: eleven of them put on their shifts, turned into birds, and flew away home. Only the eldest, Vasilissa the Wise, remained. She began praying and begged the young man.

"Please give me my shift!" she said. "You are on your way to the house of my father, the Water King. When you come, I will do you a favor."

So, the Prince gave her back her shift, and she immediately turned into a spoonbill and flew away after her companions. The prince went farther, and along the way he met the three heroes – Obedalo, Opivalo, and Moroz Treskun. He took them with him and went on to the Water King's dwelling.

The Water King saw him and said: "Hail, friend! Why have you been so long in coming to me? I have grown weary of waiting for you. Now set to work. Here is your first task. Build me a great crystal bridge in one night so that it shall be ready for use tomorrow. If you don't build it, off goes your head!"

The prince left the Water King and burst into a flood of tears. Vasilissa the Wise opened the window of her upper chamber, and asked: "What are you crying about, prince?"

"Ah! Vasilissa the Wise! How can I stop crying? Your father has ordered me to build a crystal bridge in a single night, and I don't even know how to handle an axe."

"No matter! Lie down and sleep. The morning is wiser than the evening."

She ordered him to sleep, but she herself went out onto the steps and called aloud with a mighty whistling cry. Then, from all sides, there came carpenters and workmen.

One leveled the ground; another carried bricks. Soon had they built a crystal bridge, placed cunning devices on it, and then they dispersed to their homes.

& IMMEDIATELY A MULTITUDE OF CATTLE POURED OUT

THE PRINCE SLEEPS WHILE HIS TASKS ARE PERFORMED

Early next morning, Vasilissa the Wise woke the prince and cried: "Get up, prince! The bridge is ready. My father will be coming to inspect it soon."

Up jumped the prince, seized a broom, took his place on the bridge, and began sweeping here, clearing up there. The Water King bestowed praise upon him:

"Thanks!" said he. "You've done me one service. Now do another. Here is your task. Plant me by tomorrow a green garden, – a big and shady one. There must be birds singing in the garden, flowers blossoming on the trees, and ripe apples and pears hanging from the boughs."

The prince left and could do nothing but weep tons of tears. Vasilissa the Wise opened her window and asked: "Why are you crying, prince?"

"How can I stop crying? Your father has ordered me to plant a garden in one night!"

"That's nothing! Lie down and sleep. The morning is wiser than the evening."

She made him go to sleep; but she herself went out on the steps, called and whistled with a mighty tune. From every side gardeners of all sorts arrived, and they planted a green garden, and in the garden birds sang on the trees and flowers blossomed, while apples and pears hung from the boughs of the trees,

Early in the morning, Vasilissa the Wise woke the prince:

"Get up, prince! The garden is ready: Papa is coming to see it."

The Prince immediately snatched a broom and ran off to the garden. Here he swept a path, while there he trained a twig.

The Water King praised him and said: "Thanks, prince! You've done excellent service. So choose yourself a bride from among my twelve daughters. They are all exactly alike in face, in hair, and in dress. If you can pick out the same one three times running, she will be your wife. However, if you fail to do so, I shall have you put to death."

Vasilissa the Wise knew all about that, so she found time to say to the prince: "The first time I will wave my handkerchief, the second I will be arranging my dress, and the third time you will see a fly above my head."

And so the prince guessed which maiden was Vasilissa the Wise three times running. And he and she were married, and a wedding feast was organized. Now the Water King had prepared much food of all sorts, more than a hundred men could get through. And he ordered his son-in-law to see that everything was eaten.

"If anything remains over, the worse for you!" he said.

"My father," the prince requested, "there's an old fellow of mine here. Please let him take a snack with us."

"Let him come!"

Immediately Obedalo appeared and ate up everything. Indeed, he wasn't content even then!

The Water King next set out two score tubs of all kinds of strong drinks and ordered his son-in-law to see that they were all drained dry.

"My father!" the prince requested again, "there's another old man of mine here. Please let him drink to your health."

"Let him come!"

Opivalo appeared, emptied all the forty tubs in a twinkling, and then asked for a drop more by way of stirrup-cup.

The Water King saw that there was nothing to be gained this way. So, he gave orders to prepare a bathroom for the young couple, – an iron bathroom, and to heat it as hot as possible. So the iron bathroom was made hot. Twelve loads of firewood were set afire, and the stove and the walls became red-hot – impossible to come within five steps of it.

THE HORSE WAS CHANGED INTO A WELL & THE PRINCE INTO A LITTLE OLD MAN

"My father!" the prince said. "Let an old fellow of ours have a scrub first, just to try the bathroom."

"Let him do so!"

Moroz Treskun went into the bathroom, blew into one corner, blew into another – and in one second icicles were hanging there. After him the young couple also went into the bathroom, were lathered and scrubbed, and then went home.

AN OLD PRIEST & A RUINED & MOSSCOVERED CHURCH

After a time Vasilissa said to the prince, "Let us escape my father's power. He's tremendously angry with you. Perhaps he may hurt you in one way or another."

"Let us go," said the prince.

Immediately thereafter they saddled their horses and galloped off into the open plain. They rode and rode. Many an hour went by.

"Jump down from your horse, prince, and lay your ear close to the earth," said Vasilissa. "Can you hear a sound of some pursuers?"

VASILISSA MADE A PIE

The prince bent his ear to the ground, but he couldn't hear anything. Then Vasilissa herself jumped down from her good stead, laid herself flat on the earth, and said: "Ah prince! I hear a great noise. Somebody is chasing us."

Then she turned the horses into a well, and herself into a bowl, and the prince into an old, very old man. Then the pursuers arrived right after she had done this.

"Hey, old man!" they said. "Have you seen a young man and a maiden pass by?"

"I saw them, my friends! Only it was a long while ago. I was a youngster at the time when they rode by."

The pursuers returned to the Water King.

"There is no trace of them," they said, "no news. All we saw was an old man beside a well, and a bowl floating on the water."

"Why didn't you seize them?" cried the Water King, who thereupon put the pursuers to a cruel death, and sent another troop after the prince and Vasilissa the Wise. The fugitives in the meantime had ridden far, far away. Then, since Vasilissa the Wise heard the noise made by the fresh set of pursuers, she turned the prince into an old priest, and she herself became an ancient church. Scarcely did its walls hold together, covered all over with moss when the pursuers arrived.

"Hey, old man! Have you seen a young man and a maiden pass by?"

"I saw them, my own! Only it was long, long ago. I was a young man when they rode by. It was just while I was building this church."

So the second set of pursuers returned to the Water King and said: "There is neither trace nor news of them, your Royal Majesty. All that we saw was an old priest and an ancient church."

"Why didn't you seize them?" cried the Water King louder than before, and after having put the pursuers to a cruel death, he galloped off himself in pursuit of the prince and Vasilissa the Wise. This time Vasilissa turned the horses into a river of honey with dried-fruit banks, and changed the Prince into a drake and herself into a gray duck. The Water King flung himself on the dried fruit and honey-water and ate and ate, and drank and drank until he burst! And so he gave up the ghost.

The prince and Vasilissa rode on, and soon they drew near to the home of the prince's parents. Then said Vasilissa, "Go ahead of me, prince and report your arrival to your father and mother. I shall wait for you here by the wayside. Only remember these words of mine: kiss everybody else, only don't kiss your sister. If you do, you will forget me."

The prince reached home, began saluting every one, and kissed his sister, too. No sooner had he kissed her than from that very moment he forgot all about his wife, just as if she had never entered into his mind.

Three days did Vasilissa the Wise await him. On the fourth day she clad herself like a beggar, went into the capital, and took up her quarters in an old woman's house. But the prince was preparing to marry a rich princess, and orders were given to proclaim the wedding throughout the kingdom so that all Christian people were to come to congratulate the bride and bridegroom. Each one was to bring a wheaten pie as a present. Well, the old woman with whom Vasilissa lodged prepared like everyone else to sift flour and make a pie.

"Why are you making a pie, granny?" asked Vasilissa.

"Oh, you evidently don't know then. Our king is giving his son in marriage to a rich princess. Consequently, everyone must go to the palace to serve the dinner to the young couple."

"Well then, I, too, will bake a pie and take it to the palace. Maybe the king will give me a present."

"Bake away in God's name!" said the old woman.

So, Vasilissa took flour, kneaded dough, and made a pie. And inside it she put some curds and a pair of live doves. Well, the old woman and Vasilissa the Wise reached the palace just at dinner-time where a feast was in progress, one fit for all the world to see.

Vasilissa's pie was set on the table, but no sooner was it cut in two than the two doves flew out of it. The hen bird seized a piece of curd, and her mate said to her:

"Give me some curds too, Dovey!"

"No, I won't," replied the other dove: "otherwise you'd forget me just as the prince has forgotten his Vasilissa the Wise."

All at once, the prince remembered his wife. He jumped up from table, seized her by her white hands, and seated her close by his side. From that time forward they lived together in happiness and prosperity.

Foolish John

Charles Fillingham Coxwell

This also is a Russian tale and is considered the height of wit by Russian peasants. In folk tales all over the world, foolish people often get the better of wise ones.

An old man and his wife had three sons, of whom two were sensible, but the third was foolish John. While the older sons tended sheep in the fields, the fool did nothing except sit on the stove and catch flies. Once, when the old woman had boiled some rye dumplings, she said to the fool, "Take these dumplings to your brothers, and let them have a meal."

She filled a pot with dumplings and put it into his hands. He wandered toward his brothers. It was a sunny day, and John had scarcely reached the outskirts of the village, when he saw a shadow by his side and thought, "What sort of fellow is this? He keeps by my side, and doesn't fall back a single step. No doubt he would like some dumplings."

So, he began to throw the dumplings at the shadow and didn't stop until he had thrown away all of them, even the last. Then he looked, and the shadow was still by his side. "It is impossible to satisfy such a fellow," said the fool, angrily, as he hurled the pot at the shadow so that the fragments flew about in different directions. When he came empty-handed to his brothers they asked him, "Fool, what is the meaning of this behavior?"

"I have brought you your diner."

"Where is it, then? Hand it to us quickly."

"Well you see, brothers, a strange fellow followed me closely as I came here, and I gave it to him to eat."

"What kind of fellow?"

"Well, he kept up with me all the time. It was like he glued himself to me."

The brothers abused the fool, and then thrashed him thoroughly. They told him to take care of the sheep while they themselves went to the village for dinner.

The fool began his task. When he saw that the sheep wandered about the field, he set to work to catch them and pluck out their eyes. He caught them all and removed the eyes from every one of them. Then, collecting the flock, he sat down, as delighted as if he had performed a great feat. Later, the brothers dined and returned to the field.

"What have you done, fool? Why is the flock blind?"

He answered, "Do they require eyes? When you went away, brothers, the sheep roamed about separately, and I hit on a plan; I caught them and took out their eyes. The task was exhausting."

DOI: 10.4324/9781003297536-16

"Stop, you shall get tired in a different way," said the brothers, as they beat him soundly with their fists.

In the course of time the older brothers sent John, the fool, to buy some household goods. He bought a table and spoons, and cups, and meat, and salt and heaped them all up into a load. Then he started home, but the horse was almost useless and pulled to little purpose. John thought to himself, "A horse has four legs, and a table has four legs; the table will therefore run of its own accord."

THE TABLE HAS FOUR LEGS—LET IT RUN!

He took the table out of the cart and put it on the road. Then he traveled a distance, while the crows hovered over him and cawed continually.

"It is evident the sisters would like something to eat. What a noise they are making!" reflected the fool. So, he threw the meat on the ground and let the birds regale themselves.

"Little doves! Little sisters!" said he. "Eat! And may the food do you good!"

But he himself moved on. The road led between some trees, and he found himself among a number of burnt tree-stumps. "Ah," he thought, "the children have no caps. They must be cold, the dear things!" and immediately he placed the pots and bowls upon the tree stumps.

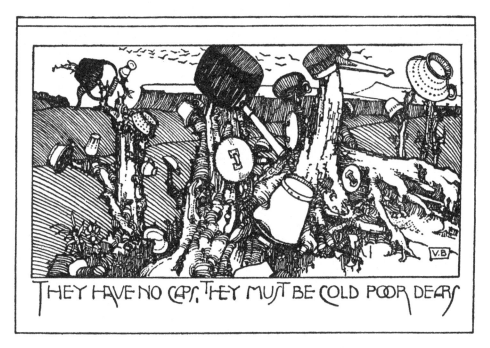

THEY HAVE NO CAPS, THEY MUST BE COLD POOR DEARS

Next John, having come to a river, sought to give his horse some water, but the horse would not drink.

"Clearly," said the boy, "he will not drink unsalted water."

The fool scattered the whole bag of salt in the water; nevertheless the horse would not drink. "Why in the world will you not drink, you wolf's flesh! Have I used up a bag of salt to no purpose?"

He seized a log, struck the horse on the head, and killed him. John possessed now only the wallet of spoons, which he carried on his person. As he went along, the spoons rattled and clattered. He thought they were saying, "John, the fool!" So, he threw them down and, trampling on them, he said in a taunting voice, "I'm John, the fool, am I? I'm John, the fool, am I? You wretched things have dared to tease me!"

HE THREW DOWN THE SPOONS & STAMPED ON THEM

Reaching home he made this announcement. "I have bought everything you needed, dear brothers."

"Thank you, fool, where are your purchases?"

"The table is running on behind, and the little sisters are eating out of the dishes. I placed the pots and bowls on the heads of children in the forest, and salted the brook with the salt, and since the spoons teased me, I threw them away on the road."

"Lose no time, fool! Go and gather everything that you scattered while on your journey."

John went into the forest, and removing the pots from the burnt tree-stumps, he knocked out their bottoms, placed about a dozen of each kind, great and small, on a stick, and carried them home where the brothers beat him. Then the brothers left him to mind the house while they went to make purchases in the town.

The fool now listened to the beer fermenting in the vat and said, "Beer, do not ferment! Do not tease me!"

Since the beer did not obey, the boy let it flow out of the vat. Afterward he sat in the trough and sang songs, or ran about in the cottage. The brothers were terribly angry. So, they grabbed hold of John, sewed him up in a sack, and dragged him to the river. Placing the sack on the shore, they went to look for an ice hole. Now, a certain lord was driving past in a troika with chestnut horses, and John cried out, "They set me in command, as a competent judge in everything; but I can neither judge nor rule."

"Stop, fool!" said the lord; "I am well able to judge and to rule. Come out of the sack!"

John came forth, sewed the lord firmly in the sack, took his seat in the conveyance and drove away rapidly. When the brothers arrived, they lowered the sack under the ice, and listened to how it gurgled in the water! But John came to meet them, from somewhere or other in the troika.

"Look," said he, "at the horses which I have captured, and there still remains a behind gray horse, such a fine one!"

The envious brothers said to the fool, "Sew us up in a sack and lower us quickly into the ice hole. The gray horse shall be ours."

John, the fool, sank his brothers down into the ice hole, and raced home to drink beer and think of them.

UNDER THE APPLE TREE

The Golden Apple Tree and the Nine Peahens

Elodie L. Mijatovich

A story from Serbia, part of the kingdom of Yugoslavia. This is one of the most beau-tiful fairy tales in the world. It is famous in Russia too, but there they call it the Fire Bird. The translation was made by a Serbian lady of great distinction, who knew all about kings and queens because she spent her life among them.

Once upon a time there lived a king who had three sons. Now, in front of the king's palace there was a golden apple tree, which blossomed, bore fruit, and lost all its fruit all in the same night though no one could tell who took the apples.

One day the king, speaking to his eldest son, said, "I should like to know who takes the fruit from our apple tree."

And the son said, "I shall keep guard tonight and shall see who gathers the apples."

So, when the evening arrived, he went and laid himself down under the apple tree on the ground to watch. Just as the apples ripened, however, he fell asleep, and when he awoke in the morning there was not a single one left on the tree. Thereupon, he went and told his father what had happened. So, the second son offered to keep watch by the tree, but he had no better success than his eldest brother.

Now, the turn came to the king's youngest son to keep guard. He made his preparations, brought his bed under the tree, and immediately went to sleep. Before midnight he awoke and looked up at the tree, and saw how the apples ripened, and how the whole place was lit up by their shining. At that minute nine peahens flew toward the tree, and eight of them settled on its branches, but the ninth alighted near him and turned instantly into a beautiful girl – so beautiful, indeed, that the whole kingdom could not produce one who could in any way compare with her. She stayed, conversing kindly with him, until after midnight and then thanking him for the golden apples, she prepared to depart. But when he begged her to leave him one, she gave him two, one for himself and one for the king, his father. Then the girl turned again into a peahen and flew away with the other eight.

Next morning, the king's son took the two apples to his father, and the king was very pleased and praised his son. When evening came, the king's youngest son took his place again under the apple tree to keep guard over it. He again conversed as he had done the night before with the beautiful girl, and brought to his father, the next morning, two apples as before. But, after he had succeeded so well several nights, his two elder brothers grew envious because he had been able to do what they could not. Finally, they found an old woman, who promised to discover how the youngest brother had succeeded in saving the two apples. So, when evening arrived, the old woman slid quietly under the bed which stood under the apple tree and hid herself.

DOI: 10.4324/9781003297536-17

And after a while the king's son came and laid himself down as usual to sleep. When it was near midnight, the nine peahens flew there as before, and eight of them settled on the branches, while the ninth stood by his bed and turned into a most beautiful girl imaginable.

Then the old woman slowly took hold of one of the girl's curls and cut it off, and the girl immediately rose up, changed back into a peahen, flew away, and the other peahens followed her. In short, they all disappeared.

THE GOLDEN APPLE-TREE & THE NINE PEAHENS

Then the king's son jumped up, and cried out, "What is that?" and, looking under the bed, he saw the old woman and dragged her out. Next morning he ordered her to be tied to a horse's tail and thus torn to pieces. But the peahens never came back. So, the king's son was very sad for a long time and wept at his loss. After some time passed, he resolved to go and search for his peahen and never to come back again unless he found her. When he told the king, his father, of his intention, the king begged him not to go away and said that he would find him another beautiful girl, and that he might choose from all those in the kingdom.

But all the king's attempts to persuade him to remain at home were useless. His son went into the world to search everywhere for his peahen, taking only one servant to serve him. After many journeys, he came one day to a lake. Now by the lake stood a large and beautiful palace. In the palace lived an old woman as queen, and with the queen lived a girl, her daughter. He said to the old woman, "For heaven's sake, grandmother, do you know anything about nine golden peahens?" and the old woman answered, "Oh, my son, I know all about them. They come every midday to bathe in the lake. But what do you want with them? Let them be, and think nothing about them. Here is my daughter. Such a beautiful girl! And such an heiress! All my wealth will be bestowed upon you if you marry her."

But he was burning with desire to see the peahens and would not listen to what the old woman said about her daughter. Next morning, when day dawned, the prince prepared to go down to the lake to wait for the peahens. Then the old queen bribed the servant and gave him a little pair of bellows, and said, "Do you see these bellows? When you come to the lake, you must blow secretly with them behind his neck, and then he will fall asleep, and not be able to speak to the peahens."

The mischievous servant did as the old woman told him. When he went with his master down to the lake, he took this opportunity to blow with the bellows behind his neck, and the poor prince fell asleep just as though he were dead. Shortly after the nine peahens came flying, and eight of them landed by the lake, while the ninth flew toward the prince, who sat on horseback, and caressed him and tried to waken him.

"Awake, my darling! Awake heart! Awake, my soul!"

But for all that, he knew nothing. It was as if he were dead.

After they had bathed, all the peahens flew away together, and after they were gone, the prince woke up and said to his servant, "What has happened? Did they not come?"

The servant told him they had been there, and that eight of them had bathed, but the ninth had sat by him on his horse and caressed and tried to waken him. Then the king's son became so angry that he almost killed himself in his rage. Next morning he went down again to the shore to wait for the peahens, and rode about a long time until the servant again found an opportunity to blow with the bellows behind his neck, so that he again fell asleep as though dead. Hardly had he fallen asleep when the nine peahens came flying, and eight of them landed by the water, but the ninth settled down by the side of his horse and caressed the prince and cried out to waken him,

"Arise, my darling! Arise, my heart! Arise, my soul!"

But it was of no use; the prince slept on as if he were dead. Then she said to the servant, "Tell your master tomorrow that he can see us here again, but never again."

With these words the peahens flew away. Immediately after the king's son woke up, and asked his servant, "Have they not been here?"

And the man answered, "Yes, they have been, and they said that you can see them again tomorrow, at this place, but after that they will not return again."

When the unhappy prince heard that he didn't know what to do with himself, and in his great trouble and misery tore the hair from his head. Now, the third day he went down again to the shore, but, fearing to fall asleep, instead of riding slowly, he galloped along the shore. His servant, however, found an opportunity to blow with the bellows behind his neck, and again the prince fell asleep. A moment later the nine peahens came, and the eight landed on the lake while the ninth landed near him, on his horse, and sought to waken him, caressing him. "Arise, my darling! Arise, my heart! Arise, my soul!"

But it was of no use, he slept on as if dead. Then the peahen said to the servant, "When your master awakens, tell him he ought to strike off the head of the nail from the lower part, and then he will find me." Thereupon all the peahens fled away. Immediately the king's son awoke and said to his servant, "Have they been here?"

And the servant answered "They have been, indeed, and the one which landed on your horse ordered me to tell you to strike off the head of the nail from the lower part, and then you will find her."

When the prince heard that, he drew his sword and cut off the servant's head. After that he traveled alone all over the world, and, after many long journeys, he came to a mountain and remained there all night with a hermit, whom he asked if he knew anything about nine golden peahens. The hermit said, "Eh, my son, you are lucky.

God has led you in the right path. From this place it is only half a day's walk. But you must go straight on, then you will come to a large gate, which you must pass through; and, after that, you must always keep to the right hand, and so you will come to the peahens' city, and find their palace there."

So next morning the king's son arose and prepared to go. He thanked the hermit, and went as he had told him. After a while he came to the large gate, and, having passed it, turned to the right, so that at midday he saw the city, and beholding how white it shone, rejoiced very much. When he entered the city, he found the palace where the nine golden peahens lived. But at the gate he was stopped by the guard, who demanded to know who he was, and where he was coming from. After the prince had answered these questions, the guards went to announce him to the queen.

HE CAME TO THE GREAT GATE

When the queen heard who he was, she came running out to the gate and took him by the hand to lead him into the palace. She was a young and beautiful maiden, and so there was a great rejoicing, and after a few days, he married her and remained there with her.

One day, some time after their marriage, the queen went to walk, and the king's son remained in the palace. Before going out, however, the queen gave him the keys of twelve cellars telling him, "You may go down into all the cellars except the twelfth which you must on no account open, or it will cost you your head."

Then she went away. The king's son stayed in the palace and began to wonder what there could be in the twelfth cellar. He soon began to open one cellar after the other, and when he came to the twelfth, he would not at first open it, but again he began to wonder very much why he was forbidden to go inside.

"What can be in this cellar?" he exclaimed to himself. Finally, he opened it. In the middle of the cellar lay a big barrel with an open bunghole, but it was tied around with three iron hoops. Out of the barrel came a voice, saying, "For God's sake, my brother – I am dying with thirst. Please give me a cup of water."

Then the king's son took a cup and filled it with water, and emptied it into the barrel.

Immediately after he had done this, one of the hoops burst asunder. Again came the voice from the barrel: "For God's sake my brother – I am dying of thirst! Please give me a cup of water."

The king's son again filled the cup, took it, and emptied it into the barrel. Then all of a sudden another hoop burst asunder. The third time the voice came out of the barrel, "For God's sake, my brother – I am dying of thirst! Please give me a cup of water."

The king's son again took the cup, filled it, and poured the water into the barrel, and the third hoop burst. Then the barrel fell to pieces, and a dragon flew out of the cellar, caught the queen on the road, and carried her away. The servant, who had gone out with the queen, came back quickly, and told the king's son what had happened, and the poor prince knew not what to do with himself, so desperate was he and full of self-reproaches.

Soon, however, he resolved to set out and travel through the world in search of her. After a long journey, he came to a lake, and near it, in a small hole, he saw a little fish jumping about. When the fish saw the king's son, he began to beg pitifully, "For God's sake, be my brother, and throw me into the water. Some day I may be of use to you. So, take a little scale from me, and when you need me, rub it gently."

Then the king's son lifted the little fish from the hole and threw her into the water, after he had taken one small scale, which he wrapped up carefully in a handkerchief. Some time later, as he was traveling about the world, he encountered a fox caught in an iron trap. When the fox saw the prince he said: "In God's name, be a brother to me and help me to get out of this trap. One day you will need me, so take just one hair from my tail, and when you want me, rub it gently."

Then the king's son took a hair from the tail of the fox and set him free. Again, as he crossed a mountain, he saw a wolf caught in a trap, and when the wolf saw him, it said, "Be a brother in God's name! Set me free, and one day I will help you. Only take a hair from me, and when you need me, rub it gently."

So, he took a hair and set the wolf free. After that the king's son traveled about a very long time, until one day he met a man to whom he said, "For God's sake, brother, have you ever heard anyone say where he palace of the dragon king is located?"

The man gave him very particular directions about which way he was to take and the amount of time he would need to get there. Then the king's son thanked him and continued his journey until he came to the city where the dragon lived. Once there, he went into the palace and found his wife. Both of them were exceedingly pleased to see each other and began to take counsel how they could escape. They resolved to run away and prepared hastily for the journey. When all was ready, they mounted on horseback and galloped away. But as soon as they were gone the dragon returned home, also on horseback, and, entering his palace, found that the queen had departed. Then he said to his horse, "What shall we do now? Shall we eat and drink, or go at once after them?"

The horse answered, "Let us eat and drink first. We shall catch them anyway. Just don't be anxious."

After the dragon had dined, he mounted his horse, and in a few moments caught up with the runaways. Then he took the queen from the king's son and said to him, "Go now, in God's name! This time I forgive you, because you gave me water in the cellar. But if your life is dear to you, don't come back anymore."

The unhappy prince went on his way for a short time, but he couldn't very long resist seeing his wife, so he came back next day to the dragon's palace and found the queen sitting alone and weeping. Then they began to plan again how they could get away. And the prince said, "When the dragon comes, ask him where he got that horse, and then you'll tell me so that I can go get another one like it. Perhaps we can escape in this way." He then went away before the dragon might come and find him.

By and by the dragon came home, and the queen began to pet him and speak lovingly to him about many things until she said, "Ah, what a fine horse you have! Where did you get such a splendid horse?"

And he answered, "Eh, where I got it, not everyone can get one! In such and such a mountain lives an old woman who has twelve horses in her stable, and no one can say which is the finest, for they are all so beautiful: But there's a horse which stands in one corner of the stable, and it looks as if he were leprous, but in truth, he is the very best horse in the whole world. He is the brother of my horse, and whoever gets him may ride to the sky. But whoever wishes to get a horse from that old woman must serve her three days and three nights. She has a mare with a foal, and whoever guards them for three nights and keeps this mare and this foal for her, will have a right to claim the best horse from the old woman's stable. But whoever commits to keep watch over the mare and does not, must lose his head."

Next day, when the dragon went out, the king's son came, and the queen told him all she had learned from the dragon. Then the king's son went away to the mountain, found the old woman, and entered her house with the greeting: "God help you, grandmother!"

And she answered, "God help you, too, my son! What do you wish?"

"I should like to serve you," said the king's son.

Then the old woman said, "Well, my son, if you keep my mare safe for three days and three nights, I shall give you the best horse, and you can choose him yourself; but if you do not keep the mare safe, you will lose your head."

THE KING'S SON SEEKS THE OLD WOMAN

Then she led him into the courtyard where the stakes were arranged all around. Each of them had a man's head on it, except one stake which had no head on it and shouted incessantly, "Oh, grandmother! Give me a head!"

The old woman showed all this to the prince and said, "Look here, all these were heads of those who tried to keep my mare, and they have lost their heads for their pains."

But the prince was not a bit afraid. So, he stayed to serve the old woman. When the evening came, he mounted the mare and rode her into the field, and the foal followed. He sat still on her, having made up his mind not to dismount, so that he might be sure of her. But before midnight he slumbered a little, and when he awoke, he found himself sitting on a rail and holding the bridle in his hand. Then he was greatly alarmed and went instantly to look about to find the mare. While looking for her, he came to a piece of water. When he saw the water, he remembered the little fish. So, he took the scale from the handkerchief and rubbed it a little. Then immediately the little fish appeared and said, "What is the matter, my half-brother?"

And he replied, "The old woman's mare ran away while under my care, and now I don't know where she is."

And the fish answered, "Here she is, turned into a fish, and the foal into a smaller one. But strike once upon the water with the bridle and cry out 'Hey, you mare of the old woman!'"

Then the prince did as he was told, and immediately the mare came with the foal, out of the water onto the shore. Then he put the bridle on her, mounted, and rode to the old woman's house followed by the foal. When he got there, the old woman gave him his breakfast. However, she took the mare into the stable and beat her with a poker, saying, "Why didn't you go down among the fish, you cursed mare?"

And the mare answered, "I have been down to the fish, but the fish are his friends, and they told him about me."

Immediately the old woman said; "Then go among the foxes."

When evening came, the king's son mounted the mare and rode to the field, and the foal followed the mare. Again he sat on the mare's back until near midnight, when he fell asleep as before. When he awoke, he found himself riding on the rail and holding the bridle in his hand. So, he was very frightened and went to look after the mare. As he went, he remembered the words the old woman had said to the mare, and he took the fox's hair from the handkerchief and rubbed it a little between his fingers. All at once, the fox stood before him and asked, "What is the matter, half-brother?"

And he said, "The old woman's mare has run away, and I don't know where she can be."

Then the fox answered, "Here she is with us. She has turned into a fox, and the foal into a cub. But strike the bridle once on the ground and cry out, 'Hey! You old woman's mare!'"

So the king's son struck the ground with the bridle and cried, "Hey, you old woman's mare!" and the mare came, followed by her foal.

Now the prince put on the bridle, mounted, and rode off toward home, and the foal followed the mare.

When he arrived, the old woman gave him his breakfast, but took the mare into the stable and beat her with the poker, crying, "To the foxes, cursed one! To the foxes!"

And the mare answered, "I have been with the foxes, but they are his friends and told him I was there!"

The old woman cried, "If that is so, you must go and mix with the wolves."

When it grew dark again, the king's son mounted the mare and rode out into the field, and the foal galloped by the side of the mare. Again the prince sat still on the mare's back until about midnight, and as he grew very sleepy, he fell into a slumber, as on the former evenings. When he awoke he found himself riding on the rail holding the bridle in his hand, just as before.

Then, as before, he went in a hurry to look after the mare. As he went he remembered the words the old woman had said to the mare, and took the wolf's hair from the handkerchief, and rubbed it a little. Then the wolf came up to him, and asked, "What is the matter, half-brother?"

And he answered, "The old woman's mare has run away, and I cannot tell where she is."

The wolf said: "Here she is with us. She has turned herself into a wolf, and the foal into a wolf's cub. Strike once with the bridle on the ground and cry out 'Hey! Old woman's mare!'"

And the king's son did so, and instantly the mare came again and stood with the foal beside her. So he bridled her and galloped home, and the foal followed.

When he arrived the old woman gave him his breakfast, but she led the mare into the stable and beat her with the poker, crying, "To the wolves, I said, miserable one."

Then the mare answered, "I have been to the wolves; but they are his friends, and told him all about me."

Then the old woman came out of the stable, and the king's son said to her, "Eh, grandmother, I have served you honestly. Now give me what you promised me."

And the old woman answered, "My son, what is promised must be fulfilled. So look here: at the twelve horses. Choose one which you like."

And the prince said, "Why should I be too particular? Give me only that leprous horse in the corner; fine horses are not suitable for me."

But the old woman tried to persuade him to choose another horse, saying, "How can you be so foolish as to choose that leprous thing while there are such very fine horses here?"

But he remained firm with his first choice and said to the old woman, "You ought to give me the horse I choose. Remember, you promised."

So, when the old woman found she could not make him change his mind, she gave him the scabby horse, and he took leave of her leading the horse by the halter. When he came to a forest, he curried and rubbed down the horse until it shone as bright as gold. He then mounted, and the horse flew as quickly as a bird, and in a few seconds brought him to the dragon's palace. Once there, the prince went in and said to the queen, "Get ready as soon as possible."

She was soon ready. Then they both mounted the horse, and began their journey home. Soon after the dragon came home, and when he saw the queen had disappeared, he said to his horse, "What shall we do? Shall we eat and drink first, or shall we pursue them at once?"

The horse answered, "Whether we eat and drink or not, it is all the same. We shall never reach them."

When the dragon heard this, he quickly mounted his horse and galloped after them. When they saw the dragon following them, they pushed on quicker, but their horse said, "Don't be afraid. There is no need to run away."

In a very few moments the dragon came very near to them, and his horse said to their horse, "For God's sake, my brother, wait a moment! I shall kill myself running after you."

Their horse answered, "Why are you so stupid as to carry that monster? Fling your heels up, and throw him off. Then, come along with me."

When the dragon's horse heard that, he shook his head angrily and flung his feet high into the air so that the dragon fell off and broke into pieces, and his horse came up to them. Then the queen mounted him and returned with the king's son happily to her kingdom, where they reigned together in great prosperity until the day of their death.

Stan Bolovan

Mite Kremnitz

Romania is next door to Serbia, on the one hand, and next door to Russia on the other. The Romanians are wonderful storytellers, as good as any in the world, because they don't only tell a good tale, but they know what you and I like to hear, which is three parts of all good tales.

Once upon a time, something happened. If it hadn't have happened, it wouldn't be told.

At the edge of the village, where the oxen of the peasants break through the hedges and the neighbors' hogs wallow in the ground under the fences, there once stood a house, and in this house lived a man, and the man had a wife; but the wife grieved all day long.

"What troubles you have dear wife that causes you to sit there drooping like a frostbitten bud in the sunlight?" her husband asked her one day. "You have all you need. So be cheerful, like other folks."

"Leave me alone, and ask no more questions!" replied the wife and became still more melancholy than before.

Her husband questioned her a second time, and received the same reply. But, when he asked again, she answered more fully. "Dear me," she said, "why do you trouble your head about it? If you know, you'll be just as sorrowful as I am. It's better for me not to tell you."

But, to this, people will never agree. If you tell a person, he must sit still, he will be more anxious to move than ever. Stan was now determined to know what was in his wife's mind.

"If you are determined to hear, I'll tell you," said the wife. "There's no luck in the house, husband – there's no luck in the house!"

"Isn't the cow a good one? Are not the fruit-trees and beehives full? Are not the fields fertile?" asked Stan. "You talk nonsense, if you complain of anything."

"But, husband, we have no children."

Stan understood; and when a man realizes such a thing it isn't well. From this time onward, a sorrowful man and a sorrowful woman lived in the house on the edge of the village. And they were sorrowful because the Lord had given them no children. When the wife saw her husband sad, she grew still more melancholy; and the more melancholy she was, the greater his grief became.

DOI: 10.4324/9781003297536-18

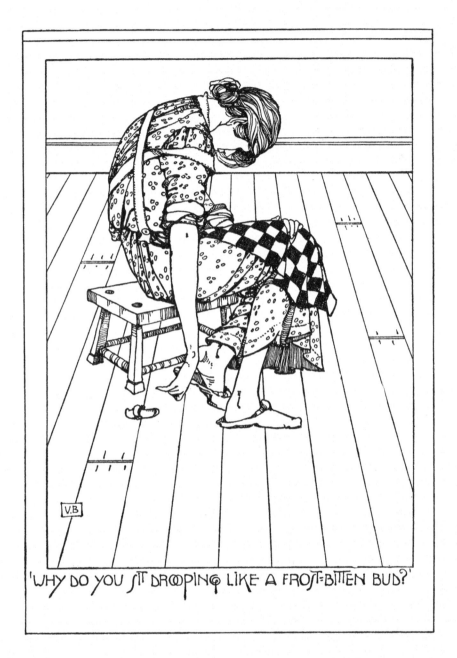

'WHY DO YOU SIT DROOPING LIKE A FROST-BITTEN BUD?'

This continued for a long time. They had masses repeated and prayers read in all the churches. They questioned all the witches, but God's gift did not come.

One day, two travelers arrived at Stan's house, and were joyfully received and entertained with the best food he had. They were angels in disguise; and perceiving that Stan and his wife were good people, one of them, while throwing his knapsack over his shoulder to continue his journey, asked his host what he most desired and said that any three of his wishes would be fulfilled.

"Give me children," replied Stan.

"What else shall I give you?"

"Children, sir, give me children!"

"Take care," said the angel, "or there will be too many of them. Have you enough to support them?"

"Never mind that, sir. Only give them to me!"

The travelers departed, but Stan accompanied them as far as the high road so that they wouldn't lose their way among the fields and woods. When Stan reached home again, he found the house, yard, and garden filled with children. Altogether there were a hundred children.

Not one was larger than the other; but each was more quarrelsome, bolder, more mischievous and noisier than the rest. And, in some way, God made Stan feel and know that they all belonged to him and were his...

"Good gracious! What a lot of them!" he cried, standing in the midst of the throng.

"But not too many, husband," replied his wife, bringing a little flock with her.

Then followed days which can only be experienced by a man who has had a hundred children. The house and village echoed with the shouts of "Father" and "Mother" and the world was full of happiness.

But taking care of children isn't such a simple a matter. Many pleasures come with many troubles, and many troubles with many joys. When, after a few days, the children began to shout, "Father, I'm hungry!" Stan began to scratch his head. There did not seem to him to be too many children, for God's gift is good, however large it may be; but Stan's barns were too small, the cow was growing thin, and the fields did not produce enough.

"I'll tell you what, wife," said Stan one day, "it seems to me that there isn't much harmony in our affairs. As God was good enough to give us so many children, He ought to have filled the measure of His goodness, and sent us food for them, too."

"Search for it, husband," the wife answered. "Who knows where it may be concealed? The Lord never does a thing by halves."

Stan went out into the wide world to find God's gift. He was firmly resolved to return home laden with food. Aha! The road of the hungry is always a long one. A man doesn't earn food for a hundred greedy children in a trice.

Stan wandered on, on, on, until he had fairly run himself off his feet. When he had thus arrived near the end of the world, where what is mixes with what is not, he saw in the distance, in the middle of a field which lay spread out flat as a cake, a sheepfold. Seven shepherds stood nearby and in the shadow within stood a flock of sheep.

"Lord help me," said Stan, and went up to the fold to see whether, by patience and discretion, he might not find some employment there. But he soon discovered that there was not much more hope here than in the other places where he had journeyed. This was the state of affairs; every night, at precisely twelve o'clock, a furious dragon came and took a ram, a sheep, and a lamb, three animals in all, from the herd. The dragon also carried milk enough for seventy-seven lambkins to the old she-dragon, so that she might bathe in it and grow young. The shepherds were very angry about it and complained bitterly. So, Stan saw that he was not likely to return home from here richly laden with food for his children. But there is no spur more powerful than for a man to see his children starving. Consequently, an idea entered Stan's head, and he said boldly, "What would you give me, if I released you from the greedy dragon?"

A SHEEPFOLD IN THE DISTANCE WITH SEVEN SHEPHERDS

One of each three rams shall be yours, one-third of the sheep, and one-third of the lambs," replied the shepherds.

"Agreed," said Stan; yet he felt rather anxious, lest he might find it too hard to drive the flocks home again. But there was no hurry about that. It was some time before midnight. And besides, to tell the truth, Stan did not exactly know how he was to get rid of the dragon.

"The Lord will send me some plan," he said to himself, and then counted the flock again to see how many animals he would have. Just at midnight, when day and night, weary of strife, for a moment, stood still, Stan felt that he was about to see something he had never beheld before. It was something that cannot be described. It is a horrible thing to have a dragon come. It seemed as if the monster was hurling huge rocks at the trees, and thus forcing a way through primeval forests. Even Stan felt that it would be wiser to take off as quickly as he could and not to enter into a quarrel with a dragon. Ah! but his children at home were starving.

"I'll kill you, or you will kill me!" Stan said to himself, and he remained where he was, close by the sheepfold.

"Stop!" he cried, when he saw the dragon near the fold; and he shouted as though he was a person of importance.

"H'm," said the dragon: "Where have you come from, and do you think it is wise to screech at me so?"

"I am Stan Bolovan, who at night devours rocks and by day grazes on the trees of the primeval forests; and if you touch the flock, I'll cut a cross in your back, and bathe you in holy water."

When the dragon heard these words, he stopped in his tracks, for he saw that he had found his match.

"But you must fight with me," replied the dragon, hesitatingly.

"I fight with you?" cried Stan. "Beware of the words that have escaped your lips. My breath is stronger than your whole body." Then, taking from his knapsack a piece of white cheese, he showed it to the dragon. "Do you see this stone?" he said. "Pick one up from the bank of yonder stream, and we'll see who is the stronger of us two."

The dragon took a stone from the shore of the brook.

"Can you squeeze buttermilk out of the stone?" asked Stan.

The dragon crushed the stone in his hand and crumbled it into powder. But he squeezed no buttermilk from it.

"It can't be done," he said rather angrily.

"I'll show you whether it can be done," replied Stan, and then squeezed the soft cheese in his hand until the buttermilk trickled down between his fingers. When the dragon saw this, he began to look around to find the shortest road to run away. But Stan placed himself before the forest. "Let us have a little reckoning about what you have taken from the fold," he said. "Nothing is given away free here."

The poor dragon would have taken flight, if he had not been afraid that Stan might blow behind him and bury him under the trees in the forest. So he stood still, like a person who doesn't know what else to do.

"Listen!" he said, after a short time had passed, "I see that you are a useful man. My mother has long been looking for a servant like you, but she has not been able to find one. Enter our service. The year has three days, and each day's wages is seven sacks of ducats!"

Three times seven sacks of ducats! A fine business! That was just what Stan needed. "And," he thought, "if I've outwitted the dragon, I can probably get the better of his mother!"

So, he didn't waste many words about the matter, but set off with the monster. A long, rough road; but still it was too short since it led to a bad end. It seemed to Stan as if he had arrived almost before he started. The old she-dragon, old as time itself, was waiting for them. She had made a fire under the huge cauldron, in which she

STAN BOLOVAN & THE DRAGON

intended to boil the milk and mix it with the blood of a lamb and the marrow from its bones because the liquid might have healing power. Stan saw her eyes glistening in the darkness when they were still three gunshots away. But, when they reached the spot and the she-dragon perceived that her son had brought her nothing, she was very angry. This she-dragon was by no means lovable. She had a wrinkled face, open jaws, tangled hair, sunken eyes, parched lips, and a breath which reeked of the smell of onions.

"Stay here," said the dragon. "I'll go and make arrangements with my mother."

Stan would willingly have stood still farther away, but he had no choice now that he had been engaged in this evil business. So he let the dragon go on.

"Listen, mother!" said the dragon, when he had entered the house. "I've brought you a man that you should get rid of. He's a terrible fellow, who eats pieces of rock and squeezes buttermilk out of stones."

Then he told her what had happened.

"Just leave him to me," she said, after hearing the whole story. "No man ever slipped through my fingers."

So the matter remained as it had first been settled. Stan Bolovan became the monster's servant and his mother was in a terrible fix! The next day, the she-dragon gave him his task. He was to give a signal to the dragon world with a club sheathed in seven thicknesses of iron. The dragon raised the club and hurled it three miles. Then he set off with Stan and challenged him also to throw it three miles, or, if possible, farther still. When Stan reached the club, he began to look at it rather anxiously. He saw that he and all his children together could not even lift it from the ground.

Why are you standing there? "asked the dragon.

"Why, you see, it's such a handsome club. I'm sorry," replied Stan.

"Sorry? Why?" inquired the dragon.

"Because," answered Stan, "I'm afraid you'll never see it again in your whole life, if I throw it; for I never know my own strength."

"Don't fear. Just throw it," replied the dragon.

"If you really mean it, we'll go and get provisions enough to last three days; for we shall have to travel at least three days, if not longer, to get it."

These words frightened the dragon, but he still didn't believe yet that it would be so bad as Stan said. So they went home to obtain the provisions, though the dragon wasn't at all pleased with the idea of having Stan serve his year by merely going after the club. When they got back again to it, Stan sat down on the bag of provisions and became absorbed in staring at the moon.

"What are you doing?" asked the dragon.

"Only waiting for the moon to sail by," replied Stan. "Don't you see that the moon is directly in my way?" he asked . "Or do you want me to fling the club into the moon?"

The dragon now began to be seriously anxious. It was a club that he had inherited from his ancestors, and he didn't like losing it in the moon.

"I'll tell you what," he said. "Don't throw the club. I'll do it myself."

"Certainly not. Heaven forbid!" replied Stan. "Only wait until the moon passes by."

Then a long conversation followed, for Stan would not consent to have the dragon throw the club again, except on the promise of seven sacks of ducats.

"Oh dear, mother! He's a tremendously strong man," said the dragon. "I could scarcely prevent him from throwing the club at the moon."

The she-dragon began to be anxious, too. Just think of it! Would it be a joke to have a person able to throw anything at the moon? She was a she-dragon of true dragon blood, and the next day had thought of a still harder task.

"Bring some water," she said early in the morning to Stan, and gave each twelve buffalo skins, ordering them to fill them by evening and fetch them home at once. So, they went to the well; and, before one could wink, the dragon had filled the twelve skins and had reached the point of carrying them back. In contrast, Stan was tired, and he had scarcely been able to drag the empty skins along. A chill ran through his veins, when he thought of the full ones. So, what do you suppose he did? He pulled a worn-out knife blade from his belt and began to scratch the earth around the well with it.

"What are you doing?" asked the dragon. "Do you think that I'm a blockhead and want to fill the skins with water?" replied Stan.

"But how will you carry the water to the house, then?"

"How? Just you see," said Stan. "I'm going to take the well, you goose!"

The dragon stood with his mouth wide open in amazement. He wouldn't let anyone do this any account, for the well was one that had belonged to his ancestors.

"I'll tell you," he said anxiously. "Let me carry your skins home, too."

"Certainly not. Heaven forbid!" replied Stan, digging on around the well. Now, another long discussion followed; and this time, too, the dragon could only persuade Stan by promising him seven sacks of ducats.

On the third day, that is, the last one, the she-dragon sent them into the forest for wood. Before one could count three, the dragon tore up more trees than Stan had ever seen before in his entire life and piled them together. But Stan began to examine the trees, chose the very finest, climbed up into one and tied its top with a wild grapevine to the next. So, without saying a word, he continued to fasten one splendid tree to another.

"What are you doing there?" asked the dragon.

"You see what I am doing," replied Stan, who continued working quietly.

"Why are you tying the trees together?"

"Why, to save myself unnecessary work in pulling them up one by one," said Stan.

"But how are you going to carry them home?"

"I shall take the whole forest, you goose! Can't you understand that?" said Stan, continuing to fasten them together.

The dragon now felt as if he wanted to take to his heels and never stop until he reached home. But he was afraid that Stan might pull down the entire forest on his head. This time, since it was the end of the year's service, it seemed as if the discussion would never cease. Stan didn't want to listen at all, but had set his mind on flinging the forest on his back at any rate.

"I'll tell you what," said the dragon, trembling with fear, "I'll make your wages seven times seven sacks of ducats. You'd better be content with that."

"Well, so be it, since I see you are a good fellow," replied Stan, who agreed that the dragon should carry the wood for him.

The year was now over. Stan was anxious only for one thing – how he was to drag so many ducats home. In the evening, the dragon and his mother sat talking together in their room while Stan listened in the entry.

"Woe betide us!" said the dragon: "This fellow upset us terribly. Give him money, even more than he has, only let us get rid of him."

Ah, yes! but the she-dragon cared for money.

"Let me tell you one thing," she said: "You must kill this man tonight."

"I am afraid of him, mother," he answered in terror.

"Have no fear," replied his mother. "When you see that he is asleep, take your club and strike him 'in the middle of the forehead."

So it was agreed. Ah, yes! But Stan always had a bright idea at the right time. When he saw that the dragon and his mother had put out the light, he took the pig's trough and laid it bottom upward in his place, covered it carefully with a shaggy coat, and lay down himself under the bed, where he began to snore like a person who is sound asleep. The dragon entered softly, approached the bed, raised his club, and struck one blow on the spot where Stan's head ought to have been. The trough sounded hollow, Stan groaned, and the dragon tiptoed back again.

Stan then crept out from under the bed, cleaned it, and lay down, but was wise enough not to close an eye all night long. The dragon and his mother were rigid with amazement when they saw Stan come in the next morning as sound as an egg.

"Good morning!"

"Good morning; but how did you sleep last night?"

"Very well," replied Stan. "Only I dreamed that a flea bit me just here on the forehead, and it seems as if it still hurt me."

"Just listen to that, mother!" cried the dragon. "Did you hear? He talks about a flea, and I hit him with my club!"

This was too much for the she-dragon. She perceived that it wasn't worthwhile to argue with such people. So they hastened to fill his sacks, in order to get rid of him as quickly as possible. But poor Stan now began to perspire. When he stood beside the bags, he trembled like an aspen leaf, because he was unable to lift even one of them from the ground. So, he stood staring at them.

"Why are you standing there?" asked the dragon.

"H'm! I'm waiting," replied Stan, "because I would rather stay with you another year. I'm ashamed to have anybody see me carry away so little at one time. I'm afraid people will say, 'Look at Stan Bolovan, who in one year has grown as weak as a dragon.' "

Now, it was the two dragons' turn to be frightened. They vainly told him that they would give him seven – nay, three times seven or even seven times seven sacks of ducats, if he would only go away.

"I'll tell you what," said Stan, at last. "Since I see you don't want to keep me, I won't force you to do so. Have it your own way. I'll go. But, since I cannot be ashamed before the people, you must carry this treasure home for me."

The words were scarcely out of his mouth than the dragon picked up the sacks and set off with Stan. Short and smooth, yet always too long, is the road that leads home. But when Stan found himself close to his house and heard his children's shouts, he began to walk slower. It seemed too near; for he was afraid that, if the dragon knew where he lived, he might come to take away the treasure. However, he was still at a loss to find a way of carrying his money home alone.

"I really don't know what to do," he said, turning to the dragon. "I have a hundred hungry children, and fear you may fare badly among them, because they are very fond of fighting. But just behave sensibly, and I'll protect you as well as I can."

A hundred children! That's no joke! The dragon – though a dragon of dragon race – let the bags fall in his fright. But, from sheer terror, he picked them up again. Yet, his fear did not overcome him until they entered the courtyard. When the hungry children saw their father coming with the loaded dragon, they rushed toward him, each one with a knife in his right hand and a fork in his left. Then they all began to whet the knives on the forks, shrieking at the top of their lungs:

"We want dragon meat!"

This was quite enough to scare Satan himself. The dragon threw down the sacks and then took to flight, so frightened that since that time he has never dared to come back to the world.

SEE WHAT YOUR WIFE HAS GIVEN YOU!

The Golden Twins

Peter Isperescu

This tale is told by many nations, but, to my mind, the Romanians tell it better than anybody. The man who wrote it down in Romanian, Mr. Isperescu, was a brilliant member of the Romanian Academy. It has been beautifully translated from his text by Mrs. Harris and her friend. She agreed to let me have it for this book if the publishers were willing, for which kindness both you and I must thank her.

Once upon a time, on his return to his own country, after having traveled all over the world, the son of a great knight passed by a hemp-dresser's hut where three pretty sisters were dressing hemp. As he trudged along, he heard some chance words from their lips that caused him to prick up his ears. So, he turned in their direction and said, "What were you talking about, my dears?"

And the eldest replied with a burst of laughter: "I said something like this: 'If the young knight who is passing by would only marry me, I could make his home beautiful even though I had nothing but a spindle full of flax.'"

The second sister in her turn replied: "I made this remark: 'If the young knight who is passing by would only marry me, I could feed all his clan, even though I had nothing but a buttered biscuit.'"

And the youngest, in her turn, said: "I was thinking out loud: 'If the young knight who is passing by would only marry me, I would give him two beautiful golden babies.'"

The young man remained silent a moment, thinking; then, approaching the sister who had spoken last, he said: "Young maiden, your words please me the best of all. If you wish to follow me, you shall be my wife, but take care that you keep your promise."

At such an offer only a simpleton would have hesitated, especially since the young man was – all joking aside – as tall and straight as a young pine tree. So, the maiden of his choice blushed like a peony, held out her hand to him, and answered: "Agreed! And may good luck follow us! If we are made for each other I will not fail you any more than you will fail me."

DOI: 10.4324/9781003297536-19

THE GOLDEN TWINS

So they set out, and the young knight led his sweetheart home to a beautiful palace, the like of which she had never seen before. There they celebrated their wedding with a splendor that was the envy of the seven surrounding kingdoms, and afterward they set up housekeeping. The husband gave his wife as waiting-maid a certain gypsy who lived in the palace and of whom he thought very highly. But the moment she laid eyes on the wife, this female crow began to wish her evil.

Months passed away, and one day the wife of the young knight told him that, according to her promise, she would soon become the mother of golden twins. He was filled with joy and ordered a beautiful cradle made for the babies. When the day of their birth approached, the husband was away on a journey. So, the gypsy servant told her mistress that, according to the custom of the country, she must go up into the topmost room of the house, far away from all her family and attendants, and depend upon her services alone to receive the beautiful golden babies (for in this way the wicked woman planned to carry out her plot in secret).

"Very well," agreed the young wife, "I shall follow the custom of the country, since custom there is."

Indeed, the innocent young creature did not suspect the plans of the gypsy; loving every body herself. So, how could she think that anyone harbored evil thoughts toward her? So she climbed up into the top most room of the house, got ready to receive the golden babies, and there they were born. But the gypsy was waiting nearby and hastily seized the little ones before their mother could so much as look at them. Then she

HE LED HER TO A BEAUTIFUL PALACE

placed them in a sieve which she had at hand, ran down the stairs to the stable-yard, and stowed them away under the dung heap, where the poor little creatures soon perished. Then she placed two newborn puppies in the sieve, ran back to her mistress, and said: "Look, mistress! Here are your babies!"

And the poor mother cried out "Oh, it's not possible!"

But the wicked woman insisted: "You have only to look and see for yourself. You are a witch and these are the children of a witch."

The arrival of the husband cut short the discussion, and the gypsy, boldly running forward, held out the sieve for him to look, and listen to the little puppies whimpering.

"Look! look!" the gypsy cried; "This is the beautiful present that your wife promised you. It was lucky, indeed, my lord that you thought of placing a discreet and devoted servant like myself near this woman; otherwise think how this story would have been spread about and how everybody would have mocked you!"

At these words, and at the sight of the ugly little beasts, the knight flew into a terrible rage, and to punish his wife, he drove her out of his house and made her become a servant, while he took the gypsy woman as wife in her place. The innocent victim of the cruel plot knew that an unjust punishment had overtaken her, but being helpless to put matters right, she kept silent and resigned herself to wait until the truth should one day be made clear.

Some time passed away, until one day, out of the dung-heap in which the gypsy had hidden the twins, two apple trees sprung up whose golden fruit shone so brightly that, even on the darkest night, a light spread all about them like the rays of the sun. These trees grew as much in one day as other trees grow in a year, and quickly became tall and strong. Therefore, the gypsy, who lived in terror that her wicked deed would be discovered, and who feared the beauty of the apple trees, said one day to the knight: "I have an idea! Let us cut down those apple trees near the stable and use them to make new slats for our bed, for the old ones are about to give way."

"Cut down those trees!" cried her husband. "Don't you see that they are as beautiful as trees in a dream and that no one else has any to compare with them? Whatever gave you such an idea?"

"As you like!" she replied, "but you will end by cutting them, for I shall never eat bread and salt with you again until you do."

Not being able to withstand the vixen for long, the knight had the trees cut down and made into two slats for the bed. Now, soon after the couple went to bed one night, the gypsy heard the slats begin to talk – for I must tell you that the souls of the golden twins had passed from the trees into the slats, that of the boy into one and that of the girl into the other.

"Dado," said the boy, "is the bed very heavy on top of you?"

"Yes, brother, very heavy, because I hold up the gypsy. Is it heavy on you, too?"

"No, not too heavy, because our father sleeps on top of me."

The gypsy realized that she would be ruined if the knight overheard the slats talking, so she dared not close her eyes all night. At daybreak, she awakened her husband and said:

"Listen! I am going to throw away these wretched slats. Because of them I have been tormented with bad dreams all night."

"What! Destroy those fine slats! You must be crazy!" cried her husband.

HE DROVE HIS WIFE OUT & TOOK THE GIPSY

"Fine slats or not, if you don't get rid of them, I will jump off a precipice!" she threatened.

So, wishing peace above all things, the knight had the slats cut up into kindling wood. Then the sly creature, having carefully closed all the windows, threw the kindling into the fire.

But two sparks flew out of the chimney and fell in the garden, and where the sparks fell there grew two tufts of basil.

Now the knight had a pet lamb which played in the court yard of the house, and one day it escaped into the garden and nibbled up the two tufts of basil. Immediately, its wool became all golden, and one could not have found such a lamb anywhere else in the entire world.

At the sight of the beautiful little animal, the gypsy turned yellow with jaundice, for she began to fear she would never escape her punishment. Nevertheless, she remained calm, waiting for a chance to do away with the lamb. One day, when the knight was in a fine humor, she said smacking her lips, "How I would like to eat the flesh of that tender little lamb."

The knight was dumbfounded and cried, "Get rid of that idea at once, woman; I will never let you kill my lamb!"

The wicked woman knew she would never get her way except by trickery, so she pretended to be very ill. For a whole week she disturbed the knight with her plaints and her groans, until one night she pretended to awaken with a start, and when her husband asked her what was the matter, she answered, "I dreamed that a magician had just told me that if I wanted to get well, I must have that lamb butchered and eat its heart and its liver."

"How you do go on, woman! Butcher my lamb, indeed! Better send for all the sorcerers in the kingdom and maybe one of them can give you a remedy that will really cure your ailment."

"I have already found a remedy," replied the gypsy stubbornly, "and if you refuse me its help, it is because you want me to die."

Being at the end of his wits, the knight gave in and ordered the lamb to be killed and sent to the kitchen. Now, the cunning gypsy, determined that every precaution should be taken this time. So, she hurried to the kitchen and took charge of the lamb herself. She seized its liver and heart, being careful not to break off even a little morsel, and, giving them into the hands of a trusted servant, she ordered her to take them to the river to wash them, and threatened her with the loss of her life should she lose even a tiny particle in the stream. But during the operation, nobody knows how, a little piece of the heart was broken off, and the servant, terribly frightened, threw the fragment into the river. Then she returned to the house, and, saying nothing about the accident, handed the heart and liver of the lamb to her mistress.

The next day the mother of the twins went down to the river to fill her pitcher, and as she sadly looked at the water flowing by, she saw, seated on a little mound near the bank, two children who were playing with golden apples. All during the afternoon, she watched them, with a strangely throbbing heart, because she felt that perhaps they might be her own little ones.

Returning late to the house, she received a cruel beating at the hands of the gypsy.

"Do not punish me, mistress," she pleaded; "I could not come back any sooner, because I was feasting my eyes on a sight that I could have gazed upon for a whole week without stopping."

Moved by curiosity, the gypsy ran to the river and, there she, too, saw the children playing. Like the mother, she could not tear her glance away. Never before had such beauty dazzled her wicked eyes. It bewitched her to see these lovely children play and dance on the little mound near the riverbank. But their beauty did not hinder her from harboring evil thoughts, and she began to plan how she could do away with them.

Now, a great crowd of people began to gather together on the bank of the river, drawn there by the sight of the golden twins, and they uttered "Oh's" and "Ah's" of admiration. Among these good folk was an old woman who was moved by a desire to adopt this wonderful boy and girl. More wary than the rest, she returned the next morning, bringing with her a little distaff and a little cane, and, advancing to the edge of the water she held them out to the children, calling to them in her sweetest tones. And the twins, seeing the toys, ran toward the old woman. The boy seized the cane and the girl, the distaff, while the good woman, delighted with her success, took each by the hand and led them to her home. She clothed them in some plain, clean garments and began to care for them as best she could.

Some time after this, the knight happened to arrange a gathering to which all the children of the village were invited. You may be sure that the old woman went and brought her beautiful twins. The reunion began with games and fortune-telling. Finally the knight arose and said: "Enough nonsense now, my children. Let us all be quiet for a while, and each one of you shall tell a story."

The boys and girls clapped their hands at this suggestion, and one by one each told his nicest story, until at last came the turn of the golden twins. But God had made them timid and they tried to excuse themselves.

"Sir Knight," said they, "what can we tell? We don't know a single story."

"My dears," he replied, "don't be afraid. It is your turn now. Tell anything you know and tell it the best you can."

Then the boy began: "Once upon a time there were three sisters who were hemp dressers, and one day a young knight passed by their hut. The eldest sister said, 'If this young knight will marry me, I will made his home beautiful even though I have only a spindle full of flax.' The next one said, 'If the young knight will marry me, I will feed all his clan, even though I have only a buttered biscuit.' And the youngest sister said, 'If the young knight will marry me, I will give him two beautiful golden babies!' And the knight took the youngest sister for his wife and gave her a gypsy woman as her servant."

Foreseeing the end of the story, the wicked gypsy interrupted the boy brusquely.

"A silver toy for your silence, boy!"

But the knight replied: "A golden toy, if you speak out, boy!"

And the child continued: "Time passed, and the hour of the babies' birth arrived, and the wife of the knight demanded a nurse. Her husband was away on a journey, so the wicked gypsy told her that she, herself, would be her nurse, and when the little ones saw the light of day, the cruel plotter stole them and carried them away in a sieve and hid them under the dung-heap, and in their place, she brought back two little puppies, which she showed to the knight on his return. telling him that his wife was a witch and these were her children. The knight was enraged and drove his wife out of the house and married the gypsy in her place, and the poor wife became the servant of the gypsy. Then from out of the dung heap into the stable yard grew two golden apple trees. Hardly had the gypsy seen them than she teased her husband until he had them cut down and made into bed slats. During the night, when the knight and his gypsy wife were asleep in the bed, the slats began to speak:

"'Dado, is the mattress heavy?'

'Yes, very heavy because the gypsy sleeps on my side.'

'And is it heavy on you?'

'No, it's not, for our father sleeps on my side.'"

Again the gypsy broke in, crying: "A silver toy for your silence, boy!"

But the knight cried, too: "A golden toy, if you speak out, boy!"

And the child continued: "The cruel woman, who alone had heard what the bed slats said, tormented her husband until he had the slats cut into little pieces which she threw into the fire. But two sparks escaped from the chimney and fell in the garden, and on this spot grew two tufts of basil. Now, the knight had a pet lamb which one day escaped into the garden, and when he came upon the two tufts of basil, he cropped them, and immediately its wool became like gold.

"When the female devil saw this fresh miracle, she fell ill and begged her husband to kill the lamb, declaring that she would die unless she were given the lamb's heart and liver to eat. Her husband was unwilling to kill his lamb, but she insisted, so much so, that to have peace, he finally consented because the wicked woman's tongue never ceased clacking. And so she sent her servant to the river to wash the lamb's entrails, cautioning her not to let the least bit of the heart or liver escape from her hands. But as the servant was washing them, she broke off a tiny piece, and it floated away in the current. The morsel was caught on a little hillock in the stream from where we sprang up, my sister and I. And, as all these words were spoken, the wicked gypsy had been crying, over and over again: "A silver toy for your silence, boy!"

But every time the knight replied: "A golden toy if you speak out, boy!"

So the child continued: "A good old woman took us home with her, where she cared for us as if we were her own children until this very evening, when she brought us to the house of my lord knight, and here we are, as beautiful and strong as when we were brought into the world by our mother."

Hardly able to believe their ears, everyone there gazed with wonder at the child who had told this strange story. Then the boy, having finished, cried out, "If you do not believe me, look and you will be convinced!"

And he and his sister stripped off their garments, and their bodies shone like gold, so that every eye was dazzled. Seeing this, their father sprang toward them, seized them in his arms, and recognized them as his children. Their mother also approached and pressed them to her heart, and all four wept with joy, blessing God for having brought them together at last. And the knight, enraged by the wicked plot of the gypsy, ordered a wild stallion to be led from his stables, and the cruel woman was fastened with a sack of nuts to the horse's tail, and the lackeys lashed the beast and set him loose on the high road, and every time a nut fell from the sack, a piece of the gypsy's flesh fell off her bones, until finally there was nothing left of her but dust.

Thus ends my tale;
And away I fly,
To gather fresh lore
'Twixt earth and sky!

& THERE THEY REMAIN ON THE HILL-SIDE TO THIS DAY

Perseus

Charles Kingsley

A fairy tale of ancient Greece. All these things happened a long while ago, when our forefathers were still troubled by dragons and mammoths in everyday life. For thousands of years this story was sung in Greek. Then several ancient Greeks wrote it down here and there, and for two thousand years it was only read by schoolboys and students. Finally, Charles Kingsley, a famous English novelist, put it into English for his young relatives

Part I – How Perseus and His Mother Came to Seriphos

Once upon a time there were two princes who were twins. Their names were Aerisius and Proetus, and they lived in the pleasant vale of Argos, far away in Hellas. They had fruitful meadows and vineyards, sheep and oxen, great herds of horses feeding down in Lerna Fen, and all that men would need to make them blessed. And yet, they were wretched, because they were jealous of each other. From the moment they were born, they began to quarrel, and when they grew up, each tried to take away the other's share of the kingdom, and keep all for himself. So. first Aerisius drove out Proetus, and he went across the seas and brought home a foreign princess for his wife, and foreign warriors to help him, who were called Cyclopes. They drove out Acrisius in his turn; and then they fought a long time up and down the land; until the quarrel was settled, and Acrisius took Argos and one-half the land, and Proetus took Tiryns and the other half. And Proetus and his Cyclopes built around Tiryns great walls of unhewn stone, which are standing to this day.

But there came a prophet to that hard-hearted Acrisius and prophesied against him, and said, "Because you have risen up against your own blood, your own blood shall rise up against you; because you have sinned against your kindred, by your kindred you shall be punished. Your daughter Danae will bear a son, and by that son's hands you will die. So the gods have ordained, and it will surely come to pass."

But he did not mend his ways. He had been cruel to his own family, and, instead of repenting and being kind to them, he went on to be more cruel than ever, for he shut up his fair daughter Danae in a cavern underground, lined with brass, so that no one might come near her. Indeed, he fancied himself more cunning than the gods, but you will soon see whether he was able to escape them.

Now it came to pass that in time Danae bore a son, so beautiful a babe that any but King Acrisius would have had pity on it. In fact, he had no pity, for he took Danae and

DOI: 10.4324/9781003297536-20

her babe down to the seashore, put them into a great chest, and thrust them out to sea for the winds and the waves to carry them wherever they would.

The northwest wind blew briskly out of the blue mountains and down the pleasant vale of Argos, and away and out to sea, and before it floated the mother and her babe, while all who watched them wept, except for the cruel father, King Acrisius.

So they floated on and on, and the chest danced up and down upon the billows, and the baby slept upon its mother's breast: but the poor mother could not sleep. She watched and wept, and she sang to her baby as they floated; and the song which she sang you will learn yourselves some day.

And now they went past the last blue headland and into the open sea. There was nothing around them but the waves, and the sky, and the wind. But the waves are gentle, and the sky is clear, and the breeze is tender and low; for these are the days when Halcyone and Ceyx built their nests, and no storms ever ruffled the pleasant summer sea.

And who were Halcyone and Ceyx? You will hear while the chest floats on. Halcyone was a fairy maiden, the daughter of the beach and of the wind. And she loved a sailor-boy and married him. Nobody on earth were so happy as they were. But at last Ceyx was wrecked, and before he could swim to the shore, the billows swallowed him up. And Halcyone saw him drowning, and leapt into the sea to him. However, it was in vain. Then the immortals took pity on them and changed them into two fair sea-birds. Then they built a floating nest every year, and sailed and lived happily ever after on the pleasant seas of Greece.

So a night passed, and a day, and a long day it was for Danae. Then another night and day beside, until Danae was faint with hunger and weeping. Yet, no land appeared. Meanwhile the babe slept quietly; and at last poor Danae drooped her head and fell asleep likewise with her cheek against the babe's.

After a while she was wakened suddenly; for the chest was jarring and grinding, and the air was full of sound. She looked up, and over her head were mighty cliffs, all red in the setting sun. Around her were rocks and breakers and flying flakes of foam. She clasped her hands together and shrieked loudly for help. And when she cried, she attracted help, for now a tall and stately man appeared over the rocks and looked down, wondering how it was that poor Danae was tossing about in the chest by the waves.

He wore a rough cloak of frieze, and on his head a broad hat to shade his face. In his hand he carried a trident for spearing fish, and over his shoulder was a casting-net. Danae could see that he was not a common man by his stature and his walk, by his flowing golden hair and beard, and by the two servants who walked behind him, carrying baskets for his fish. But she had hardly time to look at him, before he had laid aside his trident and leapt down the rocks, and thrown his casting-net so surely over Danae and the chest, that he drew it, and her, and the baby, safely upon· a ledge of rock. Then the fisherman took Danae by the hand, lifted her out of the chest, and said, "Oh beautiful damsel, what strange chance has brought you to this island in so frail a ship? Who are you, and where are you coming from? Surely, you are some king's daughter, and this boy is something more than mortal."

And as he spoke he pointed to the babe; for its face shone like the morning star. But Danae could only hold down her head and sob: "Tell me, what is this land and tell me, where am I? What country is this? What sort of men live here?"

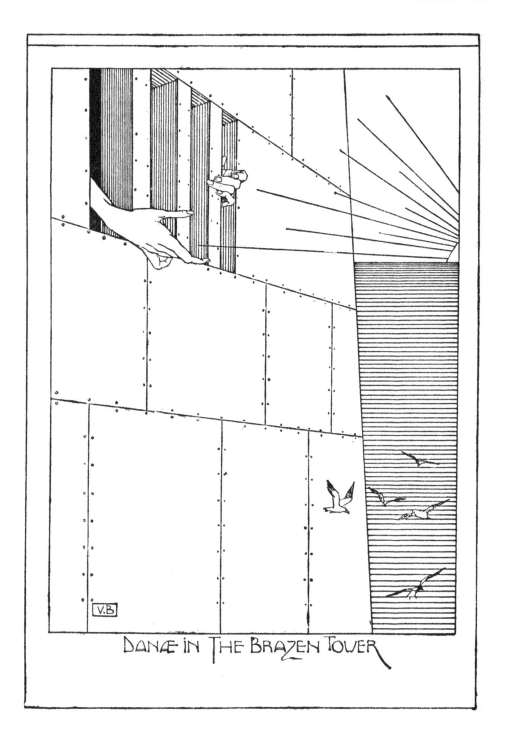

DANÆ IN THE BRAZEN TOWER

And he responded, "This isle is called Seriphos, and I am a Hellen and make my dwelling here. I am the brother of Polydectes. The king and men call me Dictys, the netter, because I catch the fish of the shore."

Then Danae fell down at his feet, embraced his knees, and cried: "Oh, sir, have pity upon a stranger, whom a cruel doom has driven to your land; and let me live in your house as a servant. I only ask you to treat me honorably, for I was once a king's daughter, and this my boy (as you have truly seen) is of no common race. I will not be a burden to you, or eat the bread of idleness; for I am more skillful in weaving and embroidery than all the maidens of my land."

And she would have gone on, but Dictys stopped her, lifted her, and said: "My daughter, I am old, and my hairs are growing gray. I have no children to make my home cheerful. So, come with me then, and you will be a daughter to me and to my wife, and this babe will be our grandchild. For I fear the gods and show hospitality to all strangers; knowing that good deeds, like evil ones, always return to those who do them."

So Danae was comforted and went home with Dictys the good fisherman, and was a daughter to him and to his wife, until fifteen years had passed.

Part II – How Perseus Vowed a Rash Vow

Fifteen years had passed and gone, and the babe had now grown to be a tall lad and a sailor, and he went on many voyages looking for merchandise on the surrounding islands His mother called him Perseus, but all the people in Seriphos said that he was not the son of mortal man, and called him the son of Zeus, the king of the immortals. Though he was only fifteen, he was taller by a head than any man in the island; and he was the most skillful of all in running and wrestling and boxing, and in throwing the quoit and the javelin, and in rowing with the oar, and in playing on the harp, and in all which befits a man. And he was brave and truthful, gentle and courteous, for good old Dictys had trained him well; and well it was for Perseus that he had done so. For now, Danae and her son faced a great danger, and Perseus had need of all his wit to defend his mother and himself.

I said that Dictys' brother was Polydectes, king of the island. He was not a righteous man, like Dictys; but greedy, cunning, and cruel. And when he saw fair Danae, he wanted to marry her. However, she did not want to wed him, for she did not love him. Indeed, she cared for no one but her boy, and her boy's father, whom she never hoped to see again. At last, Polydectes became furious, and while Perseus was away at sea, he took poor Danae away from Dictys, saying: "If you will not be my wife, you shall be my slave."

So Danae was made a slave and had to fetch water from the well, and grind in the mill, and perhaps was beaten, and wore a heavy chain, because she would not marry that cruel king. But Perseus was far away, over the seas on the isle of Samos, not thinking much about how his mother was languishing in grief.

Now one day at Samos, while the ship was loading, Perseus wandered into a pleasant forest to get out of the sun, and sat down on the turf and fell asleep. And as he slept a strange dream cane to him, the strangest dream which he had ever had in his life.

A lady came to him through the forest, taller than he was, or any mortal man, but exceedingly beautiful, with great gray eyes, clear and piercing, but strangely soft and mild. On her head was a helmet, and in her hand a spear. And over her shoulder, above her long blue robes, hung a goatskin, which bore up a mighty shield of brass, polished like a mirror. She stood and looked at him with her clear gray eyes; and Perseus saw that her eyelids never moved, nor her eyeballs, but looked straight through and through him, and into his very heart, as if she could see all the secrets of his soul, and knew all that he had ever thought or longed for since the day that he was born. And Perseus dropped his eyes, trembling and blushing, as the wonderful lady spoke. "Perseus, you must do an errand for me."

"Who are you, lady? And how do you know my name?"

"I am Pallas Athene; and I know the thoughts of all men's hearts, I discern their manhood or their baseness. And from the souls of clay I turn away, and they are blessed but not by me.

"They fatten at ease, like sheep in the pasture, and eat what they did not sow like oxen in the stall. They grow and spread, like the gourd along the ground. Yet, like the gourd, they give no shade to the traveler, and when they are ripe, death gathers them, and they go down unloved unto hell. Then their name vanishes out of the land. But to the souls of fire I give more fire and to those who are manful, I give a might more than man's. These are the heroes, the sons of the immortals, who are blessed, but not like the souls of clay. Indeed, I drive them forth on strange paths, Perseus, so that they may fight the titans and the monsters, the enemies of gods and men. Through doubt and need; danger and battle, I drive them; and some of them are slain in the flower of youth. No man knows when or where; and some of them win noble names, and a fair and green old age; but I don't know what their latter end will be, and none, save Zeus, the father of gods and men. Tell me now, Perseus, which of these two sorts of men seem to you more blessed?"

Then Perseus answered boldly: "Better to die in the flower of youth, on the chance of winning a noble name, than to live at ease like the sheep, and die unloved and unrenowned."

Then that strange lady laughed, held up her brazen shield, and cried: "See here, Perseus; dare you face such a monster as this, and slay it, so that I may place its head upon this shield?"

And in the mirror of the shield there appeared a face, and as Perseus looked at it, his blood ran cold. It was the face of a beautiful woman; but her cheeks were pale as death, and her brows were knit with everlasting pain, and her lips were thin and bitter like a snake's. Instead of hair, vipers wreathed about her temples, and shot out their forked tongues. Around her head were folded wings like an eagle's, and upon her bosom, claws of brass.

And Perseus looked awhile, and then said: "If there is anything so fierce and foul on earth, it would be a noble deed to kill it. Where can I find the monster?"

Then the strange lady smiled again and said, "Not yet, for you are too young, and too unskilled; for this is Medusa the Gorgon, the mother of a monstrous brood. Return to your home and do the work which waits there for you. You must play the man in that before I can think you worthy to go in search for the Gorgon."

Then Perseus would have spoken, but the strange lady vanished. When he awoke and realized it was a dream. But day and night Perseus saw before him the face of that dreadful woman, with the vipers writhing around her head. So he returned home; and when he came to Seripbos, the first thing which he heard was that his mother was a slave in the house of Polydectes. Grinding his teeth with rage, he went straight to the king's palace, and through the men's rooms, and the women's rooms, and so through all the house (for no one dared stop him, so terrible and fair was he) until he found his mother sitting on the floor, turning the stone hand-mill and weeping as she turned it. Immediately, he lifted her up, kissed her, and told her follow him.

But before they could pass out of the room, Polydecte entered in a rage. And when Perseus saw him, he flew at him as a mastiff would attack a boar.

"Villain and tyrant!" he cried. "Is this your respect for the gods and your mercy to strangers and widows? You shall die!"

And because he did not have a sword, he picked up the stone hand-mill and lifted it to bash out Polydectes' brains. But his mother clung to him shrieking, "Oh, my son, we are strangers and helpless in this land; and if you kill he king, all the people will attack us, and we shall both die."

Good Dictys, too, who had just entered the room, entreated him: "Remember that he is my brother. Remember how I have brought you up and trained you as my own son. So, spare him for my sake."

Then Perseus lowered his hand, and Polydectes, who had been trembling all this while like a coward because he knew that he was in the wrong, let Perseus and his mother pass.

Perseus took his mother to the temple of Athene, and there the priestess made her one of the temple-sweepers because they knew she would be safe there. Not even Polydectes would dare to drag her away from the altar. And there Perseus, the good Dictys, and his wife visited her every day. Not being able to get what he wanted by force, Polydectes cast about in his wicked heart how he might get it by cunning.

Now, he was sure that he could never get back Danae as long as Perseus was on the island. So, he made a plot to get rid of him. And first he pretended to have forgiven Perseus, and to have forgotten Danae so that, for a while, all went as smoothly as ever. Next he proclaimed a great feast and invited all the chiefs, and landowners to it, also the young men of the island, and among them Perseus so that they might all pay him homage as their king, and eat at his banquet in his hall.

On the appointed day they all came; and as the custom was then, each guest brought his present with him to the king: one a horse, another a shawl, or a ring, or a sword; and those who had nothing better brought a basket of grapes or some game, but Perseus brought nothing, for he had nothing to bring, since he was just a poor sailor lad.

He was ashamed, however, to appear before the king without a gift; and he was too proud to ask Dictys to lend him one. So, he stood at the door sorrowfully, watching the rich men enter. His face grew very red as they pointed at him, and smiled, and whispered, "Isn't that foundling going to give a gift?"

Now, this was exactly what Polydectes wanted; and as soon as he heard that Perseus stood outside his palace, he told his servants to bring him in. Then, he asked him scornfully before them all, "Am I not your king, Perseus, and have I not invited you to my feast? Where is your present, then?"

Perseus blushed and stammered, while all the proud men around laughed, and some of them began jeering him openly.

"This fellow was thrown ashore here like a piece of weed or driftwood, and yet he is too proud to bring a gift to the king."

"And though he does not know who his father is, he is vain enough to let the old women call him the son of Zeus."

And so forth, until poor Perseus grew mad with shame and hardly knowing what he said, cried out, "A present! Who are you to talk of presents? Just see if I do not bring a nobler one than all of yours together!"

He said all this boasting, and yet he felt in his heart that he was braver than all those scoffers, and more able to do some glorious deed.

"Hear him! Hear the boaster! What is it to be!" they cried, all, laughing louder than ever. ·

Then his dream at Samos came to his mind, and he cried aloud, "The head of the Gorgon."

He was half afraid after he had said the words, for everyone laughed louder than ever, and Polydectes loudest of all.

"You have promised to bring me the Gorgon's head? Then never appear again on this island without it. Go!"

Perseus ground his teeth with rage, for he saw that he had fallen into a trap; but his promise lay upon him, and he went out without a word. Down to the cliffs he went and looked across the broad blue sea; and he wondered if his dream were true, and prayed in the bitterness of his soul: "Pallas Athene, was my dream true? Shall I slay the Gorgon? If you really did show me her face, let me-not come to shame as a liar and boastful. Rashly and angrily I promised, but cunningly and patiently will I perform."

But there was no answer, nor sign. Neither thunder nor any appearance, not even a cloud in the sky. And three times Perseus called weeping, "Rashly and angrily I promised; but cunningly and patiently will I perform."

Then he saw afar off above the sea a small white cloud, as bright as silver. And it approached nearer and nearer, until its brightness dazzled his eyes. Perseus was amazed by that strange cloud, for there was no other cloud around the sky; and he trembled as it touched the cliff below. And as it touched, it broke, and parted, and within it appeared Pallas Athene, as he had seen her at Samos in his dream, and beside her a young man more light-limbed than the stag, whose eyes were like sparks of fire. By his side was a scimitar of diamond all of one clear precious stone, and on his feet were golden sandals, from the heels of which grew living wings.

They looked over Perseus keenly, and yet, they never moved their eyes. They went up the cliffs toward him more swiftly than the seagull, and yet, they never moved their feet, nor did the breeze stir the robes on their limbs; only the wings of the youth's sandals quivered, like a hawk's when he hangs above the cliff. And Perseus fell down and worshipped, for he knew that they were more than man.

But Athene stood before him and spoke gently, and told him not to have any fear. Then she said to Perseus, "He who overcomes in one trial, deserves a sharper trial still. You have overcome Polydectes, and have done so manfully. Do you dare to care Medusa the Gorgon?"

And Perseus said, "Try me; for since you spoke to me in Samas, a new soul has come into my breast, and I would be ashamed not to dare anything which I can do. Show me, then, how I can do this!"

"Perseus," said Athene, "think well before you attempt; for this deed requires a seven years' journey, in which you cannot repent or turn back nor escape; and if your

DANÆ AND THE SON OF APOLLO

heart fails you, you must die in the Unshapen Land, where no man will ever find your bones."

"Better so, than live here useless and despised," said Perseus. "Tell me, then, oh tell me, fair and wise goddess, of your great kindness and condescension, how I can do this one thing, and then, if need be, die!"

Then Athene smiled and said, "Be patient, and listen; for if you forget my words, you will indeed die. You must go northward to the country of the Hyperboreans, who live beyond the pole, at the sources of the cold north wind until you find the three Gray Sisters, who have but one eye and one tooth between them. You must ask them the way to the nymphs, the daughters of the Evening Star, who dance around the golden tree on the Atlantic island of the west. They will tell you the way to the Gorgon so that you may slay her, my enemy, the mother of monstrous beasts. Once she was a maiden as beautiful as morn, until she was too proud and sinned a sin at which the sun hid his face. From that day onward, her hair was turned to vipers, and her hands to eagle's claws; and her heart was filled with shame and rage, and her lips with bitter venom; and her eyes became so terrible that whosoever looks on them is turned to stone. Her children are the winged horse and the giant of the golden sword, and her grandchildren are Echidna the witch-adder, and Geryon the three-headed tyrant, who feeds his herds beside the herds of hell. So she became the sister of the Gorgons, Stheino and Euryte the abhorred, the daughters of the Queen of the Sea. Do not touch them, for they are immortal. I only want you to bring me Medusa's head."

"And I shall bring it!" said Perseus. "But how am I to escape her eyes? Will she not freeze me, too, into stone?"

"You will take this polished shield," said Athene, "and when you come near her, do not look at her herself, but at her image in the brass; so you may strike her safely. And when you have sliced off her head, wrap it with your face turned away, in the folds of the goatskin on which the shield hangs, the hide of Amaltheie, the nurse of the .Ægisholder. So, you will bring it safely back to me and win renown for yourself and a place among the heroes who feast with the immortals upon the peak where no winds blow."

Then Perseus said, "I will go, though I die in going. But how shall I cross the seas without a ship? And who will show me my way? And when I find her, how shall I slay her, if her scales be iron and brass?"

Then the young man spoke: "These sandals of mine will carry you across the seas, and over hill and dale like a bird, as they carry me all day long; for I am Hermes, the far-famed Argus-slayer, the messenger of the immortals, who dwell in Olympus."

Then Perseus fell down and worshipped, while the young man spoke again: "The sandals themselves will guide you on the road, for they are divine and cannot stray; and this sword itself, the Argusslayer, will kill her, for it is divine, and needs no second stroke. Now, stand up and put them on, and go forth."

So Perseus arose, and put on the sandals and the sword. And Athene cried, "Now leap from the cliff and be gone."

However, Perseus lingered and asked: "May I not bid farewell to my mother and to Dictys? And may I not offer burnt-offerings to you, and to Hermes the far-famed Argus-slayer, and to Father Zeus above?"

"You shall not bid farewell to your mother, lest your heart relent at her weeping. I will comfort her and Dictys until you return in peace. Nor shall you offer burnt-offerings to the Olympians, for your offering shall be Medusa's head. Now, leap, and trust in the armor of the immortals."

Then Perseus looked down the cliff and shuddered; but he was ashamed to show his dread. Then he thought of Medusa and the renown before him, and he leapt into the empty air.

And behold, instead of falling, he floated, and stood, and ran along the sky. He looked back, but Athene had vanished, and Hermes; and the sandals led him northward like a crane who follows the spring toward the Ister fens.

Part III – How Perseus Slew the Gorgon

So, Perseus started on his journey, going dry-shod over land and sea, and his heart was joyful, for the winged sandals carried him each day during a seven days' journey. And he went by Cythnus, and by Ceos, and the pleasant Cyclades to Attica; and past Athens and Thebes, and the Copaic lake, and up the valley of Cephissus, and past the peaks of Eta and Pindus, and over the rich Thessalian plains until sunny hills of Greece were behind him. Before him were the wilds of the north. Then he passed the Thracian mountains and many a barbarous tribe, Preons and Dardans and Triballi, until he came to the Ister stream and the dreary Scythian plains. And he walked across the Ister dry-shod, and away through the moors and fens, day and night toward the bleak northwest, turning neither to the right hand nor the left, until he came to the unshapen Land, and the place which has no name.

And seven days he walked through it, on a path which few can tell, for those who have trodden it like least to speak of it, and those who go there again in dreams are glad enough when they awake; until he came to the edge of the everlasting night where the air was full of feathers, and the soil was hard with ice. And, there at last he found the three Gray Sisters, by the shore of the freezing sea, nodding upon a white log of driftwood beneath the cold white winter moon; and they chanted a low song together: "Why the old times were better than the new."

There was no living thing around them, not a fly, not a moss upon the rocks. Neither seal nor seagull dare come near, lest the ice should clutch them in its claws. The surge broke up in foam, but it fell again in flakes of snow; and it frosted the hair of the three Gray Sisters and the bones in the ice cliff above their heads. They passed the eye from one to the other, but for all that they could not see; and they passed the tooth from one to the other, but for all that they could not eat; and they sat in the full glare of the moon, but they were none the warmer for her beams. And Perseus pitied the three Gray Sisters; but they did not pity themselves.

So he said, "Oh, venerable mothers, wisdom is the daughter of old age. You therefore should know many things. Tell me, if you can, the path to the Gorgon."

Then one cried, "Who is this who reproaches us with old age?" And another, "This is the voice of one of the children of men."

And he, "I do not reproach, but honor your old age, and I am one of the sons of men and of the heroes. The rulers of Olympus have sent me to you to ask the way to the Gorgon."

Then one, "There are new rulers in Olympus, and all new things are bad."

Another, "We hate your rulers, and the heroes, and all the children of men. We are the kindred of the Titans, and the Giants, and the Gorgons, and the ancient monsters of the deep."

And another, "Who is this rash and insolent man who pushes unbidden into our world?"

And the first, "There never was such a world as ours, nor will be. If we let him see it, he will spoil it all."

Then one cried, "Give me the eye, that I may see him."

And another, "Give me the tooth, that I may bite him."

But Perseus, when he saw that they were foolish and proud and did not love the children of men, left off pitying them, and said to himself, "Hungry men must needs be hasty. If I stay making many words here, I shall be starved."

Then he stepped close to them and watched until they passed the eye from hand to hand. And as they groped about between themselves, he held out his own hand gently, until one of them put the eye into it, fancying that it was the hand of her sister. Then he sprang back and laughed and cried: "Cruel and proud old women, I have your eye; and I will throw it into the sea, unless you tell me the path to the Gorgon and swear to me that you tell me right."

Then they wept, and chattered, and scolded. But it was all in vain. They were forced to tell the truth, though, when they told it, Perseus could hardly make out the road.

"You must go," they said, "foolish boy, to the south into the ugly glare of the sun until you come to Atlas the Giant, who holds the heavens and the earth apart. And you must ask his daughters, the Hesperides, who are young and foolish like yourself. And now give us back our eye, for we have forgotten all the rest."

So Perseus gave them back their eye, but instead of using it, they nodded and fell fast asleep and were turned into blocks of ice until the tide came up and washed them all away. And now they float up and down like icebergs forever, weeping whenever they meet the sunshine, and the fruitful summer, and the warm south wind, which fill young hearts with joy. But Perseus leapt to the south, leaving the snow and the ice behind. He flew past the isle of Hyperboreans, and the tin isles, and the long Iberian shore, while the sun rose higher day by day upon a bright blue summer sea. And the terns and the seagulls swept laughing around his head and called to him to stop and play, and the dolphins jumped joyfully as he passed and offered to carry him on their backs. And all night long the sea-nymphs sang sweetly, and the Tritons blew upon their conchs, as they played all around Galatcea their queen in her car of pearled shells. Day by day the sun rose higher, and leapt more swiftly into the sea at night, and more swiftly out of the sea at dawn; while Perseus skimmed over the billows like a seagull, and his feet were never wetted as he leapt on from wave to wave, and his limbs were never weary, until he saw far away a mighty mountain, rose-red in the setting sun. Its feet were wrapped in forests, and its head in wreaths of cloud; and Perseus knew that it was Atlas, who holds the heavens and the earth apart.

He came to the mountain, and leapt on shore, and wandered upward, among pleasant valleys and waterfalls, and tall trees and strange ferns and flowers. But there was no smoke rising from any glen, nor house, nor sign of man.

At last he heard sweet voices singing; and he guessed that he had come to the garden of the Nymphs, the daughters of the Evening Star.

They sang like nightingales among the thickets, and Perseus stopped to hear their songs, but the words which they spoke he could not understand. No, neither could any man after him for many a hundred years. So he stepped forward and saw them dancing, hand in hand around the charmed tree, which bent under its golden fruit; and around the tree-foot was coiled the dragon, old Ladon the sleepless snake, who

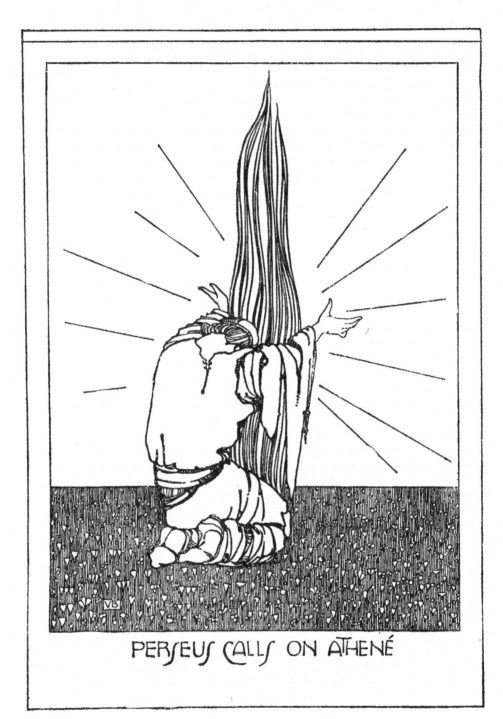

PERSEUS CALLS ON ATHENÉ

lies there forever, listening to the song of the maidens, blinking and watching with dry bright eyes.

Then Perseus stopped, not because he feared the dragon, but because he was bashful before those fair maids. However, when they saw him, they, too, stopped and called to him with trembling voices.

"Who are you? Are you Heracles the mighty, who will come to rob our garden and carry off our golden fruit?"

And he answered, "I am not Heracles the mighty, and I want none of your golden fruit. Tell me, fair Nymphs, the way which leads to the Gorgon so that I may go on my way and slay her."

"Not yet, not yet, fair boy; come dance with us around the tree in the garden which knows no winter, the home of the south wind and the sun. Come here and play with us awhile. We have danced alone here for a thousand years, and our hearts are weary with longing for a playfellow. So come, come, come!"

"I cannot dance with you, fair maidens; for I must do the errand of the immortals. So tell me the way to the Gorgon, lest I wander and perish in the waves."

Then they sighed and wept; and answered, "The Gorgon! She will freeze you into stone."

"It is better to die like a hero than to live like an ox in a stall. The immortals have lent me weapons, and they will give me wit to use them."

Then they sighed again and answered, "Fair boy, if you are bent on your own ruin, be it so. We know not the way to the Gorgon; but we will ask the giant Atlas, above upon the mountain peak, the brother of our father, the silver Evening Star. He sits aloft and sees across the ocean, and far away into the Unshapen Land."

So they went up the mountain to speak to Atlas their uncle, and Perseus went up with them. And they found the giant kneeling, as he held the heavens and the earth apart. They asked him, and he answered mildly, pointing to the seaboard with his mighty hand, "I can see the Gorgons lying on an island far away, but this youth can never get near them, unless he has the hat of darkness, which whosoever wears cannot be seen."

Then Perseus cried, "Where is that hat so that I may find it?"

But the giant smiled. "No living mortal can find that hat, for it lies in the depths of Hades, in the regions of the dead. But my nieces are immortal, and they shall fetch it for you, if you will promise me one thing and keep your faith."

Then Perseus promised; and the giant said, "When you come back with the head of Medusa, you shall show me the beautiful horror so that I may lose my feeling and my breathing, and become a stone forever, for it is weary labor for me to hold the heavens and the earth apart."

Then Perseus promised, and the eldest of the Nymphs went down and into a dark cavern among the cliffs, out of which came smoke and thunder, for it was one of the mouths of Hell. And Perseus and the Nymphs sat down seven days, and waited trembling, until the Nymph came up again; and her face was pale, and her eyes dazzled with the light, for she had been long in the dreary darkness. Nevertheless, in her hand was the magic hat.

Then all the Nymphs kissed Perseus, and wept over him a long while; but he was only impatient to be gone. And at last, they put the hat upon his head, and he vanished out of their sight.

But Perseus went on boldly, past many an ugly sight, far away into the heart of the Unshapen Land, beyond the streams of the ocean, to the isles where no ship cruises, where it is neither night nor day, where nothing is in its right place, and nothing has a name; until he heard the rustle of the Gorgons' wings and saw the glitter of their brazen talons; and then he knew that it was time to halt, lest Medusa should freeze him into stone.

He thought awhile with himself, and remembered Athene's words. He rose aloft into the air and held the mirror of the shield above his head, and looked up into it so that he might see all that was below him.

And he saw the three Gorgons sleeping, as huge as elephants. He knew that they could not see him because the hat of darkness hid him; and yet he trembled as he sank down near them, so terrible were those brazen claws. Two of the Gorgons were foul as swine and lay sleeping heavily, as swine sleep, with their mighty wings outspread; but Medusa tossed to and fro restlessly, and as she tossed, Perseus pitied her. Indeed, she looked so fair and sad. Her plumage was like the rainbow, and her face was like the face of a nymph, only her eyebrows were knit, and her lips clenched, with everlasting care and pain; and her long neck gleamed so white in the mirror that Perseus had not the heart to strike, and said, "Ah, if only it had been either one of her sisters!"

But as he looked, from among her tresses the vipers' heads awoke, and peeped up with their bright dry eyes, and showed their fangs, and hissed; and Medusa, as she tossed, threw back her wings and showed her brazen claws; and Perseus saw that, for all her beauty, she was as foul and venomous as the rest.

Then he came down and stepped to her boldly and looked steadfastly on his mirror, and struck with Herpe stoutly once, and he did not need to strike again.

Then he wrapped the head in the goatskin, turning his eyes away, and sprang into the air aloft, faster than he ever sprang before, for Medusa's wings and talons rattled as she sank dead upon the rocks; and her two foul sisters woke and saw her lying dead.

Into the air they sprang yelling and looked for the man who had done the deed. Thrice they swung around and around, like hawks who beat for a partridge; and thrice they snuffed around and around, like hounds who draw upon a deer. At last, they struck upon the scent of blood, and they checked for a moment to make sure; and then on they rushed with a fearful howl, while the wind rattled hoarse in their wings.

On they rushed, sweeping and flapping, like eagles after a hare; and Perseus' blood ran cold, for all his courage, as he saw them come howling on his track; and he cried, "Carry me well now, brave sandals, for the hounds of Death are at my heels!"

And well the brave sandals carried him in the air through cold and sunshine, across the shoreless sea; and fast followed the hounds of Death, as the roar of their wings came down the wind. But the roar came down fainter and fainter, and the howl of their voices died away; for the sandals were too swift, even for Gorgons, and by nightfall they were far behind, two black specks in the southern sky, until the sun sank, and he saw them no more.

Then, he went to Atlas again, and the garden of the Nymphs; and when the giant heard him coming, he groaned and said, "Fulfil your promise to me."

Then Perseus held up to him the Gorgon's head, and he had rest from all his toil; for he became a crag of stone, which sleeps forever far above the clouds. Then he thanked the Nymphs and asked them, "By what road shall I go homeward again, for I wandered far about in coming here?"

And they wept and cried, "Go home no more, but stay and play with us, the lonely maidens, who dwell forever far away from gods and men."

But he refused, and they told him his road and said, "Take with you this magic fruit, which, if you eat once, you will not hunger for seven days. Now you must go eastward and eastward ever, over the doleful Libyan shore, which Poseidon gave to Father Zeus, when he burst open the Bosphorus and the Hellespont, and drowned the fair Lectonian land. And Zeus took that land in exchange – a fair bargain, much bad ground for a little good, and to this day, it lies waste and desert, with shingle and rock and sand."

Then they kissed Perseus and wept over him, and he leapt down the mountain and went on, lessening and lessening like a seagull, away and out to sea.

Part IV – How Perseus Came to the Ethiops

So Perseus flitted onward to the northeast, over many a league of sea, until he came to the rolling sand hills and the dreary Lybian shore. And he flitted on across the desert: over rock-ledges, and banks of shingle, and level wastes of sand, and shell-drifts bleaching in the sunshine, and the skeletons of great sea monsters, and dead bones of ancient giants, strewn up and down upon the old sea-floor. And as he went, the blood-drops fell to the earth from the Gorgon's head, and became poisonous asps and adders, which breed in the desert to this day.

Over the sands he went – he never knew how far or how long – feeding on the fruit which the Nymphs had given him – until he saw the hills of the Psylli, and the Dwarfs who fought with cranes. Their spears were of reeds and rushes, and their house made of the eggshells of the cranes, and Perseus laughed, and continued on his way to the northeast, hoping all day long to see the blue Mediterranean sparkling so that he might fly across it to home.

But now a mighty wind erupted and swept him back southward toward the desert. All day long he strove against it, but even the winged sandals could not prevail. So he was forced to float down the wind all night, and when the morning dawned there was nothing to be seen, save the same old hateful waste of sand.

And out of the north the sandstorms rushed upon him – bloodred pillars and wreaths, blotting out the noonday sun. Perseus fled before them, lest he should be choked by the burning dust. At last the gale fell calm, and he tried to go northward again, but again the sandstorms erupted and swept him back into the waste. Then all was calm and cloudless as before. Seven days he strove against the storms, and seven days he was driven back, until he was spent with thirst and hunger and his tongue clove to the roof of his mouth. Here and there he imagined that he saw a fair lake, and the sunbeams shining on the water; but when he came to it, it vanished at his feet, and there was naught but burning sand. And if he had not been of the race of the immortals, he would have perished in the waste, but his life was strong within him, because it was more than man's.

Then he cried to Athene, and said, "Oh, fair and pure, if you hear me, are you going to leave me here to die of drought? I am bringing the Gorgon's head to you at your bidding. Up to now you have helped me in my journey. Are you deserting me in the very end? Otherwise, why won't these immortal sandals prevail against the desert storms? Shall I never see my mother again and the blue ripple around Seriphos, and the sunny hills of Hellas?"

So he prayed; and after he had prayed, there was a great silence. The heaven was still above his head, and the sand was still beneath his feet; and Perseus looked up, but there was nothing but the blinding sun in the blinding blue. And around him, there was nothing but the blinding sand. And Perseus stood still awhile, and waited, and said, "Surely I am not here without the will of the immortals, for Athene will not lie. Weren't these sandals to lead me on the right road, for the road in which I have tried to go must be a wrong road?"

Then suddenly his ears were opened, and he heard the sound of running water. Then his heart was lifted up, though he scarcely dared to believe his ears; and weary as he was, he hurried straight ahead, though he could scarcely stand upright; and within a bowshot of him was a glen in the sand, and marble rocks, and date-trees and a lawn of gay green grass. And through the lawn a streamlet sparkled and wandered out beyond the trees and vanished in the sand.

The water trickled among the rocks, and a pleasant breeze rustled in the dry date-branches; and Perseus laughed for joy and leapt down the cliff, and drank of the cool water, and ate of the dates, and slept upon the turf, and leapt up and went forward again: but not toward the north this time; for he said: "Surely Athene has sent me here and will not have me go home yet. What if there be another noble deed to be done before I see the sunny hills of Hellas?"

So he went east and went by fresh oases and fountains, date-palms, and lawns of grass, until he saw before him a mighty mountain wall, all rose-red in the setting sun. Then he towered in the air like an eagle, for his limbs were strong again; and he flew all night across the mountain until the day began to dawn, and rosy-fingered Eos came blushing up the sky. And then, behold, beneath him was the long green garden of Egypt and the shining stream of Nile. And he saw cities walled up to heaven, and temples, and obelisks, and pyramids, and giant gods of stone. And he came down amid fields of barley, and flax, and millet, and clambering gourds; and saw the people coming out of the gates of a great city, and setting to work, each in his place, among the water courses, parting the streams among the plants cunningly with their feet, according to the wisdom of the Egyptians. But when they saw him, they all stopped their work and gathered around him, and cried: "Who are you, fair youth? And what are you carrying beneath your goatskin there? Surely, you are one of the immortals for your skin is white like ivory, and ours is red like clay. Your hair is like threads of gold, and ours is black and curled. Surely, you are one of the immortals."

And they would have worshipped him then and there; but Perseus said, "I am not one of the immortals; but I am a hero of the Hellens. And I have slain the Gorgon in the wilderness and carry her head with me. Give me food, therefore, so that I may continue to finish my work."

Then they gave him food, and fruit, and wine; and they would not let him go. And when the news came into the city that the Gorgon was slain, the priests came out to meet him, and the maidens, with songs and dances, and timbrels and harps; and they would have brought him to their temple and to their king, but Perseus put on the hat of darkness and vanished away out of their sight.

Therefore, the Egyptians looked long for his return, but it was all in vain. Nevertheless, they worshipped him as a hero and made a statue of him in Chemmis, which stood for many a hundred years; and they said that he appeared to them at times, with sandals a cubit long; and that whenever he appeared, the season was fruitful, and the Nile rose high that year.

Then Perseus went eastward, along the Red Sea shore; and then, because he was afraid to go into the Arabian deserts, he turned northward once more, and this time no storm hindered him. He went past the Isthmus, and Mount Casius, and the vast Serbonian bog, and up the shore of Palestine, where the dark-faced Æthiops dwelt. Then he flew on past pleasant hills and valleys, like Argos itself, or Lacedæmon, or the fair Vale of Tempe. But the lowlands were all drowned by floods, and the highlands blasted by fire, and the hills heaved like a bubbling cauldron before the wrath of King Poseidon, the shaker of the earth.

And Perseus feared to go inland, but flew along the shore above the sea; and he continued the entire day, and the sky was black with smoke; and he went on throughout the night, and the sky was red with flame. And at the dawn of day he looked toward the cliffs; and at the water's edge, under a black rock, he saw a white image stand.

"This," thought he, "must surely be the statue of some sea-god. I will go near and see what kind of gods these barbarians worship."

So he went nearby, but when he arrived, there was no statue. Rather it was a maiden of flesh and blood; for he could see her tresses streaming in the breeze. And as he came closer still, he could see how she shrank and shivered when the waves sprinkled her with cold salt spray. Her arms were spread above her head, and fastened to the rock with chains of brass; and her head drooped on her bosom, either with sleep, or weariness, or grief. But now and then, she looked up and wailed and called her mother. Yet, she did not see Perseus, for the cap of darkness was on his head. Full of pity and indignation, Perseus drew near and looked at the maiden. Her cheeks were darker than his were, and her hair was blue-black like a hyacinth. But Perseus thought, "I have never seen so beautiful a maiden; no, not in all our isles. Surely she is a king's daughter. Do barbarians treat their king's daughters like this? She is too fair, at least, to have done any wrong. I will speak to her."

And, lifting his hat from his head, he flashed into her sight. She shrieked with terror and tried to hide her face with her hair, for she couldn't do this with her hands. But Perseus cried: "Do not fear me, fair one. I am a Hellen, not a barbarian. What cruel men have bound you? But first I will set you free."

And he tore at the fetters, but they were too strong for him. At the same time, the maiden cried: "Touch me not; I am cursed, sent as a victim to the sea-gods. They will slay you, if you dare to set me free."

"Let them try," said Perseus; and drawing Herpe from his thigh, he cut through the brass as if it had been flax.

"Now," he said, "you belong to me, and not to these sea gods, whosoever they may be!" But she only called the more for her mother.

"Why call on your mother? She can be no mother to have left you here. If a bird is dropped out of the nest, it belongs to the man who picks it up. If a jewel is cast by the wayside, it is his who dares win it and wear it, as I will win you and will wear you. I know now why Pallas Athene sent me here. She sent me to gain a prize worth all my toil and more."

And he embraced her in his arms and cried, "Where are these sea-gods, cruel and unjust, who doom fair maidens to death? I carry the weapons of immortals. Let them measure their strength against mine! But tell me, fair maiden, who you are, and what dark fate brought you here."

And she answered, weeping: "I am the daughter of Cepheus, King of Iopa, and my mother is Cassiopeia of the beautiful tresses, and they called me Andromeda, as long as my life was mine. But now, I stand bound here, hapless that I am, for the sea-monster's food to atone for my mother's sin. For she boasted of me once that I was fairer than Atergatis, Queen of the Fishes; so she in her wrath sent the sea-floods, and her brother the Fire King sent the earthquakes, and wasted all the land, and after the floods a monster bred of the slime, who devours all living things. And now he must devour me, guiltless though I am – me who never harmed a living thing, nor saw a fish upon the shore but I gave it life, and threw it back into the sea; for in our land we do not eat any fish for fear of Atergatis their queen. Yet, the priests say that nothing but my blood can atone for a sin which I never committed."

All of a sudden, Perseus laughed and said, "A sea-monster? I have fought with worse than sea-monsters! I would have faced immortals for your sake or a beast of the sea!"

Then Andromeda looked up at him, and new hope was kindled in her breast, so proud and fair did he stand, with one hand around her, and in the other the glittering sword. But she only sighed, and wept the more, and cried: "Why will you die, young as you are? Isn't there enough death and sorrow in the world already? It is noble for me to die so that I may save the lives of a whole people; but you, better than them all. Why should I slay you too? Get away; I must go my own way."

But Perseus cried, "No! You must know that the Lords of Olympus, whom I serve, are the friends of the heroes, and help them do noble deeds. Led by them, I slew the Gorgon, the beautiful horror, and it is not without them do I come here to slay this monster with that same Gorgon's head. Yet hide your eyes when I leave you, lest the sight of it freeze you too to stone."

But the maiden did not answer, for she could not believe his words. And then, suddenly looking up, she pointed to the sea, and shrieked: "There he comes, with the sunrise, as they promised. I must die now. How shall I endure it? Oh, go! Is it not dreadful enough to be torn piecemeal, without having you to look on?"

And she tried to thrust him away. But he said, "I go; yet promise me one thing before I go: If I slay this beast, promise me that you will be my wife and come back with me to my kingdom in fruitful Argos, for I am a king's heir. Promise me, and seal it with a kiss."

Then she lifted up her face, and kissed him; and Perseus laughed for joy and flew upward, while Andromeda crouched, trembling on the rock, waiting for what might happen to her.

Well, on came the great sea-monster, coasting along like a huge black galley, lazily breasting the ripple, and stopping at times by creek or headland to watch for the laughter of girls at their bleaching, or cattle pawing on the sand hills, or boys bathing on the beach. His great sides were fringed with clustering shells and sea-weeds, and the water gurgled in and out of his wide jaws, as he rolled along, dripping and glistening in the beams of the morning sun.

At last, he saw Andromeda and shot forward to take his prey, while the waves foamed white behind him, and before him the fish fled leaping.

Then down from the height of the air fell Perseus like a shooting star, down to the crests of the waves, while Andromeda hid her face as he shouted; and then there was silence for a while. Finally, she looked up trembling and saw Perseus springing toward her. Instead of the monster, she saw a long black rock, with the sea rippling quietly around it. It was proud Perseus, leaping back to the rock and then lifted his fair Andromeda in his arms and flew with her to the top of the cliff just as a falcon carries a dove.

Who could be so proud as Perseus, and who so joyful as all the Æthiop people? Indeed, they had stood watching the monster from the cliffs, wailing for the maiden's fate. And already a messenger had gone to Cepheus and Cassiopeia, where they sat in sackcloth and ashes on the ground, in the innermost palace chambers, awaiting their daughter's end. And they came, and all the city with them, to see the wonder with songs and with dances, with cymbals and harps, and received their daughter back again, as one alive from the dead.

Then Cepheus said, "Hero of the Hellens, stay here with me and be my son-in-law, and I shall give you half of my kingdom."

"I will be your son-in-law," said Perseus, "but of your kingdom. I will have none, for I long for the pleasant land of Greece, and my mother who waits for me at home."

Then Cepheus said, "You must not take my daughter away at once, for she is to us like one alive from the dead. Stay with us here a year, and after that you can return with honor."

And Perseus consented; but before he went to the palace, he asked the people to bring stones and wood, and built three altars, one to Athene, and one to Hermes, and one to Father Zeus, and offered bullocks and rams.

And some said, "This is a pious man"; yet the priests said, "The Sea Queen will be yet fiercer against us, because her monster is slain."

Yet, they were afraid to speak aloud, for they feared the Gorgon's head. So they went up to the palace; and when they entered, there stood in the hall Phineus, the brother of Cepheus, chafing like a bear robbed of her whelps, and with him his sons, and his servants, and many an armed man; and he cried to Cepheus, "You will not marry your daughter to this stranger, of whom nobody knows even the name. Was not Andromeda betrothed to my son? And now that she is safe again, has he not a right to claim her?"

But Perseus laughed and answered, "If your son is in want of a bride, let him save a maiden for himself. As yet, he seems but a helpless bridegroom. He left this one to die, and dead she is to him. I saved her alive, and alive she is to me, but to no one else. Ungrateful man! Have I not saved your land, and the lives of your sons and daughters, and will you requite me in this way? Go, or it will be worse for you!"

But all the men-at-arms drew their swords and attacked him like wild beasts. Then he unveiled the Gorgon's head and said, "This has delivered my bride from one wild beast, and now it will deliver her from many."

And as he spoke, Phineus and all his men-at-arms stopped short and were frozen and stiffened. By the time Perseus drew the goatskin over the face again, they were all turned into stone. Then Perseus asked the people to bring levers and roll them out, and what was done with them after that I cannot tell.

So, after this conflict, they made a great wedding-feast, which lasted seven whole days, and who was so happy as Perseus and Andromeda? But on the eighth night, Perseus dreamed a dream; and he saw standing beside him Pallas Athene, as he had seen her in Seriphos, seven long years, before, and she stood and called him by name, and said:

"Perseus, you have played the man, and see, you have your reward. Know now that the gods are just, and help him who helps himself. Now, give me Herpe the sword, the sandals, and the hat of darkness so that I may give them back to their owners, but I want you to keep the Gorgon's head a while, for you will need it in your land of Greece. Then you will return it to my temple at Seriphosso so that I may wear it on my shield forever, a terror to the Titans and the monsters, and the foes of gods and men. And as for this land, I have appeased the sea and the fire, and there will be no more floods nor earthquakes. But let the people build altars to Father Zeus, and to me, and worship the immortals, the lords of heaven and earth."

And Perseus rose to give her the sword, and the cap, and the sandals, but he awoke, and his dream vanished away. And yet it was not altogether a dream because the goat-skin with the head was in its place while the sword, and the cap, and the sandals were gone, and Perseus never saw them again.

Then a great awe fell on Perseus; and he went out in the morning to the people, told his dream, and requested that they build altars to Zeus, the Father of Gods and men, and to Athene, who gives wisdom to heroes; and fear no more the earthquakes and the floods, but sow and build in peace. And they did so for a while, and prospered; but after Perseus was gone, they forgot Zeus and Athene, and worshipped again Atergatis the queen, and the undying fish of the sacred lake, where Deucalion's deluge was swallowed up, and they burned their children before the Fire King, until Zeus became angry with that foolish people and brought a strange nation against them out of Egypt, who fought against them and wasted them utterly, and dwelt in their cities for many a hundred years.

Part V – How Perseus Came Home Again

And when a year had ended, Perseus hired Phoenicians from Tyre and cut down cedars, and built himself a noble galley and painted its cheeks with vermilion, and pitched its sides with pitch; and in it he put Andromeda and all her dowry of jewels, and rich shawls, and spices from the East; and great was the weeping when they rowed away. But the remembrance of his brave deed was left behind; and Andromeda's rock was shown at Iopa in Palestine until more than a thousand years had passed.

So Perseus and the Phoenicians rowed to the westward, across the sea of Crete, until they came to the blue Ægean and the pleasant Isles of Hellas, and Seriphos, his ancient home.

Then he left his galley on the beach and went up as of old, and he embraced his mother and Dictys his good foster-father, and they wept over each other a long while, for it was seven years and more since they had met.

Then Perseus went out and up to the hall of Polydectes, and underneath the goat-skin he bore the Gorgon's head. And when he came into the hall, Polydectes sat at the head of the table, and all his nobles and landowners on either side, each according to his rank, feasting on the fish and the goat's flesh, and drinking the blood-red wine. The harpers harped, and the revelers shouted, and the wine-cups rang merrily as they passed from hand to hand. And great was the noise in the hall of Polydectes.

Then Perseus stood on the threshold, and called to the king by name. But none of the guests knew Perseus, for he had changed during his long journey. He had gone out a boy, and he had come home a hero. His eye shone like an eagle's, and his beard was like a lion's beard, and he stood up like a wild bull in his pride.

But Polydectes the wicked knew him and hardened his heart still more. Scornfully he called: "Ah, foundling! have you found it more easy to promise than to fulfill?"

"Those whom the gods help fulfill their promises; and those who despise them, reap as they have sown. Behold the Gorgon's head!"

Then Perseus drew back the goatskin, and held aloft the Gorgon's head. Pale grew Polydectes and his guests as they looked at that dreadful face. They tried to rise up from their seats, but from their seats they never rose, but stiffened, each man where he sat, into a ring of cold gray stones.

Then Perseus turned and left them and went down to his galley in the bay; and he gave the kingdom to good Dictys, and sailed away with his mother and his bride.

And Polydectes and his guests sat still with the wine-cups before them on the board, until the rafters crumbled down above their heads, and the walls behinds their backs, and the table crumbled down between them, and the grass sprung up about their feet: but Polydectes and his guests sit on the hillside, a ring of gray stones until this day.

PERSEUS FLEES FROM THE DREAD SISTERS

In the meantime, Perseus rowed westward toward Argos. When he landed, he went up to the town. And when he came, he found that Acrisius his grandfather had fled. This was because Proetus, his wicked brother, had made war against him afresh; and had come across the river from Tiryns, and conquered Argos, and Acrisius had fled to Larissa, in the country of the wild Pelasgi.

Then Perseus called the Argives together and told them who he was, and all the noble deeds which he had accomplished. As a result, all the nobles and the yeomen made him king, for they saw that he had a royal heart; and they fought with him against Argos, and took it, and killed Proetus and made the Cyclopes serve them and build them walls around Argos, like the walls which they had built at Tiryns. And there were great rejoicings in the vale of Argos because they had got a king from Father Zeus.

But Perseus' heart yearned after his grandfather, and he said, "Surely he is my flesh and blood, and he will love me now that I have come home with honor: I will go and find him, and bring him home, and we will reign together in peace."

So Perseus sailed away with his Phoenicians , around Hydrea and Sumum, past Marathon and the Attic shore, and through Euripus and up the long Eubrean sea, until he came to the town of Larissa, where the wild Pelasgi dwelt.

And when he arrived there, all the people were in the fields, and there was feasting, and all kinds of games; for Teutamenes their king wished to honor Acrisius, because he was the king of a mighty land. So, Perseus did not tell his name, but went up to the games unknown, and he said, "If I carry away the prize in the games, my grandfather's heart will be softened toward me."

So he threw off his helmet, and his cuirass, and all his clothes, and stood among the youths of Larissa, while everyone wondered who he was.

"Who is this young stranger," they asked, "who stands like a wild bull in his pride? Surely he is one of the heroes, the sons of the immortals, from Olympus."

And when the games began, they were amazed even more; for Perseus was the best man of all at running, and leaping, and wrestling and throwing the javelin; and he won four crowns. When he took them, he said to himself, "There is a fifth crown yet to be won: I will win that and lay them all upon the knees of my grandfather."

And as he spoke, he saw that Acrisius sat by the side of Teutamenes the king, with his white beard flowing down upon his knees, and his royal staff in his hand; and Perseus wept when he looked at him, for his heart yearned after his km; and he said, "Surely, he is a kingly old man, and he need not be ashamed of his grandson."

Then he took the iron rings and hurled them, five fathoms beyond all the rest; and the people shouted, "Further yet, brave stranger! There has never been such a hurler in this land."

Then Perseus used all his strength and hurled. Suddenly, a gust of wind came from the sea, and carried the ring aside and far beyond all the rest; and it fell on the foot of Acrisius, and he swooned away with the pain. Immediately, Perseus shrieked and ran up to him; but when they lifted the old man he was dead, for his life was slow and feeble.

Then Perseus tore his clothes, cast dust upon his head, and wept a long while for his grandfather. Finally, he stood up and called to all the people aloud, and said: "The gods are true, and what they have ordained must be! I am Perseus, the grandson of this dead man, the far-famed slayer of the Gorgon."

Then he told them how the prophecy had declared that he would kill his grandfather, and he recounted the story of his life. So they made a great mourning for Acrisius and burned him on a right rich pile. Perseus went to the temple and was purified from the guilt of the death, because he had killed his grandfather unknowingly.

Then he went home to Argos and reigned there well with fair Andromeda; and they had four sons and three daughters, and died in a good old age. And when they died, the ancients say, Athene took them up into the sky, with Cepheus and Cassiopeia. And there on starlit nights you may see them, shining still; Cepheus with his kingly crown, and Cassiopeia in her ivory chair, plaiting her star-spangled tresses, and Perseus with the Gorgon's head, and fair Andromeda beside him, spreading her long white arms across the heaven, as she stood when chained to the stone for the monster. All night long they shine as a beacon to wandering sailors; and all day long they feast with the gods on the still blue peaks of Olympus.

Tom, Dick, and Harry

Ignacz Kunos

What Tom told Dick and Harry,
And what Dick told Harry and Tom,
What Harry told Tom and Dick,
And what Tom said in the end.

"This a very old story," said Tom, "and you may have heard it before, but at any rate this is the first time I've ever told it. A man told me, and a Turk told him, but where the Turk heard it, I don't know."

An old woman longed for a piece of liver. So, she gave a girl a few pence and said: "Go to the market place and buy me some liver. Wash it in the market trough and bring it to me."

The girl went to the market, bought the liver, and washed it in the trough.

As she was washing it down, a stork flew by and snatched the liver out of the girl's hand and flew away again.

"Stork, stork, give me my liver. I must take it to the old woman, or she will beat me."

"Fetch me a barley ear, and I'll give you back the liver," said the stork.

The girl went to the straw and said: "Straw, straw, give me a barley ear, so that I may give it to the stork, so that he may give me back my liver, that I may give it to the old woman, or the old woman will beat me."

"Pray to Allah for rain, and I will give you a barley ear," said the straw.

"So the girl prayed for rain and said. "Oh Allah, give me rain that I may give rain to the straw, so that the straw may give me a barley ear, so that I may give the barley ear to the stork, that the stork may give me back my liver, that I may give it to the old woman, or the old woman will beat me."

But while she was praying, a priest came along and said: "What good are prayers without a censer? Go to the bazaar keeper and get a censer."

So she went to the bazaar and asked the merchant there: "Sir, sir, give me a censer that I may burn incense to Allah, so that Allah may give me rain, that I may give rain to the straw, so that the straw may give me a barley ear, so that I may give the barley ear to the stork, so that the stork may give me back my liver so that I may give it to the old woman, or the old woman will beat me."

"Bring me a boot from the cobbler." said the merchant.

So she went to the cobbler and said: Cobbler, cobbler, give me a boot so that I may give it to the merchant so that he may give me a censer, so that I may burn incense to Allah, so that Allah may give me rain, that I may give rain to the straw, so that the straw may give me a barley ear, that I may give the barley ear to the stork, that

DOI: 10.4324/9781003297536-21

the stork may give me back my liver, that I may give it to the old woman, or the old woman will beat me."

"Bring me leather from the tanner, and I will give you a boot," said the cobbler.

So she went to the tanner and said: "Tanner, tanner, give me leather so that I may give it to the cobbler so that the cobbler may give me a boot, that I may give it to the merchant, so that he may give me a censer, that I may burn incense to Allah, so that Allah may give me rain, so that I may give rain to the straw, so that the straw may give me a barley ear, that I may give the barley ear to the stork, so that the stork may give me back my liver, so that I may give it to the old woman, or the old woman will beat me."

"Go to the ox and get me a hide, and I will make you a boot," said the tanner.

So she went to the ox and said: "Ox, ox, give me a hide so that I may give it to the tanner, so that he may give me leather, so that I may give it to the cobbler, so that the cobbler may give me a boot, that I may give to the merchant, so that he may give me a censer, so that I may burn incense to Allah, so that Allah may give me rain, that I may give to the straw, so that the straw may give me a barley ear, that I may give the barley ear to the stork, so that the stork may give me back my liver, so that I may give it to the old woman, or she will beat me."

"Get me fodder, and I'll give you a hide," said the ox.

So the girl went to the farmer, and said: "Farmer, farmer, give me fodder so that I may give it to the ox, so that the ox may give me a hide, that I may give it to the tanner, so that he may give me leather, that I may give it to the cobbler, so that the cobbler may give me a boot, that I may give to the merchant, so that he may give me a censer, so that I may burn incense to Allah, so that Allah may give me rain, that I may give to the straw, so that the straw may give me a barley ear that I may give the barley ear to the stork, so that the stork may give me back my liver so that I may give it to the old woman, or she will beat me."

"I'll give you fodder if you'll give me a kiss," said the farmer.

"Well," thought the girl, "a kiss is cheap," so she kissed the farmer, and he gave her the fodder, and she gave the fodder to the ox, who gave her a hide for the tanner, who gave her leather for the bootmaker, who gave her a boot for the merchant, who gave her a censer for her prayers to Allah, who gave rain to the straw, who gave the barley ear to the girl, who gave it to the stork, who gave her back her liver. So, she gave the liver to the old woman who cooked and ate it for supper, and no doubt the girl married the farmer.

"I don't think much of your story," said Dick. "I know one that's worth ten of your pieces of nonsense."

"All right," said Tom, "fire away."

"An old woman was sweeping her house," began Dick, "and she found a little crooked sixpence. 'What,' she said, 'shall I do with this little sixpence? I think I will go to market and buy a little pig.' As she was coming home, she came to a stile. The piggy would not go over the stile. She went a little farther, and she met a dog. So she said to the dog:

'Dog, dog, bite pig.
Piggy won't get over the stile
So I won't get home tonight!'

"But the dog would not. On she went a little farther, and she met a stick. So she said:

> 'Stick, stick, beat dog. Dog won't bite pig;
> Piggy won't get over the stile,
> And I won't get home tonight!'

"But the stick would not. On she went a little farther, and she met a fire. So she said:

> Fire, fire, burn stick;
> Stick won't beat dog; -
> Dog won't bite pig;
> Piggy won't get over the stile,
> And I won't get home tonight!'

"But the fire would not. On she went a little farther, and she met some water. So she said:

> 'Water, water, quench fire;
> Fire won't burn stick;
> Stick won't beat dog;
> Dog won't bite pig;
> Piggy won't get over the stile,
> And I won't get home tonight!'

"But the water would not. On she went a little farther, and she met an ox. So she said:

> Ox, ox, drink water;
> Water won't quench fire;
> Fire won't burn stick;
> Stick won't beat dog;
> Dog won't bite pig;
> Piggy won't get over the stile,
> And I won't get home tonight!'

"But the ox would not. On she went a little farther, and she met a butcher. So she said:

> Butcher, butcher, kill ox,
> Ox won't drink water,
> Water won't quench fire.
> Fire won't burn stick·
> Stick won't beat dog,
> Dog won't bite pig,
> Piggy won't get over the stile,
> And I won't get home tonight!'

"But the butcher would not. On she went a little farther, and· she met a rope. So she said:

Rope, rope, hang butcher.
Butcher won't kill ox.
Ox won't drink water.
Water won't quench fire.
Fire won't burn stick.
Stick won't beat dog.
Dog won't bite pig; ·
Piggy won't get over the stile.
And I won't get home tonight!'

"But the rope would not. Then she went a little farther, and she met a rat. So she said:

Rat, rat, gnaw rope.
Rope won't hang butcher.
Butcher won't kill ox.
Ox won't drink water.
Water won't quench fire.
Fire won't burn stick.
Stick won't beat dog.
Dog won't bite pig.
Piggy won't get over the stile.
And I won't get home tonight!'

"But the rat would not. On she went a little farther, and she met a cat. So she said:

Cat, cat, kill rat.
Rat won't gnaw rope.
Rope won't hang butcher.
Butcher won't kill ox.
Ox won't drink water.
Water won't quench fire;
Fire won't burn stick.
Stick won't beat dog.
Dog won't bite pig.
Piggy won't get over the stile.
And I won't get home tonight!

"Then the cat said to her, 'If you will go to yonder cow, and fetch me a saucer of milk, I will kill the rat.'
    "So away went the old woman to the cow, and said:

Cow, cow, give .me a saucer of milk;
Cat won't kill rat.
Rat won't gnaw rope;
Rope won't hang butcher;
Butcher won't kill ox;
Ox won't drink water;
Water won't quench fire;

Fire won't burn stick;
Stick won't beat dog;
Dog won't bite pig;
Piggy won't get over the stile,
And I won't get home tonight!'

"But the cow said to her, 'If you will go to yonder haymakers and fetch me a wisp of hay, I'll give you some milk.'

"So away went the old woman to the haymakers, and said:

Haymakers, give me a wisp of hay;
Cow won't give milk;
Cat won't kill rat;
Rat won't gnaw rope;
Rope won't hang butcher;
Butcher won't kill ox;
Ox won't drink water;
Water won't quench fire;
Fire won't burn stick;
Stick won't beat dog;
Dog won't bite pig;
Piggy won't get over the stile,
And I shan't get home tonight!'

"But the haymakers said to her, 'If you will go to yonder stream, and fetch us a bucket of water, we will give you the hay.' So away the old woman went. But when she got to the stream, she found the bucket was full of holes. So, she covered the bottom with pebbles, and then filled the bucket with water, and she went back with it to the haymakers, and they gave her a wisp of hay.

"As soon as the cow had eaten the hay, she gave the old woman the milk, and away she went with it in a saucer to the cat. As soon as the cat had lapped up the milk. The cat began to kill the rat. The rat began to gnaw the rope. The rope began to hang the butcher. The butcher began to kill the ox. The ox began to drink the water. The water began to quench the fire. The fire began to burn the stick. The stick began to beat the dog. The dog began to bite the pig. The little pig in a fright jumped over the stile. And the old woman got home that night!"

When Dick had finished, Harry piped up: "I know a tale that's worth hundreds of yours."

"Let's hear it," said Tom and Dick.

"It was a dark and stormy night," said Harry, "and twelve robbers sat around a fire in a cave and the robber chief said to the second robber, 'Tell us a story.'"

"The second robber said, 'I will. It was a dark and stormy night, and twelve robbers sat around a fire in a cave, and the robber chief said to the second robber, "Tell us a story." The second robber said "I will" and began by saying, "it was a dark and stormy—"

"Oh," cried Tom in a loud roaring voice, "I can't stand any more of this."

And to be quite sure, no one would tell anymore tales that night, he added fiercely:

"Silence in the pig market, for a donkey's about to speak."

Bibliography

Hans Christian Andersen (1805–1875)
"The Shirt Collar"
Source: *Fairy Tales and Other Stories*
Editors: W. A. and J. K. Craigle
Oxford: Oxford University Press
"The Nightingale"
Source: *Fairy Tales from Hans Christian Andersen*
Ed. Ernest Rhys
London: Everyman's Library
Andersen was a Danish novelist, playwright, and poet whose fame is based on his
    fairy tales. He had a great gift for transforming Danish folk tales into unusual
    literary tales. He added a personal and modern touch to old stories that made
    everyday life more startling. Moreover, his social-political perspective exposed the
    hypocrisy of his times.

Peter Christen Asbjørnsen (1812–1885) and Jørgen Moe (1813–1882)
"The UT-Röst Cormorants"
Source: *Norwegian Fairy Tales from the Collection of Asbjørnsen and Moe*, tr. Helen
    and John Gade
Oxford: Oxford University Press,
Asbjørnsen, a zoologist, and Moe, a bishop, met in their college years and remained
    friends for the rest of their lives. They both collected Norwegian folk tales by taking
    journeys through the countryside. Their first publication of tales was in 1843 and
    was followed by another in 1844 and 1871. George Dasent translated the tales into
    English in 1859.

Charles Marius Barbeau (1883–1969) and Gregory MacDonald (no dates available)
"The Round Castle of the Red Sea"
Source: *Journal of American Folklore* XXX (1917)
Barbeau was a Canadian folklorist and ethnographer, who founded Canadian anthro-
    pology. Though controversial because of his unconventional theories and his refusal
    to include indigenous informants in his works, he contributed to a recognition of
    original Québecois customs and traditions.
Violet Brunton (1878–1951), also known as Victor du Lac, was born in Brighouse,
    Yorkshire. She studied woodcarving, miniature painting, and illustration at the
    Liverpool School of Art and the Royal School of Art in London. A multi-talented

artist, she created all the illustrations for Romer Wilson's *Green Magic* (1928) and *Silver Magic* (1929). She captured the humorous and provocative aspects of most of the fairy tales in these two collections. Her black and white illustrations are particularly striking and tend to underline the major themes of the tales.

Charles Fillingham Coxwell (1856–1940)
"The Man Who Understood Animals' Conversation"
"The Brotherless Girl"
"Foolish John"
Siberian and Other Folk Tales: Primitive Literature of the Empire of the Tsars
London: C. W. Daniel, 1925.
Coxwell was a British translator and folklorist. During World War I he traveled widely in Russia and collected numerous folk tales which formed the basis for his book *Siberian and Other Folk Tales*. In addition to his work on Russian tales, he also translated Goethe's *Faust*.

Antoine Galland (1763–1881)
"The History of Ali Baba, and of the Forty Robbers
Who Were Killed by One Slave"
Source: *Dalziel's Illustrated Arabian Nights*
London: Ward L, Lock, & Co. 1865.
Galland was a prominent French orientalist and was the first European translator of *The One Thousand and One Nights* (1704–1717). Altogether there were fourteen volumes. The Syrian storyteller Hanna Diyab contributed an oral version of "Ali Baba and the Forty Thieves" to Galland in 1709.

Herbert Giles (1845–1935) and Pu Singling (1640–1716)
"The Lake Princess"
Source: "The Princess of Tung T'ing Lake"
Strange Stories from a Chinese Studio
Trans. Herbert Giles
Shanghai: Kelly & Walsh, 1916.
Herbert Allen Giles was a British diplomat and sinologist, who was the professor of Chinese at the University of Cambridge for thirty-five years. Giles was educated at Charterhouse School before becoming a British diplomat in China. He is the author of over fifty books dealing with the Chinese language and literature. His translation of Songling's collection of seventeenth-century Chinese tales was one of the first ever published in English.

Jacob Grimm (1785–1863) and Wilhelm Grimm (1786–1859)
"The Musicians of Bremen"
"Rapunzel"
Source: *Fairy Tales*, Everyman's Library
Editor Ernest Rhys (1859–1946)
Jacob Grimm (1785–1863) and Wilhelm Grimm (1786–1859)
"The Six Swans"
The Grimm Brothers were German philologists who pioneered the development of folklore in Europe. They published numerous folk tales which originated in Europe

and the Middle East in seventeen editions during their lifetime. Today their tales are generally considered the most significant folk and fairy tales in the world.

Diamond Jenness (1886–1969)
"The Wolf's Bride"
Source: *Eskimo Folklore,* XIII (1917–18)
Born in New Zealand. Jenness later became one of Canada's greatest early scientists and a pioneer of Canadian anthropology. He tried carefully, but with mixed success, to improve the knowledge and welfare of Canada's aboriginal peoples. Between 1920 and 1970, Jenness authored more than 100 works on Canada's Inuit and First Nations people. Chief among these are his scholarly government report, *Life of the Copper Eskimos* (published 1922), his ever-popular account of two years with the Copper Inuit, *The People of the Twilight* (published 1928).

Charles Kingsley (1819–1875)
"Perseus"
Source: *The Heroes*
London: Macmillan, 1856.
Charles Kingsley was a broad church priest of the Church of England, a university professor of history, social and reformer, historian, novelist, and poet. He is particularly associated with Christian socialism. Kingsley's interest in history is shown in several of his writings, including *The Heroes* (1856) about Greek mythology, He was sympathetic to the idea of evolution and was one of the first to welcome Charles Darwin's book *On the Origin of Species.*

Ignacz Kunos (1860–1945)
"Tom, Dick, and Harry"
Source: *Turkish Fairy Tales*
Trans. R. Nisbet Bain
London: George Garrap, 1896.
Ignác Kúnos was a Hungarian linguist and folklorist. During his lifetime, he was one of the most established scholars of linguistics and Turkish folk literature. He collected an impressive amount of folk tales and anecdotes that were published in Hungarian as well as many other European languages.

Mite Kremnitz (1852–1916)
"Stan Bolovan"
Source: *Romanian Fairy Tales*
New York: Henry Holt, 1885.
Kremnitz was a German writer who spent many years in Romania, where she collaborated with Queen Elizabeth in the writing of short stories and novels. She is specifically notable for the sketches she wrote in Romania and Germany.

Elodie L. Mijatovich or Elodie Lawton Mijatović (1825–1908)
"The Golden Apple Tree and the Nine Peahens"
Source: *Siberian Fairy Tales*
London: William Heinemann

Mijatovich was a British author who translated various Serbian works into English. In 1899 she published *Serbian Folk*-lore, and in 1917, *Serbian Fairy Tales*, which includes "Bash-Chalek," and was published posthumously.

Peter Isperescu (1830–1887)
"The Golden Twins"
Source: *The Foundling Prince and Other Tales*
Adapted by: Julia Collier and Rea Ipcar
Boston: Houghton Mifflin, 1917.
Isperescu was encouraged to become a priest during his teenage years, but after working with printers, he decided in 1862 to write and publish tales and novels. In particular, he was drawn to folk and fairy tales and became renowned for his unusual mix of folk tales, legends, and myths.

Charles Perrault
"Puss in Boots"
Source: *The Old, Old Fairy Tales*
Mrs. Valentine, editor
The Old, Old Fairy Tales
London: Frederick Warne, 1890.
A French poet, Charles Perrault is the foremost writer of literary fairy tales, perhaps in the world. His 1697 book, *Histoires ou contes du temps passé* (Stories or Tales from Past Times) includes such classics as "Cinderella," "Little Red Riding Hood," "Puss in Boots," "Sleeping Beauty," and other classics. There is probably not one single author of fairy tales whom he has not influenced.

William Ralston (1828–1889)
"The Water King and Vasilissa the Wise"
Source: *Russian Folk Tales*
London: Smith, Elder & Co., 1873.
Ralston studied Russian at the University of London and also traveled to Russia. By the time he accepted and worked at the British Library, he became one of the foremost scholars of Russian folklore and literature. He was also a talented storyteller and often performed Russian tales on various occasions.

Laura Valentine (1814–1899)
"Fortunatus and the Wishing Cap"
Source: *The Old, Old Fairy Tales*
London: Frederick Warne, 1890.
Laura Belinda Charlotte Jewry's married name was Laura Valentine, and her pen names were Mrs. Valentine and Aunt Louisa. She was a Victorian English writer primarily known for her children's literature. However, her book, *The Old, Old Fairy Tales* contains classical fairy tales for young and old and is also notable for the illustrations.